African Francophone Writing
A Critical Introduction

Edited by
Laïla Ibnlfassi and Nicki Hitchcott

BERG
Oxford • Washington, D.C.

First published in 1996 by
Berg
Editorial offices:
150 Cowley Road, Oxford, OX4 1JJ, UK
13950 Park Center Road, Herndon, VA 22071, USA

Berg is an imprint of Oxford International Publishers Ltd.

Library of Congress Cataloguing-in-Publication Data

A catalogue record for this book is available from the Library of Congress.

British Library Cataloguing-in-Publication Data

A catalogue record for this book is available from the British Library.

Cover photograph: by Ernest Cole and supplied, with kind permission, by
Mayibuye Centre, South Africa. © Mayibuye Centre.

ISBN 1 85973 009 4 (Cloth)
1 85973 014 0 (Paper)

Printed in the United Kingdom by WBC Bookbinders, Bridgend, Mid-Glamorgan.

African Francophone Writing

Berg French Studies

General Editor: John E. Flower

ISSN: 1354-3636

John E. Flower and Bernard C. Swift (eds), *François Mauriac: Visions and Reappraisals*

Michael Tilby (ed.), *Beyond the Nouveau Roman: Essays on the Contemporary French Novel*

Richard Griffiths, *The Use of Abuse: The Polemics of the Dreyfus Affair and its Aftermath*

Alec G. Hargreaves, *Voices from the North African Immigrant Community in France: Immigration and Identity in Beur Fiction*

Colin Nettlebeck, *Forever French: The French Exiles in the United States of America during the Second World War*

Bill Marshall, *Victor Serge: The Uses of Dissent*

Allan Morris, *Collaboration and Resistance Reviews: Writers and the Mode Rétro in Post-Gaullist France*

Malcolm Cook, *Fictional France: Social Reality in the French Novel 1775–1800*

W.D. Halls, *Politics, Society and Christianity in Vichy France*

David H. Walker, *Outrage and Insight: Modern French Writers and the 'Fait Divers'*

H.R. Kedward and Nancy Wood, *The Liberation of France: Image and Event*

David L. Looseley, *The Politics of Fun: Cultural Policy and Debate in Contemporary France*

This book is dedicated to the memory of
Haj El-Khayatti Ibnlfassi

Contents

Notes on Contributors   ix

Introduction
Laïla Ibnlfassi and *Nicki Hitchcott*   1

1   The Institutional Framework of *la Francophonie*
    Anne Judge   11

    Part I: North Africa   31

2   Writers of Maghrebian Immigrant Origin
    in France: French, Francophone, Maghrebian
    or Beur?
    Alec G. Hargreaves   33

3   Points of View: Looking at the Other in
    Michel Tournier's *La Goutte d'or* and Rachid
    Boudjedra's *Topographie idéale pour une agression
    caractérisée*
    Carys Owen   45

4   Chraïbi's *Le Passé simple* and a Theory of Doubles
    Laïla Ibnlfassi   59

5   Unmasking Women: The Female Persona in
    Algerian Fiction
    Farida Abu-Haidar   69

6   Commuting the 'Sentences' of Malek Haddad
    Sara Poole   83

7   'Don't Look Back': Albert Memmi's *La Statue
    de sel*
    Seán Hand   93

8   To be a Poet in Morocco
    Jacqueline Kaye   103

Part II: Sub-Saharan Africa   123

9   Linguistic and Cultural Heterogeneity
and the Novel in Francophone Africa
Madeleine Borgomano   125

10   'Confidently Feminine'? Sexual Role-Play in
the Novels of Mariama Bâ
Nicki Hitchcott   139

11   Tradition and Continuity: The Quest for
Synthesis in Francis Bebey's *Le Fils d'Agatha
Moudio*
Abimne D. Njinjoh   153

12   Marxist Intertext, Islamic Reinscription? Some
Common Themes in the Novels of Sembène
Ousmane and Aminata Sow Fall
Peter Hawkins   163

13   Amadou Hampaté Bâ's *Amkullel*: A Malian
Memoir and its Contexts
Andrew Manley   171

Afterword: Homecoming
Mongo Beti   181

Chronology   189

Index   209

Notes on Contributors

Farida Abu-Haidar is a sociolinguist and researcher at the Universities of Nijmegen and Tilburg. She has published numerous articles on the Algerian novel. She is currently working on mother-tongue maintenance by Maghrebian immigrants in Europe.

Mongo Beti is the pen-name of Cameroonian novelist and essayist, Alexandre Biyidi (b. 1932). His many works include *Ville cruelle* (1954), *Le Pauvre Christ de Bamba* (1956) and *Remember Reuben* (1974). He has recently published *La France contre L'Afrique: Retour au Cameroun* (1993).

Madeleine Borgomano is Associate Professor at Université de Provence Aix-Marseille I. She taught at different universities in Africa for 20 years. Her publications include *Lecture de 'L'Appel des arènes' d'Aminata Sow Fall* (1985) and *Voix et visages de femmes* (1989). She is currently working on a critical study of Ahmadou Kourouma, *Les Soleils des Indépendances*.

Seán Hand is Reader in French at London Guildhall University. He is General Editor of the Longman series, 'Modern Literatures in Perspective'. He has published on contemporary writers and theorists such as Leiris and Levinas.

Alec G. Hargreaves is Professor of French and Francophone Literature at Loughborough University. He is a specialist on the Maghrebian population in France. His numerous publications on the Beurs include *Voices from the North African Immigrant Community in France: Immigration and Identity in Beur Fiction* (1991). He is also the author of *The Colonial Experience in French Fiction* (1981).

Peter Hawkins is Lecturer in French at the Universities of Bristol and La Réunion. He has published widely in the field of African literature and is co-editor of *Protée noir: essais sur la littérature francophone* *de l'Afrique noire et des Antilles* (1992) as well as editor of the African section of *The New Oxford Companion to Literature in French* (1995).

Nicki Hitchcott is Lecturer in French at the University of Nottingham. She has published articles on francophone African women's writing and is currently completing a book entitled *The Unspoken Self: Feminism and Cultural Identity in African Women's Writing in French*.

Laïla Ibnlfassi is Lecturer in Francophone Literature at London Guildhall University. She has published articles on Chraïbi and Ben Jelloun as well as translated extracts of texts by Mimouni and Djaout. She is currently finishing a doctoral thesis on the francophone Moroccan novel.

Anne Judge is Senior Lecturer in French and Linguistics at the University of Surrey. She is co-author of *Reference Grammar of French* and is currently working on the impact of legislation on the development of the French language.

Jacqueline Kaye is Senior Lecturer in Literature at the University of Essex. She is co-author of *The Ambiguous Compromise: Language, Literature and National Identity in Algeria and Morocco* (1990) and editor of *Maghreb: New Writing from North Africa* (1992).

Andrew Manley covers francophone Africa for *The Economist* Intelligence Unit. He is currently completing a doctoral thesis on African Islamic history.

Abimne D. Njinjoh is Lecturer in African Literature at the Ecole Normale Supérieure, University of Yaoundé I. He is the author of several poems as well as numerous articles on the West African novel.

Trevor Norris is Lecturer in French at London Guildhall University where he teaches contemporary French literature.

Carys Owen is Lecturer in French at the University of Leeds. She is a specialist in the twentieth-century French novel and has published articles on Céline and Robbe-Grillet.

Sara Poole is Lecturer in French Studies at the University of Reading. She has published on D.H. Lawrence and has recently completed a critical guide to Etcherelli, *Elise ou la vraie vie*.

Acknowledgements

The Editors wish to acknowledge the financial support of the Faculty of Human Sciences and the Department of Language Studies, London Guildhall University, and the British Academy.

We would also like to thank Andrea Barnard, Neil Carruthers, Peter Coates, Andrew Crompton, Rima Dapous, Kathryn Earle, Anna Hitchcott, Deian Hopkin, Roger Middleton, Connie Ostmann, Tony Sayers and Mike Saward.

Introduction

Laïla Ibnlfassi and Nicki Hitchcott

Historical Background

Early Maghrebian literature written in French[1] was defined by critics such as Khatibi as 'ethnographic', providing the reader with a colourful account of everyday life in the French colonies.[2] Such writing followed the style of travel/oriental literature by depicting exotic native locations for the benefit of an essentially French audience. This naïve literature was soon to be replaced by a more critical, powerful and dynamic writing, that of the so-called 1950s generation (Memmi, Chraïbi and Yacine). The writers of this generation, for many, are the forefathers of what is now known as 'francophone Maghrebian literature'.

After the independence of the three countries of the Maghreb (Algeria, Morocco and Tunisia) and the establishment of Arabic as their official language, those who were in favour of the continuation of French supremacy were pessimistic about the future of francophone North African literature. Amongst those was Isaac Yétiv, who predicted that: 'Après avoir fleuri pendant la dernière décade de la colonisation et suscité beaucoup d'éspoir, [la littérature maghrébine] semble aujourd'hui appartenir à l'histoire.'[3] His prediction has proved inaccurate. Over the decades following the independence of the Maghreb and up to the present, the number of writers who write in French has grown considerably.[4]

---

1. E.g. Mouloud Feraoun (1950), *Le Fils du pauvre*, Paris: Seuil, and Ahmed Sefrioui (1954), *La Boîte à merveilles*, Paris: Seuil.
2. Cf. Abdelkebir Khatibi (1968), *Le Roman maghrébin*, Rabat: SMER.
3. Isaac Yétiv (1972), *Le Thème de l'aliénation dans le roman maghrébin d'expression française*, Quebec: Editions Naaman, p.227.
4. E.g. Abdelwahab Meddeb, Tahar Ben Jelloun, Assia Djebar, Mohammed Khaïr-Eddine, Abdellatif Laâbi, Rachid Mimouni, Tahar Djaout.

South of the Sahara, the first black African novel in French is generally acknowledged to be *Batouala* (1921) by René Maran (although Maran was actually from Martinique). Like their North African counterparts, the first examples of sub-Saharan African writings in French were largely descriptive and tended to imitate European literary forms and styles; for example, Paul Hazoumé was strongly criticized for painting too rosy a picture of the colonial experience in his novel, *Doguicini* (1938), as was Camara Laye in the 1950s for his novel *L'Enfant noir* (1954).

The 1950s saw a politicization of the francophone West African text, a development which coincided with the move towards independence (all the French sub-Saharan colonies were independent by the early 1960s). Novelists such as Oyono, Sembène and Beti began to produce anticolonial novels which questioned France's presence in the sub-Saharan colonies and put black African writing in French on the literary map.

Anticolonial Struggle

Both north and south of the Sahara, francophone African literature was born out of the struggle against colonialism.

In 1930s Paris, the development of the American Harlem Renaissance movement inspired a group of young black intellectuals to come together under the literary and political banner of Negritude.[5] Negritude has been described as a literary movement, an aesthetic tool and a political weapon. The emphasis is on the positivization of being black, in other words, the reaffirmation of the humanity of an oppressed and dehumanized people. The first generation of Negritude poets (Senghor, Birago Diop, Alioune Diop and the Martinican, Aimé Césaire) was soon followed by a number of key anticolonial writers,[6] represented in this collection by Mongo Beti, whose postscript serves as a poignant reminder of both the horrors of European colonialism and its contemporary neocolonial mutations.

Maghrebian literature also emerged as an anticolonial literature, namely in Algeria, where novels advocating the national liberation

---

5. The Negritude movement has been well documented by critics of African literature in French. See, for example Dorothy Blair (1976), *African Literature in French*, Cambridge: CUP; Jacques Chevrier (1974), *Littérature Nègre*, Paris: Armand Colin; and Lilyan Kesteloot (1963), *Les Ecrivains noirs de langue française*, Brussels: Editions de l'Université de Bruxelles.
6. E.g. Ferdinand Oyono, Bernard Dadié and Tchicaya U'Tamsi.

movement flourished. In fact, pro-FLN[7] novels played a major role in unifying the Algerian people in their struggle for independence. However, what is noticeable in such literature is the writer's shift of position; from the late 1960s onwards the kind of literature produced expresses the Algerian people's disillusionment with the aftermath of independence and the establishment of the FLN-controlled single-party state.

The Literary Genre

The novel as a genre in francophone literature is more popular than drama and poetry. The latter are well-established genres in both traditional African and Arabic literature. They are historically bound to Arabic literary tradition and to the oral tradition of story-telling which pre-existed Arabic in the Maghreb. South of the Sahara, oral literature is expressed in African tribal languages, although some of the traditional African stories have now been translated into French by writers such as Birago Diop.[8]

Poetry, according to Sartre, was the most suitable genre for the expression of Negritude, as he explains in his famous essay, 'Orphée noir', the preface to Senghor's *Anthologie de la poésie Nègre et malgache* (1948). However, although the first generation of Negritude writers were indeed poets, subsequent generations have tended to opt for the novel as the genre for black African literature in French.

The novel developed alongside the policy of assimilation under French rule in Africa. After the Second World War, North Africa was on the agenda on the international political scene. This coincided with the emergence of the first novels which voiced the anticolonial protest. The novel as a genre was then the perfect medium to portray life in the French colonies in a more realistic way. The novel became the carrier of a message of protest to the Western world, and a means of communication and solidarity between Africans living under colonial rule.

The Language Question

The decision of whether of not to write in French has always been fraught with political problems, and perspectives differ slightly on

---

7. Front de Libération Nationale (National Liberation Front).
8. *Les Contes d'Amadou Koumba*, Paris: Présence Africaine, 1947, is Birago Diop's best-known collection of stories.

either side of the Sahara.

In sub-Saharan Africa, the bilingual (or often multilingual) writer is forced to choose between his or her native African language and the language of the colonizer and oppressor, i.e. French. However, the choice is not as straightforward as this rather schematic description suggests. For the multiplicity of native languages in Africa is such that a decision to write in, for example, Bambara would immediately restrict one's audience to a very small area of the African continent.

The question of literacy is also a contributing factor. Even if a writer such as Senghor had opted to write in Wolof (his mother tongue and the major – and now official – language in Senegal), the high level of illiteracy would have limited the number of readers. It is only in recent years that indigenous governments have established comprehensive literacy programmes so that even contemporary authors are obliged to take this factor into account.

For the North African writer, beside the Berber languages, the situation is further complicated by the distinction between classical and vernacular Arabic. Classical Arabic is only accessible to a literate audience. Dialectal Arabic varies from region to region and, like the native languages of sub-Saharan Africa, is a spoken language which is rarely written down.

For a long time, the French language was almost an inevitable choice. That is not to say that it was an easy one. The ambivalence of the African writer towards French is the subject of a number of important essays[9] and opinions are often divided. However, a common thread appears in the increasing attempts to undermine the very fabric of the language, through, for example: the fragmentation of syntax; neologisms; the literal translation of African and Arabic idioms into French; or the proliferation of violent and obscene vocabulary.[10]

More recently, African writers have been moving towards a reappropriation of the vernacular as a medium for artistic expression. There is, however, an important difference in that these authors tend to opt for a genre other than the traditional novel. One of Senegal's best-known writers and film-makers, Ousmane Sembène, has produced filmic texts[11] in his native Wolof as well as French.

---

9. E.g. Albert Memmi (1957), *Portrait du colonisé*, Paris: Seuil; Léopold Sédar Senghor's essays in *Liberté I, II, III, IV* (1964–83); and Abdelkebir Khatibi (1983), *Maghreb pluriel*, Rabat: SMER.
10. For example, in works by writers such as Rachid Boudjedra, Driss Chraïbi, Sony Labou Tansi and Werewere Liking.
11. E.g. *Ceddo* (1976).

In the Maghreb, for different reasons, some writers have turned to writing in their dialectal Arabic. Kateb Yacine, one of the pioneers of francophone writing, and whose novel *Nedjma* is a canonical text in Maghrebian literature, was reluctant to accept the institutionalization of *francophonie* in the 1980s, which he considered to be cultural imperialism.[12] To the dismay of his readers and contemporaries, who nevertheless expressed their respect for his decision, Kateb Yacine no longer wrote in French. Instead, he turned to writing plays in Algerian Arabic.[13] Such a shift in genre and language was Yacine's attempt to reach the illiterate masses.[14] Likewise, Assia Djebar, while still producing novels in French, also writes film scripts in her vernacular language (in 1975 she won the Venice Biennial prize for her film *Les Femmes du Mont Chenoua*), in which she directly addresses women, amongst whom the rate of illiteracy is even higher.

It is therefore in the visual arts that African and Arabic languages are beginning to play an important role. There are not yet any examples in francophone Africa of novelists who have followed the path of Kenyan writer Ngugi Wa Thiongo, who wrote *Caitaani Mutharabaini* (1980) in his native language, Kikuyu.[15]

Publishing

The economic climate in most African countries makes *in situ* publishing difficult, if not sometimes impossible.

For the first generation of writers in both North and sub-Saharan Africa, there was no alternative but to publish in France, as local publishing houses did not exist. Indeed, some French publishers such as Le Seuil and L'Harmattan have played an important role in the promotion and distribution of African literature in French.[16]

---

12. See Judge's account of Algeria's policy of non-involvement in *francophonie* in Chapter 1.
13. For a useful study of African drama in French, see John Conteh-Morgan (1994), *Theatre and Drama in Francophone Africa*, Cambridge: CUP.
14. Ironically, most of Kateb's work in Arabic was censored by the State and none of his plays have appeared on national television.
15. The title means 'Devil on the Cross'.
16. Although it should of course be stressed that French publishers are market-led and are therefore not always totally receptive to texts by African authors.

More recently, African publishers have established themselves, some with sizeable lists and representatives in more than one country.[17] However, most indigenous publishers are partly (or more often completely) financed by the State, which can make freedom of expression very difficult indeed. Mongo Beti's 32-year exile from Cameroon is a case in point.

Freedom of expression, State censorship and self-censorship help to explain the number of writers living and publishing in European French-speaking countries and mainly in France. In the countries of the Maghreb, most of the major publishing houses are State-controlled.[18] Consequently, most writers are forced to live in exile, where they do not risk being silenced for upholding freedom of speech. However, those who choose to stay in their countries, especially Algeria, risk imprisonment or face the permanent threat posed by anti-intellectual fundamentalists. The latter is what has become known as 'censorship by the bullet', whereby those who challenge the ideology of Muslim fundamentalism do so by risking their own life (such was the fate of a number of Algerian intellectuals and writers, among them the writer Tahar Djaout, who was assassinated in 1993).

Women's Writing

In 1977, the Senegalese sociologist Awa Thiam published a ground-breaking study, *La Parole aux Négresses*, in which for the first time African women were given the chance to speak about such taboo subjects as genital mutilation and polygamy. The publication of this book coincided with the emergence of francophone literary texts by black African women.[19]

African women came to writing much later than men for a number of social and cultural reasons. Historically, only boys were educated, whether at traditional Koranic schools or in the French school system implanted under colonial rule. Gradually, women's education became

---

17. E.g. Les Nouvelles Editions Africaines, which has offices in Dakar, Abidjan and Lomé.
18. E.g. SNED in Algeria and Dar-el-Kitab in Morocco.
19. E.g. Mariama Bâ (1979), *Une si longue lettre*, Dakar: Les Nouvelles Editions Africaines; Nafissatou Diallo (1975), *De Tilène au plateau*, Dakar: Les Nouvelles Editions Africaines; Aminata Sow Fall (1975), *Le Revenant*, Dakar: Les Nouvelles Editions Africaines, and (1979) *La Grève des bàttu*, Dakar: Les Nouvelles Editions Africaines.

an issue and girls were encouraged to attend school. However, these girls were very much in the minority and were generally from wealthy families.

Although women's writing in North Africa has not been (and is still not) given the prominence it deserves, women began publishing as early as 1947 (the year that saw the publication of Djamila Debèche's *Leila, jeune fille d'Algérie* and Marguerite Taos Amrouche's *Jacinthe noire*). Early francophone women's literature tends to be *récits* or *témoignages* which are straightforward accounts of life experiences. The writers of this type of novel often share the same sociopolitical concerns, generally lapse into silence after their first publication and therefore never attain their full capacities as writers.

Because of State censorship and social, religious and familial constraints, women's writing is impregnated with silences, omissions and gaps. However, today's women writers (especially with the rise of fundamentalism, of which they are the prime victims) are more eager to voice themselves and be heard. Such is the case of Fatima Mernissi, whose non-fiction writing advocates women's rights in Muslim societies,[20] and Assia Djebar's novels, which are aimed at depicting the multiplicity of women's voices in writing.

Women writers are generally concerned with women's issues. Unlike such contemporary male authors as Sony Labou Tansi and Abdelkebir Khatibi, African women tend not to focus on the political implications of the use of French as a means of expression. The French language is still viewed as a tool which will give these women a voice. Only very recently have the texts of such writers as Werewere Liking and Assia Djebar begun to subvert what Djebar describes as 'the stepmother tongue' of Africa.[21]

The aims of this collection are twofold. Firstly, for the new reader of African francophone writing, the book will provide an introduction to an exciting new literature which is increasingly taught and researched in British and American universities. The panoramic essays do not confine themselves to the field of early writings from the 1950s. These have already been discussed at some length in critical introductions to francophone literature in Africa.[22] Indeed, the focus

20. Mernissi (1987), *Le Harem politique*, Paris: Albin Michel, was censored because it suggests that women can be leaders in Islam.
21. In Assia Djebar (1985), *L'Amour, la fantasia*, Paris: Editions J.-C. Lattès.
22. See the studies of African literature in French by, for example, Dorothy Blair and Jacques Chevrier (sub-Saharan Africa); Jacqueline Arnaud and Jean Déjeux (North Africa).

of Borgomano's chapter on linguistic and cultural heterogeneity (Chapter 9) is on new writings from sub-Saharan Africa in the last twenty years. Likewise, Abu-Haidar (Chapter 5) considers a new literature from the Maghreb – literature by women – and maps the rise of feminist writing in North Africa, a subject which is rarely, if ever, given the critical attention it deserves. Hargreaves's essay (Chapter 2) on so-called Beur literature discusses the new generation of writers from North African immigrant families and highlights the movement forward of francophone African literature, a direction we wish to emphasize in this collection.

The texts discussed in this collection are defined not just geographically, but also within the cultural context of *francophonie*. In situating the literature and providing the student and the scholar with details of precisely the kind of cultural framework which many of the writers are challenging in their writings, Anne Judge's essay (Chapter 1) explains the way in which France has tried to maintain links with her former colonies. The traditional African historical context is also considered in Andrew Manley's essay (Chapter 13) on Amadou Hampaté Bâ.

The second aim of the collection is to suggest a number of new approaches to the study of African literature in French. Different chapters demonstrate the use of such theoretical apparatuses as: feminist theory (Hitchcott, Chapter 10); psychoanalysis (Ibnlfassi, Chapter 4); Orientalism (Owen, Chapter 3); theories of autobiography (Hand, Chapter 7); and Marxist theory (Hawkins, Chapter 12). In discussing the 'canonical authors' of francophone Africa (Bâ, Chraïbi, Boudjedra, Memmi and Sembène), each of these chapters provides both an introduction and a refreshing new approach to a developing field of critical enquiry. These new perspectives are intended both to stimulate the new reader and to inspire further scholarship in an ever-expanding field.

Although the dominant genre in francophone writing is that of the novel, a chapter on Maghrebian poetry (Kaye, Chapter 8) has also been included to demonstrate the diversity of this literature and to provide points of comparison with the novels we discuss.

Finally, we have included discussions of works by writers who, although widely read in their native countries, have been less often the focus of critical enquiry in Europe and America. Malek Haddad, Francis Bebey and Amadou Hampaté Bâ are all major figures in the African literary world. Chapters 6, 11 and 13 by Poole, Njinjoh and Manley redress the critical imbalance by examining the writer in question from an Afrocentric rather than a Eurocentric point of view.

African Francophone Writing offers new perspectives on African literature. Recognizing the need to break the mould of Eurocentric 'images of Africa'-style criticism and deliberately moving away from well-worn discussions of the colonial experience and the Algerian war, the emphasis here is on implicit rather than explicit meaning. The collection is inspired by the innovation of francophone literature from Africa and this is reflected in its engagement with current literary debates both in Africa and in Europe.

This is the first work of its kind to consider francophone African literature from both sides of the Sahara. Francophone Africa is fascinating because of the differences emerging from two corners of a shared continent which have experienced similar colonial histories, albeit in slightly different forms.[23] It is hoped that the essays in *African Francophone Writing* will highlight the similarities in literary expression from North and sub-Saharan Africa, but also that they will illustrate the wealth and diversity of these writings issued from a common historical experience and expressed in a common language – French.

23. We are referring to the distinction between colonies and protectorates.

– 1 –

The Institutional Framework of *la Francophonie*

Anne Judge

To understand the role and importance of North and West African francophone literature it is necessary to examine it in the context of *la francophonie*, which is usually translated rather inadequately as 'the French-speaking world', inadequately because the English term is too vague and has none of the connotations of the French term.

Traditionally the rarely used term *francophonie* referred to the countries or regions in the world where, for historical reasons usually associated with colonialism, French was spoken. Nowadays *la francophonie* also refers to a set of countries or regions which have agreed to become part of an official francophone community. In some cases it is the near totality of the population of the member state which is francophone, but in other cases it may be no more than a tiny percentage (e.g. 0.5 per cent in Egypt). In other words the degree to which a state belonging to *la francophonie* is francophone varies considerably from country to country. There are also some francophone countries which are absent from this community, having refused to join, such as Algeria.

Nowadays *la francophonie* also has a geographical dimension. This is illustrated by the fact that at the end of each issue of *L'Année francophone internationale*, the official publication on the subject, there is a set of tables entitled 'Géographie de la francophonie'. These list the states or regions where French is spoken, their size, their capital city, the size of their population and its life expectancy (but not the proportion of francophone speakers), their GNP and their main exports.

The new *francophonie* is associated with the emancipation of the countries which set it up. This is because over the last thirty years – particularly in Africa – eminent francophones have claimed that the use of French in the countries concerned has created links between them which go beyond the end of colonialism. Thus in 1962 the most eminent of them all, Senghor, spoke of 'le merveilleux outil trouvé dans les décombres du régime colonial: la langue française'.[1] They have pointed to a rich and interesting francophone literature which reflects both their diversity and a common cultural heritage as embodied by the French language. For them *la francophonie* refers to a postcolonial community. This was clearly stated again recently by the president of the Conseil permanent de la Francophonie: 'La Francophonie est un espace de dialogue et de coopération basé sur une communauté de valeurs et une communauté de langage. Assurer l'unité de cet ensemble diversifié est un défi porteur d'avenir.'[2]

The second statement, made some thirty years after the first, demonstrates a belief in the existence of a genuine community of ideas and ideals as symbolized and expressed by the French language. It is this belief which led members of the francophone intelligentsia to campaign for this to be recognized at an international level through the creation of francophone institutions, grouping them for cultural, economic and – more recently – political purposes. At first France refused to cooperate for fear of being accused of colonialism, but this is no longer the case since Mitterrand came to power.

The future of francophone literature is clearly dependent on the success of the francophone movement, and it is difficult to predict whether this has a long-term future or not (the case of Algeria leads to pessimism but the goodwill and enthusiasm of the participating member states are positively infectious). It is possible, however, to analyze the characteristics and the strengths of the institutions which have been established and which are essential to the survival of a Francophone Community as it is understood at present. To do so it is necessary to consider briefly the traditional linguistic policies of France, their extension to the colonial empire and their impact on the francophone entity which emerged in the 1960s, and which has, in the 1980s and 1990s, developed into a powerful movement with its own institutional framework and a continuously evolving network of international institutions.

The relatively new and significant role played by France is examined, as is the problem of assessing whether for France these institutions are an unconscious form of neocolonialism or a new

1. In *Esprit*, 1962, quoted in 'Francophonie et Francité', a paper given by M. Piron to the Académie royale de langue et de littérature françaises de Bruxelles on 21 October 1970.
2. Leaflet published by the Conseil permanent de la Francophonie for the Mauritius Summit.

'vision' of the world. The future of francophone literature in North and West Africa may depend on the answer to this question.

Traditional French Linguistic Policies, Their Extension to Her Colonial Empire and Their Legacy Today

French in France

In France, French has gone through various stages: it became the king's language in the tenth century and became a famous literary language between the twelfth and fifteenth centuries, by which time it was also a lingua franca for the whole Mediterranean area. It became the administrative language of France in the sixteenth century and the language of the European élite in the eighteenth century, a position that was maintained in Russia until the Revolution and in Poland until the outbreak of the Second World War. French was not in those days the language of the people but of the intelligentsia, a language polished by writers and various intellectuals in the context of salons and academies. It was only during the last seventy years or so that French may really be said to have become the language of the people. Its aristocratic antecedents are at the root of both its present strengths and its weaknesses.

The most famous date in the history of the French language is probably 1539, when the Edict of Villers-Cotterêts made it the official administrative and legal language in France. A second significant date is 1635 with the founding of the French Academy. This marked the beginning of the systematic standardization of French and its development into a 'classical language'. The third important date is 1790, when the Abbé Grégoire organized the first ever full linguistic questionnaire. This questionnaire revealed that numerous languages and dialects were spoken in France, and the revolutionaries decided that they should be suppressed in the name of equality of opportunity. This began a movement to establish state schools primarily for the teaching of French. These only became a reality in the 1880s, when Jules Ferry created state primary schools with compulsory attendance. Another important factor in spreading the use of French in France was the First World War, with the army acting as a melting-pot. By the end of the war most people spoke French, although many were bilingual, and by the end of the Second World War most people only spoke French.

The most important recent date is 23 June 1992, when, for the first time, French was stated as the official language of France in its constitution. This statement is included in its second article: 'La langue de la République est le français.' This means that all communications between the citizens of France and the State have to be in French, whatever the context and in all forms of civil life. This constitutional change was brought in to protect French from English in the context of the European Union, but it could have major consequences in terms of the regional languages and other languages transported to France by immigrants. In other words French linguistic policy in France corresponds to a long march towards monolingualism.

French Abroad

The implantation of French abroad is tied up with the development of the colonial empire, which corresponds to two quite different phases of expansionism. The first (sometimes called the first colonial empire) happened in the seventeenth and eighteenth centuries in North America (mainly Canada and Louisiana), in the West Indies and in various trading posts in India. French people went and settled in these areas, which offered new opportunities and an escape from political problems at home. The move was therefore mainly from east to west, but it included also the transfer of African slaves. In these regions French was the natural language of the settlers and those joining the community later had to learn it, unless they outnumbered the French speakers *in situ* (as was the case in areas of Canada other than Quebec and in Louisiana). Not surprisingly, in these areas, French is the normal mother tongue. In modern-day terms, French is classified either as the only official language, as in the West Indies and in Quebec (this is disputed from a constitutional point of view), or it is a co-official language, as in the rest of Canada, where the State recognizes two languages in all official contexts.

The second phase (or second colonial empire) took place in the nineteenth and twentieth centuries in the Maghreb, Africa and the Far East. This time the movement was mainly from north to south, but it did not lead to so many people leaving France. The aim of French governments was to impose the French language for the good of France and for the good of the people concerned. Their motives were basically those which pushed the revolutionaries of 1792 to reject regional languages in the name of equality of opportunity. Indeed, Onésime Reclus, a geographer of the late nineteenth century, who is the first known to have used the term *francophonie* in a book on Algeria, stated that the Arabs and Berbers would become francophone in the same way as the Bretons and the Basques. Despite this assertion, today, the populations in these areas – with the exception of the

Maghreb – are bilingual or multilingual, French being very often the language of education, social contracts and foreign diplomacy, but not the language spoken in the home. French has therefore the status of a privileged foreign language, in which case it is sometimes labelled 'langue administrative' or 'langue supplétive'.

For a list of francophone countries (or regions) and the status occupied by French in these areas see Table 1.1.

There is therefore a parallel to be drawn between the development of French in France and in the colonial empire: in both cases French was first used as a tool for domination, and then as a way of ensuring equality of opportunity by offering these countries an opening into the Western world. Although such a point of view is no longer explicitly acceptable today, there is none the less in France a tendency to unconsciously confuse the concepts of French as a tool for nationalistic expansion and as the expression of an 'advanced' civilization. It is precisely because of this confusion of aims that some countries like Algeria have refused to participate in *la francophonie* – discouraging French in favour of English – while others have joined mainly for the practical advantages they can reap in the short term. But these are exceptions. Nowadays francophones from countries other than France are trying to develop a new role for French, centred on the concept of solidarity embodied by a number of international institutions. This new role and the institutions upon which it is dependent are examined below.

La Francophonie: a New Ideal

Connotations of 'Francophone'

The word 'francophone' has different connotations nowadays from when it was first used by Onésime Reclus, for whom it was no more than a word describing people who spoke French outside France and areas of the world apart from France where French was spoken. The connotations implicit in the term since it was 'recoined' by Senghor in an article published in 1962 in a special number of *Esprit* on 'Le français dans le monde' are new. The term itself refers to what was later defined as 'les pays ayant en commun l'usage du français', an expression which does not imply francocentrism but the regrouping of countries having something – the French language - in common, which is no longer seen as the property of France alone but as a common vehicle of ideas and ideals. This concept has been expressed even more clearly since then: since the Mauritius Summit of 1993,

Table 1.1: List of Countries and Regions in which French has a Special Status

	Countries in which French is the official language	Regions in which French is the official language	Countries in which French is co-official	Regions in which French is co-official	Countries in which French is co-official in certain areas only	Regions in which French is co-official in certain areas only	Countries in which French is the administrative language
Africa 27 countries and regions	Benin Burkina Faso Congo Ivory Coast Gabon Guinea Mali Niger Central African Republic Senegal Togo Zaïre	Mayotte Reunion	Burundi Cameroon Comoro Islands Djibouti Rwanda Seychelles Chad		Mauritius		Madagascar Morocco Mauritania Tunisia
Europe 6 countries and regions	France Monaco		Belgium Luxemburg Switzerland	Val d'Aoste			

	Countries in which French is the official language	Regions in which French is the official language	Countries in which French is co-official	Regions in which French is co-official	Countries in which French is co-official in certain areas only	Regions in which French is co-official in certain areas only	Countries in which French is the administrative language
America 11 countries and regions	Haiti	Guadeloupe Guyana Martinique Quebec St Pierre and Miquelon	Canada	New Brunswick North-West Territories Yukon		Manitoba	
Oceania 4 countries and regions		New Caledonia French Polynesia Wallis and Futuna	Vanuatu				

the term refers to 'les pays ayant le français en partage'. Sharing the same language and the values and ideals conveyed by this language, as well as sharing similar problems in the aftermath of decolonization and emancipation, leads to the logical conclusion that such countries should feel solidarity for one another and should cooperate.

The reason this word with its new connotations established itself so successfully in the 1960s (until then its use was very rare) is because the whole concept was very much of the time: the same publication included other articles expressing similar points of view to those of Senghor, in particular those expressed by Norodom Sihanouk of Cambodia and Jean-Marc Léger of Quebec, who later became the General-Secretary of the ACCT (defined below). Following this, Habib Bourguiba of Tunisia, Diori Hamani of Niger, Charles Hélou of Lebanon and many other political figures joined together to promote the idea of establishing internationally recognized institutions grouping all countries having French as a common language.

There were various but connected reasons for such a general movement. Senghor, who has claimed many times that 'l'avenir est au métissage' (meaning 'the future is to cross-cultural breeding') and who himself represents the perfect symbiosis of French and African culture, saw the possibility of using French to create 'une communauté exemplaire' among those from different cultures who spoke it. Similarly, Hélou of Lebanon saw the use of a common language as a means to common aspirations; Bourguiba considered French to be 'le véhicule de la modernité'; Quebec saw the newly emerging international francophone community as offering an opportunity to develop at an international level; some countries, such as Egypt, Cambodia and Vietnam, saw it as a neutral international language ('la langue du non-alignement'); others claimed to be the co-owners ('co-propriétaires') of French. A number of countries also joined for purely practical reasons: they saw it as the only way of dealing with multilingualism in their own country and the need to speak an international language to communicate with other nations.

Originally the countries involved were situated in Africa, America, the Middle East and Asia. Gradually, however, European countries, such as Belgium, Switzerland and Luxemburg, became interested in establishing cultural links. This general desire for links led in the first instance to the creation of a large number of francophone associated bodies: the Association des universités partiellement ou entièrement d'expression française (AUPELF) in 1961 (predating the issue of *Esprit* referred to above); the Groupe des délégations d'expression française à l'Organisation des Nations Unies in 1966; the Association internationale des parlementaires de langue française (AIPLF) in 1967 (from October 1993 the Assemblée des parlementaires de langue française); the Conseil de la langue française (CILF) in 1967, responsible for the standardization of French at an international level; the Fédération internationale des professeurs de français (FIPF) in 1969; and the Association internationale des maires francophones (AIMF) in 1979. In recent years there has been a remarkable increase in the number of associations created for francophone members of the same profession (dentists, doctors, specialists, nurses, etc.).

Development of the Francophone Ideal

The history of the development of the francophone ideal in institutional and political terms came about as follows. In 1962, Senghor proposed to his partners in the Union Africaine et Malgache (or UAM) to promote the idea of a Francophone Community. The UAM was dissolved in 1964 but reconstituted as the Organisation Commune Africaine et Malgache (OCAM), which became the starting-point for the development of the whole project as conceived by Senghor, Bourguiba and Diori. The original project of the OCAM was extremely complex since it distinguished between four kinds of states. Group 1 comprised those states with French as their only language (e.g. France, Haiti); group 2 comprised those for whom French was one of two or more official languages (e.g. Switzerland, Canada, Belgium, Luxemburg); group 3 comprised those states for whom French was their official language (the member states of the OCAM); and group 4 those countries using French as a 'langue d'usage' mainly in educational and cultural contexts, without it being the official language of the land (Lebanon, the Maghreb). 'Francophonia A' comprised states in groups 1 and 3 in order to cooperate in cultural, educational and economic fields; 'Francophonia B' comprised states in groups 1, 3 and 4 for cultural and, to a lesser extent economic, matters; 'Francophonia C' included all states for cultural pursuits. In June 1966 the conference of the OCAM held in Madagascar gave its support to the project and delegated to Senghor and Diori the task of making contact with all francophone countries in order to initiate the process.

It is at this stage that efforts were made to include France in the project; it was presented to de Gaulle in September 1966, but he showed a distinct lack of enthusiasm, probably for fear of being accused of colonialism. Jean de Broglie, on the other hand, the Minister for Foreign Affairs, expressed 'interêt et sympathie' for this project and founded the Association de Solidarité francophone in

1967. But this was no more than a private organization and the ambassadors of the project expressed their disappointment at the lack of official support. The project did, however, get some governmental support, but in a different way. Already the Haut Comité pour la Défense et l'Expansion de la langue française, created in 1966, included a Commission de la coopération culturelle et technique involving all countries with French as a common language. The Prime Minister, Pompidou, expressed his approbation of the project and, finally, de Gaulle joined in with his famous 'Vive le Québec libre' in 1967 in the course of his official visit to Quebec. This, according to many, put the idea of a francophone entity on the world agenda.

The efforts of Presidents Senghor and Diori led to the first conference of francophone states at Niamey, in Niger, in February 1969, at which a resolution was adopted expressing a common desire to see the creation of an agency for francophone cooperation, the Agence de Coopération Culturelle et Technique, or ACCT, which was established in 1970 at the second conference of francophone states with the motto: 'Egalité, Complémentarité, et Solidarité.' It was based on the principle of a general fund to which countries would contribute according to their means: 'Ça vient de tous les côtés. Ça va de tous les côtés. De tous pour un à tous pour tous.'[3] Twenty-one countries joined, the most obvious absentees being Algeria, Guinea and Switzerland. Some countries expressed disappointment in the new structure, however, because the principle of groups of countries with different points in common had been replaced by the principle that all states had the same interests. Subsequently, it was noted in 1973 at the third conference that the monolithic nature of the ACCT had precluded it from being able to address the differing needs of the countries concerned. Moreover, the then President of France, Giscard d'Estaing, showed little enthusiasm for the project. He declared somewhat paradoxically that: 'La langue française est le bien commun de tous ceux qui la parlent et nous avions tort d'enfermer sa défense et illustration dans les limites de la France.' This declaration is interesting in that it reveals a new attitude in relation to the French language which is no longer seen as the sole property of the French, but at the same time he uses terms such as 'défense et illustration' which go back to Villers-Cotterêts and typify a traditional approach to the sanctity of the French language and the need to protect it. Such confusion of attitudes is still endemic in France today.

Thus the first important institution, the ACCT, was in place but in an imperfect state and without being received with general

3. In *La Lettre de la Francophonie*, 20 March 1992, published by the ACCT.

enthusiasm; however, it gradually saw its importance increase. In 1978 it was granted the status of observer at the United Nations and in 1991, at the Chaillot Summit (see below for the creation of Summit meetings), it became the only official international organization to represent the Francophone Community. A new educational establishment dependent on the ACCT, the Ecole internationale de Bordeaux, was created in 1990, and organized in that year alone 50 seminars for the improved training of some 800 managers and technicians, mainly in those sectors given priority at the Summit meetings. The ACCT also opened an office in Geneva acting as a secretariat and an information bureau for francophone countries without a permanent delegation at the United Nations.

As a result, by 1991 more than 50 per cent of projects planned by the ACCT were realized, mainly in the fields of education, culture, the media, energy, environment and agriculture.

Matters improved for the ACCT and for the Francophone Community in general in the 1980s. This was partly due to the election in 1981 of Mitterrand as President of the French Republic, which signalled a change in France's attitude towards *la francophonie*. Mitterrand announced that it was his intention to deal personally with the development of institutions relating to the Francophone Community, declaring himself to be passionately interested in the topic. His first act was the creation in 1984 of the Haut conseil de la francophonie, presided over by the head of the French state and with a foreign vice-president (Senghor since its foundation). This council represented a new departure as regards French institutions, since it is an official French body composed mainly of foreign members. It is financed by the French Ministry for Foreign Affairs and its aim is 'de préciser le rôle de la francophonie et de la langue française dans le monde externe. Il rassemble les données et confronte les expériences, notamment dans le domaine de l'enseignement, de la communication, de la science et des techniques nouvelles.' Each year a theme is discussed in a plenary session; these have included so far 'La Francophonie et l'opinion publique' in 1986, 'L'Espace économique francophone' in 1988, 'La Pluralité des langues en francophonie' in 1989 and 'La Francophonie dans la communauté scientifique mondiale: la responsabilité partagée des politiques et des scientifiques' in 1992, a subject of particular importance to the French at the moment.

The Haut conseil de la francophonie is in constant communication with two other new French linguistic bodies. The first is the Conseil supérieur de la langue française, responsible for the development of the French language, particularly in terminological matters (each ministry in France has its own terminological commission and since

June 1990 representatives of various francophone countries have sat on these commissions and reported back to their country on the decisions taken, to ensure the standardization of vocabulary). The second is the Délégation générale à la langue française, which is responsible for the application of the decisions taken by the Conseil, and in particular for the harmonization of their application abroad. In other words, in France, there has been an important move towards consideration of the *dimension francophone* and the establishment of a far more aggressive political agenda on linguistic policies. One of the most publicized of these has been the passing of the *loi Toubon*, which aims at protecting French in France and which, at least partly, owes its origins to a movement started in Quebec demanding that France should do more to protect the French language. This illustrates the fact that the Francophone Community can now exert pressure on France.

Mitterrand also initiated in 1986 the principle of the Summits of Heads of State, which take place every two years. Since the first Summit merely established the ground rules, it was followed by the second Summit the following year in Quebec, which was devoted to assessing the needs and interests of the participating states; the third in Dakar in 1989 examined a specific sector, education, setting the goal of a book for every schoolchild by the year 2000. The fourth Summit held in Chaillot in 1991 led to the strengthening of the ACCT. The fifth took place in Mauritius, named the 'rainbow island', because it symbolized racial harmony.

On the same model, there are Summits of specific ministers, such as the Ministers of Foreign Affairs, the Ministers of Education and the ministers dealing with the media, which have led to the setting up of francophone programmes (TV5 Europe in 1979, TV5 Quebec-Canada in 1988, TV5 Africa in 1991 and TV5 Latin America in 1992).

The most recent creation was the Conseil Permanent de la Francophonie in 1992 as a result of the Fourth Francophone Summit of Heads of State, which is concerned with the implementation of decisions taken at the Summit meetings. According to its president, Shrin Aumeeruddy Cziffran, 'Le Conseil Permanent incarne et exprime la volonté de nos Chefs d'Etats et de Gouvernement de faire de la communauté francophone un ensemble géopolitique de coopération dans des projets multilatéraux concrets qui répondent aux besoins des populations: la Francophonie, c'est la mise en commun des ressources de chacun au profit de l'ensemble.'[4] It now includes two committees, a Comité de quinze, which prepares and organizes the Summits of Heads of State, and a Comité de onze, also called Comité

4. Leaflet published by the Conseil permanent de la Francophonie.

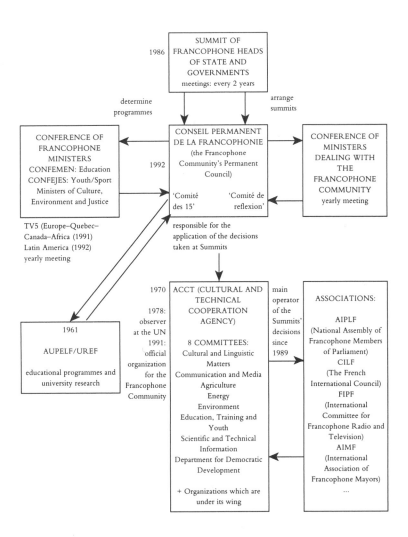

Figure 1.1: Main Organizations Defining the Francophone Community (in view of the constantly evolving situation, this chart is provisional)

de réflexion (basically a think-tank). The members of these committees are chosen at the Summits of Ministers for Francophone Affairs (there is some confusion here in the context of France, since three French ministers attend these conferences: the *Ministre de la Culture et de la Francophonie*, the *Ministre de la Coopération* and the *Ministre des Affaires Etrangères*).

See Figure 1.1 for a diagram of the main organizations defining the Francophone Community politically and institutionally.

If belonging to the Francophone Community is defined as belonging to the ACCT or the Summits of Heads of State (see below), there are now 47 participating countries. A recent development has been the participation of countries from Eastern Europe, with Romania and Bulgaria among the 47 participating states (see Table 1.2). The obvious absentee is Algeria, with over 6 million French speakers. Algeria, according to a statement by President Boumediene in 1979, sees the francophone world as no more than political colonialism transformed into economic colonialism.

Table 1.2 gives the names of the countries or regions which have attended the various Summits and belong to the new 'Conseil permanent de la francophonie' and to the ACCT.

The Ambiguous Role of France

It may be seen from the previous sections that the position of France has shifted in terms of her attitude towards the setting up of a formal Francophone Community. French people, on the other hand, usually feel less committed to the idea than most politicians, who sometimes see the Francophone Community as a counterbalance to the European Community. Thus Senator Deniau, in the context of a discussion on an amendment to the constitution to replace the article on the defunct *Communauté* (set up by de Gaulle) by an article on the Francophone Community, declared: 'Il m'a paru en effet anormal, alors que nous visons, par l'examen de ce texte, à établir une solidarité européenne plus précise et plus complète, de ne pas rappeler qu'il existe un autre système de solidarité très actif, dans lequel la France joue un rôle majeur, celui de la francophonie.'[5] The proposed new article to be added to the constitution when French was added as the official language of France, in 1992, was to read: 'La France participe à la construction d'un espace de solidarité et de coopération.' That the

5. *Journal Officiel, Débats, Assemblée nationale*, 12 May 1992, p.1059.

Table 1.2: Main Organizations Defining the Francophone Community Politically and Institutionally

	1986 Paris	1987 Quebec	1989 Dakar	1991 Paris	1993 Mauritius	CPF[a] 1994	ACCT[b] status
Belgium	X	X	X	X	X	X +	MS
Fr. Comm. of Belgium		X	X	X	X	X	MS
Benin	X	X	X	X	X		MS
Bulgaria				X (OBS)	X (OBS)		OBS
Burkina Faso	X	X	X	X	X	+	MS
Burundi	X	X	X	X	X	X	MS
Cambodia				X (OBS)	X (OBS)		OBS
Cameroon				X	X	X +	MS
Canada	X	X	X	X	X	X +	PG
Canada Quebec	X	X	X	X	X	X +	PG
New Brunswick	X	X	X	X	X		PG
Cape Verde Islands				X (OBS)	X		MS
Central African Republic	X	X	X	X	X		MS
Chad	X	X	X	X	X		MS
Comoro Islands	X	X	X	X	X		MS
Congo	X	X	X	X	X		MS
Ivory Coast	X	X	X	X	X	X	MS
Djibouti	X	X	X	X	X		MS
Dominican Republic	X	X	X		X		MS
Egypt	X	X	X	X	X	X	ASS

	1986 Paris	1987 Quebec	1989 Dakar	1991 Paris	1993 Mauritius	CPF[a] 1994	ACCT[b] status
France	X	X	X	X	X	X +	MS
Gabon	X	X	X	X	X	+	MS
Guinea	X	X	X	X	X		MS
Guinea-Bissau	X	X	X	X	X (ASS)		ASS
Equatorial Guinea				X (OBS)	X		MS
Haiti	X	X	X	X	X		MS
Laos	X (OBS)	X (OBS)	X (OBS)	X	X	X	MS
Lebanon	X	X	X	X	X	X	MS
Luxemburg	X	X	X	X	X		MS
Madagascar	X	X	X	X	X		MS
Mali	X	X	X	X	X	X	MS
Morocco	X	X	X	X	X (ASS)	+	ASS
Mauritania	X	X	X	X	X (ASS)		MS
Mauritius	X	X	X	X	X	X +	ASS
Monaco	X	X	X	X	X		MS
Niger	X	X	X	X	X		MS
Romania				X (OBS)	X (OBS)	+	OBS
Rwanda	X	X	X	X	X	X	MS
Saint Lucia	X	X	X		X		ASS
Senegal	X	X	X	X	X	X +	MS
Seychelles	X	X	X	X	X		MS
Switzerland	X (OBS)	X (OBS)	X (OBS)	X	X		
Togo	X	X	X	X	X		MS

	1986 Paris	1987 Quebec	1989 Dakar	1991 Paris	1993 Mauritius	CPF[a] 1994	ACCT[b] status
Tunisia	X	X	X	X	X		MS
Vanuatu	X		X	X	X		MS
Vietnam	X (OBS)	X (OBS)	X (OBS)	X	X	+	MS
Zaïre	X	X	X	X	X		MS

a. X, Comité des 15
   +, Comité de réflexion or think-tank
b. MS, member state
   ASS, associate state
   PG, provincial government
   OBS, state present as an observer

NB: Associate states have the same duties as member states, but their legal bonds are more restrictive.

amendment was defeated shows either a lack of commitment to the Francophone Community, a lack of belief in its survival, or, more positively, a feeling that France should not interfere too much in these matters but leave the initiative to the francophone nations.

Similarly the *projet de loi Tasca*, proposed by the previous government but replaced by the *loi Toubon*, stated:

> La France assume d'importantes responsabilités internationales. Un quart des pays membres des Nations-Unies appartiennent à la Communauté francophone. Ces pays placent dans la langue française une part de leur présent et de leur avenir. Certains d'entre eux ont adopté des dispositions strictes afin de défendre l'usage du français. La France doit, au premier rang, conduire la promotion de la langue française et assurer son rayonnement.[6]

Such a statement is absent from the *loi Toubon*, perhaps because of the unfortunate wording of the last sentence, which seems to have definite neocolonial tones. This wording is all the more surprising as the new mood in France is to push plurilingualism in Europe as a means of fighting the perceived influence of English, and moreover plurilingualism is fundamental to the Francophone Community. Indeed, the secretary-general of the Haut conseil, Stelio Farandjis, has often stated his preference for the term 'polyphony' or even 'francopolyphony' to the term *francophonie* to avoid all suspicion of expansionism or paternalism. This seems to indicate either a lack of consultation with the Haut conseil when drawing up the new law, or the force of habit in linguistic matters in France.

Absence of formal recognition, both in the constitution and the Toubon law, of the francophone dimension does not mean that it does not exist in practice. On the contrary: there are innumerable links tying France to her francophone partners – cultural and economic in the first instance. Farandjis, for his part, explains the deterioration in the economic situation of the francophone Third World countries by the survival of financial structures which go back to colonial days. His aim is to use the Francophone Community as a pressure group to bring about change in this domain. He favours the setting up of 'co-enterprises' linking North and South in order to channel more money from the North to the South (at present, according to him, more money flows from South to North). This would not be an act of charity on the part of France for it is the success of the whole Community which will ensure the well-being of each individual country, including France.

6. The proposed Tasca bill, section 1 on 'Les fondements de la nouvelle loi'.

There are also political links, in the sense that France is supposed to help some of these countries in their efforts to set up democratic states. Concrete help includes providing them with judicial and administrative documentation, giving them access to data banks, helping to train their magistrates and keeping their members of parliament generally informed on world developments. The result is supposed to be complete emancipation from the structures of the past. But this is an almost impossible task without France appearing to act in a paternalistic fashion. Therein lies the probable reason for France's hesitation to spell out her commitment to the Francophone Community in her constitution. On the other hand, France's call (which was answered) to the Francophone Community to help uphold her demand for her cultural industries to be excluded from the Uruguay round of the GATT negotiations shows that the relationship can work both ways, which is very encouraging.

Conclusion

As far as literature is concerned, being part of the Francophone Community is a way of 'being different together' – or, to quote Lopes, a Congolese writer, 'j'écris en français sans écrire en français'. The whole point is to create a meeting of Western and other cultures. In the words of Senghor: '[la tradition gréco-latine] nous apporte l'esprit de méthode et d'organisation tandis que le Sud, et singulièrement l'Afrique Noire, nous apporte l'esprit d'intuition et de création'.[7] The expression of the Arab and Berber cultures through the medium of French is particularly important in this respect.

Writing in French has the practical advantage of providing the writer with a large potential readership, although it is regrettable that more is not done to encourage publishing firms to help struggling francophone writers. The institutionalization of the Francophone Community also makes it easier to function in French in distant parts of the globe, even when French is not the dominant language, by according it a certain status. It also diminishes the sense of individual artistic isolation by offering membership of a cultural community and creates a wider market for spreading diverse cultural influences. The idealistic motivation of the institutions is unique, and the fact that the movement was initiated outside France has the advantage of placing cultural, economic and political initiative in some of the developing

---

7. *Africa Scope, Rapport mondial sur la francophonie*, 1986, p.12.

areas of the world. From that point of view, it would possibly be best for France to remain peripheral and not to be too interventionist.

From a French point of view, francophone writers could do for French what American literature did for English. As Lopes, put it:

> elle [la langue française] est très belle, il n'y a rien à ajouter à cela, mais c'est une erreur pour nous que de vouloir l'imiter. . . A vouloir trop imiter nous nous ridiculiserions. . . Ce n'est pas parce que nous avons le goût du beau qu'il convient de mettre, par exemple, un fauteuil Louis XVI sous une véranda des tropiques. Il faut mettre le fauteuil qui s'y adapte et on est assis quand même. De la même façon, il ne faut pas exprimer son pays dans la manière qui ne convient pas à ce climat là. . . L'essentiel est de se faire comprendre non seulement par les gens de son pays, mais par tous les autres.[8]

The possibilities for the development and enrichment of French are unlimited in this context.

8. Ibid., p.15.

Part I

North Africa

– 2 –

Writers of Maghrebian Immigrant Origin in France: French, Francophone, Maghrebian or Beur?

Alec G. Hargreaves

Introduction

Authors of Maghrebian immigrant origin in France pose a difficult classificatory problem. They are popularly known as Beurs, and I have used this label myself in earlier analyses,[1] but for reasons which I will explain later in this chapter I have growing doubts about its suitability. Critics, librarians and booksellers are divided and often confused on this matter. Most of the authors with whom I am concerned are to be found on the 'Maghrebian literature' shelves of the L'Harmattan bookstore in Paris. A few blocks away at the FNAC, in contrast, some are classified as 'French literature', while others are in a section marked 'Immigration'. Charles Bonn devotes the final pages of his *Anthologie de la littérature algérienne* to a selection of these writers, but in introducing them he warns the reader that they

> n'ont probablement pas leur place dans une anthologie de la littérature algérienne, car la plupart d'entre eux ne se reconnaissent plus que de très loin dans l'identité culturelle de leurs parents, mais plutôt dans une identité de banlieues des grandes villes européennes où les 'origines' ethniques ou culturelles cèdent souvent la place à une conscience de marginalité qui n'a que peu de points communs avec les définitions identitaires consacrées.[2]

---

1. See, for example, Alec G. Hargreaves (1991), *Voices from the North African Immigrant Community in France: Immigration and Identity in Beur Fiction*, Oxford/New York: Berg.
2. Charles Bonn (1990), *Anthologie de la littérature algérienne*, Paris: Livre de poche, p.227.

Abdelkader Djeghloul locates them in a veritable no man's land:

> Ces textes ne se situent pas dans le prolongement d'une accumulation littéraire antérieure, qu'elle soit à proprement parler française ou maghrébine de langue française. Ils constituent, en quelque sorte, le degré zéro d'une capitalisation hypothétique fait de français scolaire, de bribes langagières arabo-berbères et d'emprunts éclectiques, le tout bricolé dans un effort d'élaboration d'un nouvel imaginaire à même d'intégrer les multiples différences dont ils sont porteurs.[3]

In contrast, Jean Déjeux takes the view that writers of immigrant origin have a legitimate place in the cultural spaces on both sides of the Mediterranean, since they are contributing to 'un processus d'élargissement et d'enrichissement de la littérature maghrébine et de la littérature française'.[4]

At first sight, it might appear tempting to sidestep this issue by labelling them simply as francophone authors. In its most literal sense, 'francophone' serves simply to designate the fact of speaking or writing in French. Defined thus, it would apply to all authors writing in French, regardless of whether their origins are inside or outside France. In reality, of course, the term 'francophone' is reserved for authors originating outside metropolitan France. Even in this more restricted sense, the word is of little help in the present context, for the classificatory problems associated with writers of immigrant origin spring precisely from the fact that they straddle this seemingly neat territorial divide. While raised and in many cases born in France (which might be held to disqualify them from 'francophone' status), they share to a considerable extent in the cultural heritage of their parents (and might by the same token be placed outside the dominant cultural space of metropolitan France). The real issue we have to confront, therefore, is whether these writers belong more to French or to Maghrebian literature, or perhaps to some intermediary or marginal space. It is impossible to answer this question without first defining the corpus with which we are concerned. This task will be tackled in the first part of my analysis. I will then go on to consider how such a corpus may best be classified.

3. Abdelkader Djeghloul (1989), 'L'Irruption des Beurs dans la littérature française', *Arabies*, May, pp.80–1.
4. Jean Déjeux (1992), *La Littérature maghrébine d'expression française*, Paris: PUF, p.88.

Defining the Corpus

The word Beur is now widely used to described young people descended from Maghrebian immigrants in France. Its first recorded public usage came with the creation of a local radio station, Radio Beur, in a Paris suburb in the autumn of 1981. That same autumn saw the publication of Hocine Touabti's novel *L'Amour quand même*.[5] The novel passed almost unnoticed at the time, but in retrospect it can now be seen to be the first work of fiction to fall within our corpus. Touabti was born in Algeria in 1949, but was only a few months old when his family settled in France, and subsequently became the first person brought up in France by Maghrebian immigrant parents to publish a full-length work of literature.

It will be observed that, in identifying Touabti as the first Beur author, I am proceeding on the basis of biographical criteria. Other approaches are, of course, possible. Michel Laronde, for example, opts for a thematic approach. In a recent study entitled *Autour du roman beur: immigration et identité*, he defines Beur fiction as narrative works dealing with young Maghrebians in France, regardless of the author's origins. Among the authors included in Laronde's corpus are several who was born and raised in the Maghreb, such as Slaheddine Bhiri and Ahmed Zitouni, the French novelist Michel Tournier and a writer who has made a point of emphasizing her *métissage*, Leïla Sebbar. None of the writers I have just listed could be classed as a Beur. They are included in Laronde's study, however, on the ground that they have written about the Beurs. Although this is not strictly true of either Bhiri in *L'Espoir était pour demain* or of Tournier in *La Goutte d'or* – in both cases, the young protagonist has spent his formative years on the southern side of the Mediterranean – it is certainly the case that Sebbar has written extensively about the Beurs, while often acknowledging that she is not herself a Beur.[6] Laronde therefore includes her in his corpus, which is defined by reference to 'un certain *contenu* (ingrédients géo-historiques, personnages, situations) [qui] donne au terme *beur* le sens d'un *esprit* particulier'.[7] At the same time, Laronde excludes from his corpus several writers of Maghrebian immigrant origin on the grounds that they do not display what he calls 'l'esprit beur',[8] by

5. Hocine Touabti (1983), *L'Amour quand même*, Paris: Belfond.
6. Leïla Sebbar and Nancy Huston (1986), *Lettres parisiennes*, Paris: Barrault, p.125.
7. Michel Laronde (1993), *Autour du roman beur: immigration et identité*, Paris: L'Harmattan, p.6; author's italics.
8. Ibid.

which he appears to mean that they do not write directly about their experiences within the immigrant community.

While Laronde's study contains many interesting insights, the criteria by which his corpus is defined are not altogether convincing. According to Laronde 'le terme *beur* est à prendre dans le sens ethnique (les romans écrits par des *Beurs*) et à élargir dans le sens d'une dialectique: celle qui *parle* de la situation du jeune Maghrébin dans la société française contemporaine'.[9] Jean-Marie Le Pen talks a great deal about young Maghrebians in France. Are we to infer from this that Le Pen is an example of 'l'esprit beur'? One of his supporters, Jean Raspail, has written a novel dramatizing the collapse of France under the weight of an immigrant invasion.[10] Should we therefore classify him as a Beur writer? Aberrations of this kind can be avoided if we stipulate that 'l'esprit beur' presupposes a sympathetic attitude towards Beur subject-matter. However, as Laronde excludes from his corpus a number of immigrant-born authors (who can scarcely be accused of being out of sympathy with themselves), a significant element of purely personal taste seems to be involved in the selection process.

A strictly thematic definition of Beur writing would include works by authors who biographically, ideologically and formally are very diverse indeed. There is little point in asking whether a corpus defined in this way belongs to one literary tradition rather than to another. If the defining feature is purely thematic, the corpus is bound to be extremely heterogeneous in other respects. A parallel case is that of literature dealing with the Algerian war of independence. Numerous authors on both sides of the Mediterranean have written about this theme, but that does not suffice to make them into a coherent literary community. On the contrary, the ethnic and ideological divisions which characterized the war of independence are reproduced in the literary corpus inspired by the conflict. The most important fault line is that dividing authors who belong unequivocally to the literature of France from those who belong rather to the field of Algerian francophone literature. A novel like Jean Lartéguy's *Les Centurions* has very little in common with one such as Mouloud Mammeri's *L'Opium et le bâton*. The literary community to which a writer belongs is defined far less by the themes which are treated than by the author's origins and the readership which he or she seeks to address. The very title of *Les Centurions* reflects the Eurocentric mould in which it is cast. Brought up to share the cultural and historical reference points of metropolitan France, Lartéguy sees the war through the eyes of a

9. Ibid.; author's italics.
10. Jean Raspail (1985), *Le Camp des saints*, Paris: Laffont.

Frenchman and addresses his novel to a purely French readership. The mental reference points of Mammeri's novel, in contrast, are those of an Algerian, and the readership at which he aims is at least partly Algerian. Conceived as a community of writers and readers, no literary space is entirely isolated or complete in itself. There are crossover points of various kinds between the literature of France and that of Algeria. There is nothing to prevent a francophone Algerian from reading *Les Centurions* but, compared with a French reader, he or she will find it a very alien experience. Algerians who write in French often have a French readership in mind, but, as their origins and mental baggage place them in a different community, their works cannot be said to be belong wholly to the literature of France.

If we define the corpus of Beur literature biographically rather than thematically, we have a much firmer base on which to situate writers of immigrant origin in relation to the literary communities of France and the Maghreb. As we shall see, this relationship depends far less on dieretic content than on the implied position from which texts are narrated and the kinds of readership at which they are aimed.

Classifying the Corpus

It is often said that second-generation members of the Maghrebian population in France are torn between two cultures. The children of immigrants certainly participate in a variety of cultural traditions, which sometimes conflict with each other. Many conflicts of this kind are described in the creative works produced by authors of immigrant origin, but it would in my view be wrong to overplay these fault lines. Three different dimensions of the literary process may be usefully distinguished, and if we examine each in turn we shall see that the writings of immigrant-born authors are more coherently structured than is sometimes thought.

Let us consider first of all the dieretic dimension, that is to say the events recounted by these authors. The protagonists whom they depict often experience identity crises, particularly when they are children. The most acute crises tend to be associated with the transition from home to school, when the child discovers that the cultural codes which he or she has learnt within the family environment are inoperative or positively counterproductive in the world outside. Narratives such as Azouz Begag's autobiographical *Le Gone du Chaâba*[11] and

11. Azouz Begag (1986), *Le Gone du Chaâba*, Paris: Seuil.

Farida Belghoul's *Georgette!*[12] are typical in this respect. In each case, the child protagonist becomes hopelessly (and often comically) confused as he or she attempts to comprehend and manipulate the conflicting cultural imperatives received on the one hand from their Maghrebian parents and on the other from their French teachers and friends. But as young Maghrebians advance in years, contradictions of this kind generally become less acute, even if they do not disappear altogether (adolescence often brings a recrudescence of them). By the time they reach adulthood, most are committed far more to French norms than to those inherited from their parents.

The effects of this sedimentation are clearly felt at a second level, that of the narrative viewpoint adopted in the text. The position from which the narrator speaks is seldom defined explicitly, but almost always he or she narrates the story retrospectively.[13] This is the case, for example, in *Le Gone du Chaâba*, where Begag, the narrating 'I', is clearly distanced in time and space from Azouz, the dieretic 'I' whose experiences he recounts. This spatiotemporal distance is associated in turn with an important mental gap. The more mature narrator often pokes fun at his younger self and the scrapes he got into. As a boy, he caused embarrassment and pain to himself and others by attempting to transplant the norms of one sociocultural milieu into another. His older self is far less mixed up. Instead he occupies a self-confident position of stability from which he playfully underlines the foolishness and naïvety of his younger self. That position is never explicitly defined, but it owes far more to the secular culture of France than to the Arabo-Islamic traditions of the Maghreb.

An analysis by Jamila Boulal of ten novels by writers of immigrant origin has found that a total of 138 Arabic or Berber words are used in them.[14] Boulal did not add up the number of French words used, but this was quite unnecessary. Immigrant-born authors are insufficiently versed in Arabic or Berber to be able to write in the language of their parents. As a consequence, none has any choice but to write in French, and the Arabic or Berber terms included here or there are no more than linguistic spice added to the main ingredients.

It is true that, even while writing in French, these authors could in theory address themselves to an audience outside France – most obviously, the francophone reading public in the Maghreb. However,

12. Farida Belghoul (1986), *Georgette!*, Paris: Barrault.
13. *Georgette!* is a rare exception to this. It uses a stream-of-consciousness technique.
14. Jamila Boulal (1989), 'Introduction à la littérature française d'expression immigrée', thèse de doctorat, Université de Paris VII, pp.273 *et seq.*

they are relatively unfamiliar with that public and have no easy means of access it. Even for writers who have lived all their lives in the Maghreb, finding a publisher there is no easy task. It is even more difficult for writers based outside the Maghreb. From the point of view of a commercial publisher, the Maghrebian population in France is too small and too poorly educated to constitute a financially viable market. Most of the older generation are illiterate, and young Maghrebians have particularly high failure rates at school. In practice, therefore, the French public is the only commercially viable audience available to immigrant-born authors.

If French editors are to be persuaded to take the risk of publishing unknown authors, their texts must be accessible to a French audience. It was for this reason that Seuil asked Begag to provide a glossary of slang and foreign terms, as a reassuring gesture aimed at French readers of *Le Gone du Chaâba*. The step was hardly necessary in fact, for the text was already implicitly structured with a French readership in mind. Like almost all the works produced by authors of immigrant origin, it is peppered with explanations designed to assist French readers, who are assumed to know little about the Maghreb; in contrast, there are practically no explanations of the kind that non-French readers (including Maghrebians) may need when faced with some of the more allusive references to aspects of contemporary French society.

In structuring the narration in this way, immigrant-born writers adopt a position which is similar to what Anne Roche has called the ethnographic posture.[15] The defining feature of that posture lies in the condition of ethnic alterity characterizing the relationship between the people described in the text and those to whom it is addressed. In conventional works of ethnography, the narrator is usually situated in the same cultural community as the reader; he or she tries to convey to the reader an understanding of that other culture by drawing on information supplied by people inside it. In francophone Maghrebian literature, the roles of informant and narrator are often combined, for the narrator is someone whose roots are in the Maghreb, but who is sufficiently versed in French culture to be able to serve as an intermediary between the two. By writing in French, early Maghrebian writers, such as Mouloud Feraoun, tried to render the land in which they were born and brought up intelligible to an

15. Anne Roche (1984), 'La Posture ethnographique dans quelques textes à compte d'auteur de Français sur l'Algérie', *Revue de l'occident musulman et de la Méditerranée*, vol. 37, no. 1, pp.165–74.

audience on the northern shore of the Mediterranean. The new generation of immigrant-born writers is engaged in a similar project. Born of Maghrebian parents, they have been educated in French state schools and have largely internalized the culture of France, enabling them to serve as interpreters between the two communities. They are, as Jean-Robert Henry has put it, 'hommes- [and, we might add, *femmes-*] frontières'.[16]

There are many ambiguities in this role of go-between, and they vary from one group of writers to the other. While francophone authors socialized on the southern shore of the Mediterranean tend to be distanced from the precolonial cultures of the Maghreb, they never identify themselves with the French national collectivity. They stand, rather, between two Maghrebian camps, one of which emphasizes the precolonial legacy, while the other is committed to a more modern stance; where their audience is concerned, the tension is more between the needs of a French readership on the one hand and those of Maghrebians on the other. Immigrant-born authors are torn not between two different versions of Maghrebian culture, but between the Maghrebian heritage of their parents and the full force of French society, and the audience at which they aim is clearly French. There is in this sense a greater proximity to the cultural community of France among this new generation of authors when compared with those born and raised in the Maghreb.

It seems likely that the ethnographic characteristics of these two literary currents will tend to decline, but for different reasons. As the colonial period recedes into history and the reading public within the Maghreb grows in size, authors based on the southern shore of the Mediterranean may feel less inclined to direct their writings towards the former colonial motherland. Young authors born and raised in France tend to internalize its cultural norms far more than those of the Maghreb; in this sense, as they advance in years they tend to become closer to their French audience. In contrast with conventional ethnographic texts, the writings of immigrant-born authors often aim to demonstrate that the Maghrebian presence in France is far less alien than is commonly thought. Far from constituting a separatist community, young Maghrebians long to be recognized as a legitimate component of French society.[17] One of the most recent narratives by an author of this kind, Brahim Bennaïcha, typifies this stance when,

16. Jean-Robert Henry (1993), 'Introduction', in Alec G. Hargreaves and Michael J. Heffernan (eds), *French and Algerian Identities from Colonial Times to the Present: A Century of Interaction*, Lewiston, NY/Lampeter: Edwin Mellen Press, pp.1–18.

for example, the narrator turns directly to his French readers and exclaims:

> Oh! Français, nous sommes bel et bien ici, juste à côté de vous. Beaucoup d'entre vous ignorent que nous sommes enterrés là dans ce trou, au pied de votre Palais des Expositions. Et pourtant, il faudra bien qu'un jour nous vivions tous ensemble dans un monde moderne.[18]

A similar sentiment inspired Mehdi Charef. Explaining his intentions in writing *Le Thé au harem d'Archi Ahmed*,[19] Charef has commented: 'J'ai voulu que le lecteur soit impliqué. . . J'avais toujours l'impression qu'ils nous regardaient de loin. C'est comme si je disais aux gars de l'extérieur, aux Français: "On n'est pas des bêtes, nous aussi on cherche quelque chose, on veut vivre."'[20] It is no accident that Charef's novel places two co-protagonists on a par: Madjid, the son of an Algerian immigrant, and Pat, a French youth. 'Je voulais tout simplement montrer', explains Charef, 'que dans une famille française et une famille immigrée, on vit toujours la même chose.'[21] Neither is it surprising that immigrant-born authors such as Ramdane Issaad and Jean-Luc Yacine have moved steadily away from Maghrebian themes, focusing instead on French protagonists. Significantly, Yacine's first novel, *L'Escargot*,[22] was published in L'Harmattan's 'Ecritures arabes' collection, whereas his latest narrative, *La Mauvaise Foi*,[23] was included by the same publisher in the collection 'Voix d'Europe'.

Conclusion

Instead of French, Maghrebian or francophone, would Beur be a better label for the writings of immigrant-born authors? There are two

17. Cf. Samia Mehrez (1993), 'Azouz Begag: Un di Zafas di Bidoufile (Azouz Begag: Un des enfants du bidonville) or The *Beur* Writer: A Question of Territory', *Yale French Studies*, vol. 1, no. 82, pp.25–42.

18. Brahim Benaïcha (1992), *Vivre au paradis: d'une oasis à un bidonville*, Paris: Desclée de Brouwer, p.58.

19. Mehdi Charef (1983), *Le Thé au harem d'Archi Ahmed*, Paris: Mercure de France.

20. Interview of Mehdi Charef by Alec G. Hargreaves, 17 September 1987.

21. Ibid.

22. Jean-Luc Yacine (1986), *L'Escargot*, Paris: L'Harmattan.

23. Jean-Luc Istace-Yacine (1993), *La Mauvaise Foi*, Paris: L'Harmattan.

main reasons why this term seems increasingly inappropriate: its rejection by many of those to whom it is applied and the misleading impression of separatism which it might be taken to imply. A back-slang adaptation of *Arabe*, the word was adopted as a self-designation by young Maghrebians in the Paris suburbs during the 1970s. One of its main attractions was that it enabled them to escape the pejorative connotations associated with everyday French usage of *Arabe*. During the 1980s, the word Beur was taken up by the French media, and many young Maghrebians felt that it was being turned against them in journalistic usage; hence their growing reluctance to accept it. This resistance to finger-pointing categorization is itself symptomatic of a deep desire to be accepted as an integral part of French society instead of being singled out as a stigmatized subgroup. Most immigrant-born writers identify with this dynamic. Beur was initially valued as a self-designation not only because it released young Maghrebians from the stigma of being labelled as an *Arabe*, but also because it created a breathing-space beyond the polarized antinomy of France and the Maghreb. In the long run, however, a wholly separate space seems unsustainable, and immigrant-born writers appear increasingly concerned to secure a stake within the French cultural field, rather than outside it.

Jean Déjeux rightly observes that the imagination of these writers 'est autre que celui d'un écrivain français nourri [uniquement] de l'histoire française. Les racines des parents parlent donc quand même d'une façon ou d'une autre. Des noms, expressions, bribes d'histoire algérienne, rappels de la guerre, etc., se remarquent ici et là.'[24] The fragile hold of these authors over their Maghrebian heritage is, however, clearly alluded to by Déjeux, and it seems destined to grow weaker still with the passage of time. The ethnic gap between the position from which they speak and that of the audience which they address therefore seems set to decline. With hindsight, Touabti's novel may be felt to have presaged all this. As Salim Jay observed in an article contrasting *L'Amour quand même* with *Le Thé au harem d'Archi Ahmed*, Touabti was remarkably self-effacing where his Maghrebian origins were concerned.[25] Apart from the author's name, there is no indication in the title or on the cover of the book that it might contain a significant Maghrebian dimension. On the contrary, the cover presents a photograph of the quintessentially French Fontaine Saint-Michel, in the heart of the Latin Quarter of Paris. It is there that the

24. Déjeux, *La Littérature maghrébine*, pp.86–7.
25. Salim Jay (1983), 'Mehdi Charef, *Le Thé au harem d'Archi Ahmed*', *L'Afrique littéraire*, no. 70 (October–November), p.106.

narrator, whose name we never learn, becomes besotted with a young French woman called Sylvie, who occupies centre stage throughout the text. Occasional trips to the multiethnic Goutte d'or district serve to establish the narrator's Maghrebian background, but the novel's centre of gravity lies on the Left Bank, where, significantly, the French publishing industry has its heartland.

Unable to write in Arabic or Berber, immigrant-born authors have no alternative but to write in French. With only one or two exceptions,[26] all their works are published in France and they address an essentially French audience. While it is theoretically conceivable that a 'minor literature', as defined by Gilles Deleuze and Félix Guattari,[27] might one day emerge as a distinct immigrant-based enclave within the language of the former colonial motherland, the corpus which has so far been produced, like the word Beur itself, seems more likely to prove a transitional step along the road towards incorporation into the mainstream of French cultural production.

26. Kamal Zemouri (1986), *Le Jardin de l'intrus*, Algiers: Entreprise Nationale du Livre; Ahmed Kalouaz (1987), *Celui qui regarde le soleil en face*, Algiers: Laphomic.
27. Gilles Deleuze and Félix Guattari (1975), *Kafka: pour une littérature mineure*, Paris: Minuit. For a wider discussion of this problematic, see Abdul R. JanMohamed and David Lloyd (eds) (1990), *The Nature and Context of Minority Discourse*, New York/Oxford: Oxford University Press.

3

Points of View: Looking at The Other in Michel Tournier's *La Goutte d'or* and Rachid Boudjedra's *Topographie idéale pour une agression caractérisée*

Carys Owen

Knowledge of the Orient first reached the West via travellers' tales. The Western world formed its notions about its Other through accounts of journeys and later through fiction which nevertheless often fed on the writers' personal experience of travel. And yet how reliable were the travellers as reporters? Many traversed considerable distances, staying in only a handful of places. An account of an itinerary was at the most a schematic framework straddling the country or countries visited. It was, moreover, a grid given substance largely by visual detail. Traditionally most Western travellers have had little knowledge of local languages along their route. For want of means of insight, they recorded what ordinary sight made available to them: costume, architecture, customs, flora and fauna. Interestingly, sight is the one sense where one commonly uses the terminology of journeying; one's gaze travels, wanders, roams. Just as the Western traveller has roved, so his eye has roved, skimming the surface of reality, unable to go beneath that surface. Both the journey and the use of sight may be considered flawed as attempts to engage fully with the truth of the Other.

The flaws are not simply those of physical limitation. Travel by individuals led to colonization, the successors of the early explorers claiming dominion over lands the explorers had merely traversed. Sight, too, is no longer considered an innocent sense, disinterested in its wanderings. We may be said to colonize what we see. We look, it is suggested, via distorting lenses, seeing what we think might be there. Visual perceptions are not welcomed for their novelty; they are fed into pre-existing codes which enable us to 'read' them. In the case of the East, the Westerner has not gone on his travels with open eyes and mind; he has taken his viewpoint with him. Critics like Edward Said have further argued that the Western way of looking at the Orient incorporates structures of hierarchy and domination. The Westerner does not even wish to look on his Other as an equal; he looks down on him. The insistent portrayal, in writing about the East, of picturesque externals, of what is called 'couleur locale', does not reduce the distance between West and East. 'Couleur locale', with its predilection for quaint detail and its smattering of local terms selected for their outlandish spelling, increases the distance by underlining the alien nature of what is on the Other's side.

The convention of 'couleur locale' is still very much alive in modern Western writing about distant lands. A sense of place is still a priority in the entertainment of Western readers. But there is, of course, a problem for those writers who are not themselves Westerners, who are writing about their own peoples, but who do so in a Western language and in literary forms which come from Western culture. To what extent is it possible for them to avoid reproducing the assumptions long entrenched in those languages and forms and convince the Western reader (for whom they must still largely be writing if they resort to his language) that there are other ways of writing about what is not the West?

The difficulty is already apparent in the works of the Maghrebian writers who emerged around 1950. The socioethnic concerns of Feraoun and Mammeri produced in their novels a degree of material detail that could be dismissed by European readers as particularly strenuous accumulations of 'couleur locale' and no more. It is noticeable that later writers of the 1950s, Memmi, Chraïbi and Kateb Yacine, largely forsake pictorial representation to direct their energies elsewhere. Nevertheless, Chraïbi's first novel, *Le Passé simple* (1954),[1] is also the first novel by a Maghrebian writer to take up the question of Orientalism and, in doing so, to associate the themes of travel and sight. At one point the young protagonist, Driss Ferdi, goes to see his European headmaster, named – with every intention of irony – Joseph Kessel, after the real-life writer and traveller. The headmaster explains that his obsession with North Africa stemmed from his early travel as an aviator, but also that, for a European, such an obsession only concerns externals: 'De la couleur locale, voilà ce qui intéresse le

---

1. Driss Chraïbi (1954), *Le Passé simple,* Paris: Denoël. All references are to the 1986 Folio edition, Paris (title abbreviated to *PS*).

lecteur européen, il est fixé, les mousmés, les casbahs' (*PS,* p.214). The young Driss exacts his revenge when, about to leave his headmaster's study, he requests a couple of favours:

> La première consisterait à jeter un coup d'oeil sur l'ameublement de ce bureau, j'ai oublié de la faire, tant je vous écoutais. . . Voyons, un bureau en acajou, des chaises à haut dossier, des bibelots kabyles, l'ordinaire paperasse chère aux proviseurs, volets tirés – vieille habitude –, un syphon d'eau de Seltz sur un guéridon, le pastis est quelque part dans ce placard. . . et quelques mouches, une odeur de cire, de carton chaud et de très vieilles souris. Comprenez-moi! je suis obligé de *situer*. (*PS,* pp.215–16)

For once, the Easterner's gaze travels around the European's habitat as if to say: 'How curious! how amazing!', but with the banality of the enumerated items making it clear that this 'couleur locale' is a time-wasting digression.

This phenomenon of the East looking at the West has reappeared in other texts by Maghrebian writers but it is given particularly extensive treatment in Rachid Boudjedra's *Topographie idéale pour une agression caractérisée* (1975).[2] For the purposes of this study, however, Boudjedra's novel will be examined in conjunction with a novel by a French writer: *La Goutte d'or* (1986) by Michel Tournier.[3] The two novels have a remarkable number of ingredients in common. On the other hand, those ingredients may be exploited in very different ways.

Unlike Chraïbi, whose narrator as yet views Europe only through the microcosm of his headmaster's study, Boudjedra and Tournier invert the tradition of journeys by Westerners to the East, and bring their Maghrebian protagonists to the heart of an ex-colonizing power, Paris. This time, the East comes to the West. In Boudjedra's novel, we are given the final lap of that journey; his Maghrebian travels through the Paris Metro system, from the railway station of his arrival to the stop closest to his destination, where he at last emerges into the open air. Tournier's central character has a much fuller journey, all the way from the Sahara to Paris and then extended by his peregrinations around Paris. In keeping with the conventions of the journey, both protagonists encounter a number of 'natives' and witness various types of behaviour or phenomena peculiar to the 'foreign

2. Rachid Boudjedra (1975), *Topographie idéale pour une agression caractérisée,* Paris: Denoël. All references are to the 1986 Folio edition, Paris (title abbreviated to *TIAC*).

3. Michel Tournier (1985), *La Goutte d'or,* Paris: Gallimard. All references are to this edition (title abbreviated to *GO*).

land'. Both characters are from remote areas in their own country; they have not therefore undergone the same relentless media-operated exposure to the West as city-dwellers. Boudjedra and Tournier thus ensure that when their characters venture into the unknown, their gaze is relatively fresh. As in traditional Western travelogues, sight is the major vehicle of perception, hardly a page in either novel not drawing attention to the activity of looking. As the protagonists journey, so vision is constantly at work. But there are also, in both novels, repeated references to processes whereby visual data undergo transformations: photographs, advertising images, films. The initial viewing experience is reconstructed. Whatever the reality viewed, perceptions are organized into a code of interpretation. The specificity of the data disappears to permit the approved reading.

It would nevertheless be unrealistic to expect Tournier and Boudjedra to produce a simple inversion of the traditional Westerner's journey to the East, however assiduously they exploit conventions of the genre. One major reason for their not doing so is the identity of their readership. Their novels, written in French, target principally, not the reading public of the travelling protagonists' own country, but that of the country in which the travel takes place. The topographical realities they evoke do not possess the seductiveness of the unknown; they are realities which are totally familiar to the majority of readers. What is more, French readers are being put in a situation which requires them to share the viewpoint of protagonists with whom they may feel little drawn to identify, not simply because they are of a different 'race' and continent but also because of powerful prejudices existing in their own cultural context against those originating from that 'race' and continent. Tournier and Boudjedra have therefore a project in their novels which is very different from that of the traditional Westerner writing about travels in the East. It is necessary at this point to start considering the two writers separately in order to see how that project materializes.

La Goutte d'or is not the first of Tournier's novels in which a non-European is a key figure. In *Vendredi ou les limbes du Pacifique* (1969), the stranded traveller, Crusoe, decides that what he sees as the natural existence of Vendredi is superior to his own arid, organized existence. Because, on all but a few occasions, Tournier refrains from portraying Vendredi's point of view, whether to justify his actions or interpret his feelings, it is not possible to know whether Crusoe is simply constructing a myth about his Other. Vendredi eventually departs for Europe on the rescue ship and the reader is left to speculate about what happens to him on arrival. Meanwhile, Tournier dedicates the novel to the hosts of modern Vendredis, the migrant workers who have also made that journey. In *La Goutte d'or*, however, he actually shows that journey being made. His fifteen-year-old protagonist, Idriss, is inspired to leave his Saharan home when a French woman tourist takes his photograph. She fails to send him a copy of the photograph and so Idriss resolves to go and get it himself. The reader follows him systematically along his itinerary, up through Algeria, across to Marseilles, and then on to Paris, where he continues his wanderings, this time around the city. Tournier relates the journey with a certain amount of realism. Indeed, he adds a postscript at the end of the novel to underline how exhaustively he has researched his material; he cites readily his various sources of information, the majority of names clearly belonging to Maghrebians.

Even so, Idriss's journey, whether to Paris or around Paris, may be thought to be highly unrealistic, particularly as regards the absence of practical problems. This Saharan Berber understands and communicates with everyone he meets. There is no suggestion within the Algerian section of his journey that there are language differences that might impede his progress. Thanks to his Uncle Mogadem, who served in the Allied Armies' campaign in Italy, the goatherd Idriss already speaks and even writes French before ever leaving his oasis and never appears to attract attention through any accent or limitation of vocabulary. Other practical difficulties also evaporate. There are no problems with papers or passport. People seem to go out of their way to help Idriss on his journey; he is given lifts, offered money, food, useful addresses. And, most remarkably, this Maghrebian encounters little overt racist behaviour, his main experience of rejection occurring when, still in Algeria, he is told, ironically, by a black hotel servant that his presence is unwelcome. In France, however, most people positively want to meet and entertain Idriss. Indeed, it is only through Idriss's cousin, Achour, that the reader learns that the same welcome does not await all Maghrebians and that exploitation, unemployment and isolation really do exist.

However, the elimination of the difficulties that a real-life Idriss might encounter enables Tournier to pursue his real business in this novel. The multiple encounters made by Idriss along his route are designed to let him hear what others have to say. For example, the meals that seem to flow so freely in Idriss's direction are occasions, as in any television soap opera, for acquaintances to launch into accounts of their interests and experiences. The accounts nevertheless have one thing in common; they all have a bearing on Idriss because they all propose a representation of the Other.

It is true that Tournier is not only concerned with Orientalist representations. *La Goutte d'or* illustrates a number of ways in which people try to transform others to match an image. Even before leaving Algeria, Idriss encounters an elderly woman who develops the delusion, and does her best to make him share it, that he is a member of her family. In Paris, Mage, the film director, confides to Idriss his difficulty in identifying with the stereotype of the homosexual propagated by the teenagers he frequents. Idriss himself may lend a hand in similar processings. Told to get rid of the camel filmed in an advertising sequence, he fails to get it dispatched at the abattoir and leaves it instead at the Jardin des Plantes, where, harnessed and pompommed, it immediately trots away with a load of children. Tournier suggests that we are all guilty of processing the Other. We change the Other to fit our requirements. Thus the camel escapes the abattoir only to be consumed in another way. The meals offered so generously to Idriss are perhaps eventually less occasions for him to eat than opportunities for others to eat him. His cousin, Achour, complains too, but for different reasons, that he has been 'bouffé par Paris' (*GO*, p.147).

It is nevertheless the case that the majority of representations in *La Goutte d'or* concern Idriss as Maghrebian. The people he meets already have their point of view ready; they 'know' what a Maghrebian must look like, what he eats, how he speaks.

If Idriss does not wish to be annihilated, then he must learn to resist the assumptions that others persist in thrusting upon him. Thus, when Sigisbert de Beaufond tells him to look at the scars on his wrists, Idriss does not pretend to see them, refusing to give substance to the story of European heroism in the Maghreb (*GO*, pp.156–7); when Mage and his cameraman invent nonsense etymologies for the words 'chameau' and 'dromadaire', he shows he does not understand them (*GO*, p.176). Dissatisfaction with the expectations everyone has of him eventually pushes Idriss to seek out the cultural roots that can provide an identity and to learn calligraphy (conveniently, this goatherd seems to know classical Arabic) in order to write that identity himself. When last seen, he is dancing with his pneumatic drill in front of the shop-window where he has glimpsed the gold bead that has come to symbolize his ethnic context. His dance suggests that Idriss's casual perambulations have at last become organized as an abstract pattern of the Orient, the arabesque.

Like *Vendredi ou les limbes du Pacifique*, *La Goutte d'or* leaves the reader with a number of problems as regards interpretation. The reader recognizes without difficulty that the plethora of episodes and subsidiary narratives in *La Goutte d'or* is intended to train him to recognize the Eurocentric thought patterns that constantly inform them. Other things are less easy to establish, particularly the degree to which Tournier is able to liberate himself from those thought patterns. It is noticeable that Tournier seems particularly assiduous in amassing 'couleur locale' in the early chapters, in describing the vegetation or fauna of the Sahara or the paraphernalia of a wedding feast. Marseilles, too, is worthy of description because it looks like North Africa. On the other hand, Paris as a topographical reality is given little attention, quaintness being restricted to the practices of some of its inhabitants. Idriss, however, never actually seems surprised by what he sees. The reader may well feel that it is still the Eastern world that comes over as the curiosity, not the Western world visited by the travelling Idriss. It can be noted, too, that the two Oriental narratives that Tournier includes in his novel, the story of Barberousse being the first story told to Idriss and that of the Reine Blonde being the last, are both given a Western slant. Barberousse is reconciled with his image by a Nordic weaver and the portrait of the Reine Blonde is rendered harmless by the discovery that her face is composed of a number of configurations of both Eastern and Western origin. It might appear that the European writer cannot leave the Oriental narratives alone; they must in some way be Westernized. Even the postscript seems to underline the predilection for the European. Acknowledgements of sources conventionally appear at the beginning of a book. Occurring in Tournier's at the end, they may suggest a somewhat defensive last-minute assertion that his material is rooted in solid fact authenticated by actual Maghrebians. Yet by far the longest acknowledgement is to a French source, the original hero of the crash landing in the desert related by Sigisbert de Beaufond, its very length making it appear that it is the European experience that interests Tournier. Finally, what is the reader to make of Achour's account of life in Paris? It is Achour who describes what it is like to be a migrant worker and who inverts a traditional European justification of colonization – that is, that it was Europeans who created everything of worth in the colonies – by stating: 'La France moderne, c'est nous les bougnoules qui l'ont faite' (*GO*, p.142), going on to list the railways, roads and buildings constructed by migrant labour. Yet Tournier also allows Achour to match the Maghrebian of racist mythology by appearing lazy, uncommitted, living off France instead of repaying dues.

However, it is not impossible that Tournier intends to trap the reader into thinking that he is prioritizing a European viewpoint. The point is to provoke debate about that viewpoint. At the same time, there is reason to think that he does not intend to make any affirmation about the viewpoint of the Easterner; as a European, he cannot say what that viewpoint might be. This might well explain his handling of his protagonist. Idriss can seem a rather unsatisfactory creation. To begin with, he is a figure well in keeping with the Sahara 'couleur locale', able to 'read' the desert for information he needs. The further he proceeds on his journey, the more he seems to fade. The elimination of practical difficulties naturally helps this process since no self-assertion is required of him. He is also a listener, with some part in conversations but never with the same degree of access to the first person as his interlocutors, who may therefore come across as much more substantial individuals. The reader, however, is expected to believe that, in addition to his physical journey, which is seen in some detail, Idriss makes a journey in self-knowledge and responsibility for self. Of this journey the reader knows less. Idriss gradually discovers what he is not but it is less easy for the reader to understand what he is. At one point in the novel, he explains to an acquaintance that he learned the word 'Sahara' in France: 'Chez nous y a pas de mot pour désert' (*GO*, p.151), perhaps because, for those who live there, the desert is a plenitude, not an emptiness. May the reader assume that Tournier recognizes that, however hard he tries to express the Other, his words cannot reach that Other? Perhaps, at the most, Tournier and the reader still journey around the Other, attempting to map him out but with little faith in the available points of reference. Like the gold bead, Idriss remains an inviolable secret.

Much in *La Goutte d'or* is metaphorical and capable of multiple readings. The 'goutte d'or', which so neatly evokes the migrant-dominated area of Paris, has a number of possible interpretations. At the end of the novel, Idriss dances in front of the shattered shop-window, heedless of the consequences. The arrival of the police, however, ensures arrest and imprisonment (confirming Idriss's earlier fear of 'la fantasmagorie qui. . . menace de l'emprisonner, comme dans un filet d'images' (*GO*, p.164)). The round gold jewel thus becomes the full stop of his journey and of the text; it also signals a stop to understanding.

It has already been suggested that Boudjedra's novel has many ingredients in common with Tournier's. Boudjedra, however, uses them differently and makes different demands on the reader. Like Idriss, the Maghrebian peasant who is the central figure in *Topographie* is both 'voyageur' and 'voyeur'.[4] He is presented in the process of making a physical journey but also makes a visual journey around an

4. The terms 'voyageur' and 'voyeur' can usually be understood as applying to the Maghrebian. However, since Boudjedra deliberately exploits ambiguous phrasing (e.g. 'selon le voyeur' (p.13)), they may also often be read as references to other peoplein the Metro. It is even possible that Boudjedra

unfamiliar world, this second journey consisting partly of his looking at other people but even more of his examination of the pictures that line the walls of the Paris Metro system. That his acquaintance with the country into which he has set foot is limited to the visual is explained by the fact that, more realistically than with Tournier's Idriss, Boudjedra's Maghrebian speaks no French. His one linguistic bridge to the new world is the slip of paper he clutches in his hand and on which a schoolgirl from his village has written, in French, an address. He is thus a bearer of signs but has no understanding of those signs and it will be seen that this ignorance of the visual representation of language leads eventually to the erasing of the Maghrebian. He cannot read the signs that might get him safely to his destination. Boudjedra reinforces the sense of linguistic non-existence by showing his protagonist to be unable to understand the dialect of a fellow-Maghrebian who tries briefly to facilitate his journey.

Unable to know what the Other might tell him about his world, Boudjedra's Maghrebian can only look as he travels, a truer parallel with the European traveller of old than Idriss could be. Boudjedra's decision to limit his account of the Easterner's journey to the West to the traversing of the Metro system is clever because it enables him to suggest how extensively the Western world relies on pictorial representation. His protagonist spends a lot of time gazing at the pictures on the walls of the Metro platforms and corridors, not just because he is there for such a long time anyway, but also because their number and endless repetition are key elements in the confusion that keeps him there. The problem is that, however much the Maghrebian looks, he has no access to the truth. The pictures he examines belong to advertisements and they are constructed to carry messages. But to decipher the messages the accompanying text must be read and this the Maghrebian cannot do. In his day-long misery in the Metro, he gains a momentary comfort from the picture of a woman who seems to be smiling a welcome at him; what is missing is the understanding that she is advertising female sanitary products (*TIAC*, pp.219–24).

---

as writer or the reader is a 'voyeur'. In the following example, however, the 'voyageur' clearly does not have the same identity as the 'voyeur': 'Et lui se demandant s'il n'avait pas déjà vécu cette situation hallucinante, mélangeant la topographie de l'espace et celle de la mémoire, les confondant même et les malaxant à travers une chose bizarre que le voyeur s'empresse d'appeler, pompeusement: paramnésie, mais qui échappe au voyageur à moitié assommé, épongé et paniqué par l'odeur de la femelle imprégnant son corps, ses vêtements, sa valise' (*TIAC*, p.143).

But, if a large part of the text of *Topographie* shows the Maghrebian looking at this deceptive 'couleur locale' of the Western world, considerable space is also given to the images of him created by other 'voyeurs'. Indeed, some of the Metro advertisements for tourism already show what the West makes of oriental landscapes. Just as in *La Goutte d'or*, there is the sense in *Topographie* that the Other persists in journeying around the traveller. The reason why this happens is that, when the Maghrebian finally reaches the stop closest to his destination, he is murdered within a few yards of the Metro exit by thugs wielding bicycle-chains. In the course of the police investigation, various people who claim to have seen the Maghrebian are interviewed and their testimonies are included in the text, along with the speculations of the police inspector, who did not himself see the Maghrebian but who is trying to construct a picture of him. All these accounts are partial, in both senses of the word. In some cases, the way the witnesses view the Maghrebian is blinkered by their private preoccupations. In other cases, the visual memory is vague; did they see the Maghrebian in question or was it someone else? There is clearly lack of familiarity with the differentiating characteristics of another ethnic group. Thus, 'they' all look alike. The witnesses' accounts can be partial because of distractions or lack of information, but in the case of the police inspector the partiality is that of racial prejudice. He attempts to reconstruct the Maghrebian's day in the Metro but it is a reconstruction not just in the sense of piecing together the events that led to a crime but also in that the inspector reads the Maghrebian according to a code. This symbol of authority in the context into which the Maghrebian ventured is clearly a boor and a bigot, bullying his subordinates and offensive in his use of innuendo against those he does not wish to understand. His is a mentality little different from that of the thugs who commit the murder. His obsession, ill-justified since the point would seem to be to identify the murderers, is with trying to plot the movements of the victim, with the fact that he did not start from the Gare de Lyon and that he spent some twelve hours in the Metro. He cannot, however, piece together this outsider because he does not know what explains the difference in behaviour. The spatial and temporal structures that contain his own universe cannot be made to encompass the Other.

Like Tournier, Boudjedra uses a number of strategies to reinforce the reader's sense that representations by Westerners displace the reality of the Maghrebian. The protagonist is presented solely via the third person; it is the witnesses and police inspector who express themselves via the first person, revealing the points from which they view him. And yet what is there to see? As with Tournier's Idriss,

Boudjedra's Maghrebian appears to be a nonentity. He has no name; he is only ever 'il' or 'l'autre'.[5] If elements of his external aspect are described, it is a question of items of clothing, his suitcase, his manner of walking or the piece of paper in his hand, most of which simply underline his function as a traveller. It is only at a very late stage in his novel, four-fifths of the way through, that Boudjedra slides a couple of extra details into his text, to the effect that his character is 'svelte, ébène' (*TIAC*, p.191), details which at this stage startle the reader who may well have decided long ago how to picture the Maghrebian – brown-skinned, perhaps, but not pitch-black, and certainly not the silhouette of willowy elegance suggested by 'svelte'. Boudjedra reminds the reader that he too may have slotted the protagonist into a pictorial stereotype.

Yet, while it is as important to Boudjedra as to Tournier to show how the Western world views the representative of the East, he is also much more concerned than Tournier to suggest the nature of the actual viewing experience of his protagonist. To reproduce what the unhabituated eye of the Maghrebian sees not only conveys the raw horror of the lost traveller but also exposes the separate elements of the viewing experience. Boudjedra deconstructs vision to show that it is not a natural whole but composed of structures based on relationships and oppositions. Just as the Maghrebian's journey falls apart, so his organizing vision goes to pieces. Light and line are prominent victims. It is, in any case, part of Boudjedra's scheme of things that the ethnic opposition of white and black means that the protagonist spends his day in Paris on its underside, in the Metro system, only emerging when it is already dark outside. But Boudjedra also describes extensively and disturbingly, both for the eye of the Maghrebian and the imagining eye of the reader, the effect of artificial light in the Metro, reflecting off tiled surfaces or the metallic strips of the escalator steps. The seeming disintegration of light means the destruction of perspective and proportion, so that the Maghrebian can no longer clearly establish his relationship to the physical context around which he moves. Line, too, loses its property of delineating and containing space. *Topographie* endlessly evokes the complexity of linear patterns: the weave of the Maghrebian's trousers, the creased

5. The repeated use of 'l'autre' in connection with the Maghrebian underlines the fact that, despite being the central figure, he is forced by his context to remain the Other. However, Boudjedra also uses 'l'autre' in referring to other characters, thus obliging the reader to switch viewpoints, sometimes within the space of a few lines (e.g. *TIAC*, p.36).

surface of his suitcase, the girders of the bridge over the Seine or, most frequently of all, the map of the Metro. All these complex patterns that dance before the Maghrebian's eye suggest that human beings have woven a system of control over their universe, but their very complexity ends by inducing confusion and a sense that the control was only ever an illusion anyway. The Metro map is an admirably neat construct but does not correspond to the real Paris in terms of distances and points of the compass. Like light, line does not ease the Maghrebian's apprehension of space.

The Metro map has other uses, too, for Boudjedra, most particularly in that it raises questions of reading and writing. Like Tournier, Boudjedra exploits the idea that the opposition of East and West is concretized most effectively in the fact that their writing systems progress in opposite directions. Phrases like 'écriture à l'envers' (e.g. *TIAC*, pp.16, 25, 79) occur repeatedly in *Topographie*, underlining the fact that, for this Maghrebian, this new world is written back to front just as he is back to front for all who view him. The police inspector, who works his way back over the day of the murder victim, is indeed writing him the other way round. Boudjedra himself does not include any Arabic writing in *Topographie* as he does in others of his French-language novels, but he is manifestly concerned to disturb his reader's confidence in the 'rightness' of Western patterns of expression, concentrating his subversion on those elements that most visibly indicate structure, whether in the arrangement of chapters or that of material within chapters. Again it is the ideogram of the Metro map that comes automatically to the imagining eye of the reader.

The sections that comprise *Topographie* are numbered according to the sections of the Metro network on which the Maghrebian travels. The first chapter is therefore Ligne 5 (note the 'ligne' again), the second Ligne 1, followed by Ligne 12, Ligne 13 and Ligne 13 bis. A logic certainly exists, but one which conflicts with the order the reader normally expects chapter numbers to possess. A similar disorientation comes from the narrative structure of *Topographie*. The text incorporates extensive digressions, one distracting item leading into another and then on to more again, before an abrupt return to the point of departure, the process suggesting excursions along branch lines or side corridors, only to encounter a dead end. The same effect is achieved by the proliferation of parentheses. Parentheses conventionally add information or modifications that cannot be placed in the proper syntactical structure of the sentence, but their deliberate overuse in *Topographie*, sometimes with parentheses within already lengthy parentheses, ends by causing total disarticulation of the sentence (e.g. *TIAC*, pp.69–71).

Full stops also have their role in the syntactical disruption. Whereas Tournier's 'goutte d'or' is only interpreted as a stop, here, in *Topographie*, the full stop is visibly used to disconcert the reader. At frequent points along his journey, the Maghrebian thinks of the telegram he will send his friends to announce his safe arrival. Admittedly, Boudjedra is not totally logical since the Maghrebian has to think the telegram in French: 'ARRIVE. STOP. SAIN. STOP. SAUF. STOP.' But the point is that the Maghrebian does not understand the word STOP because each word, including the word STOP, is followed by a full stop. Punctuation, the visible indicator of structure in written expression, here becomes meaningless. Inappropriately used full stops also occur in Boudjedra's text. Sentences come to an abrupt end, incomplete, or else a stop is placed within a sentence which appears to continue because the word following the full stop does not have a capital letter. Most frequently, these disruptive full stops occur after connecting words like 'ou' or prepositions, parts of speech that most clearly point to relationships and require other words to follow them.[6] The full stops can remind the reader of the little circles that punctuate the lines on the Metro map, indeed the stops, but they are also a visible sign of what Boudjedra's novel is all about. His Maghrebian comes to a full stop, a dead end. But it should be noted that Boudjedra does not place the account of the murder at the end of the novel. Instead it occurs halfway through the text and even then Boudjedra does not intend

6. The disruptive full stops number at least a few dozen. The following are representative examples:

'desquels ils avaient extrait méticuleusement des photos dont la gelatine. Cela ne l'avancera pas beaucoup' (*TIAC*, p.25).

'comme une plaie vive s'entêtant à ne pas s'enfermer, à. Se disant calamiteux' (*TIAC*, p.154).

'le foulard coquin et la pochette rouge comme un signe de ralliement ou un étendard minuscule ou. vendant à tour de bras de pauvres fleurs' (*TIAC*, p.188).

The sense that parts of the text have been obliterated is even more marked when words are truncated:

'cette histoire d'empreinte de chaussures dont la photographie a été rempl. mais qui a dit qu'il s'est évanoui?' (*TIAC*, p.101).

to surprise since hints have already been given. In the last two pages of the novel, however, he returns to the beginning of the Maghrebian's journey in the Metro, a beginning already marked by stops: the physical stop, the ticket barrier over which the Maghrebian vaults, but also the mental barrier, constituted by the behaviour of the station personnel, the embodiments of Western authority, which he will never get over. The full stop is, in fact, already in place at the very start of the Maghrebian's Metro journey.

Like Tournier, Boudjedra intends the title of his novel to carry various layers of meaning. The Paris Metro is indeed an ideal place for grievous bodily harm to be inflicted. But the aggression also comes from visual characteristics of the environment, of which the Maghrebian has no previous experience and which he cannot control. Finally, the 'idéale' and 'caractérisée' point to mental and written encodings that ensure the Maghrebian's obliteration.

Tournier ends *La Goutte d'or* by citing his authorities, for the most part Maghrebians. Oddly enough, Boudjedra also cites his authorities, also Maghrebians, but this time dead ones. He inserts into his text a page bearing a statement from the Amicale des Algériens en Europe and listing, without comment, eleven violent or mysterious deaths of Algerians in France (p.161). Boudjedra's very harrowing book itself becomes the missing comment; his nameless protagonist could be any one of them.

Both Tournier and Boudjedra, in writing journeys from East to West, preserve characteristics of traditional travelogues. However, they lend the journey and its accompanying visual experience interpretations which belong to the twentieth century, underlining the existence of structures that make it impossible to move and look freely. Indeed, Tournier's novel suggests that only the nomad escapes these structures but he sacrifices human society to do so. But the saddest difference between these two modern novels and traditional tales of travel is that the traveller who comes from the East to view his Western Other may find that the Other views him even more ferociously. Tournier, the French writer, can only think of giving Idriss a one-way ticket back to his own expressive system for safety, with no suggestion of viewpoints ever coinciding. Boudjedra, Algerian but bilingual in Arabic and French and writing in both, at least demonstrates that different writing systems can coexist, and that he can travel in the direction he chooses.

4

Chraïbi's *Le Passé simple* and a Theory of Doubles

Laïla Ibnlfassi

According to Charles Mauron, 'Au drame, apparemment objectif, qu'un auteur nous raconte, peut correspondre un autre drame intérieur, personnel, dont il ne nous dit rien.'[1] In other words, the writer, through different means, reveals to us different aspects of his personality that are not obvious in his explicit story. The silent and implicit drama of the writer appears to us somehow disguised by different rhetorical figures, such as metaphors. These metaphors, which in turn will show the split personality of the writer, are to be seen as a means of distancing by which the author lays claim to his detachment from the events of his stories. In so doing, Driss Chraïbi opts for, to borrow Genette's term, the 'autodiégétique' method of enunciation by which he keeps himself distant from the narrator, but which simultaneously implies a certain self-observation.

In the novel under study the narrator bears the same first name as the author: Driss. But to differentiate himself from the narrator, Chraïbi gives him the surname Ferdi. The name is very relevant as well as suggestive, for the word 'ferdi' has a double meaning in Arabic. In classical Arabic it means 'solitary', while in Moroccan Arabic it means 'pistol'. In both cases the allusion is striking. Driss Ferdi is a long-suffering and lonely character as well as unique compared with the rest of his family. He also bears a destructive element. Death is constantly present in the circle in which he evolves. In *Le Passé simple*, those who are too close to him, like his younger brother and his mother, die. His father, 'le Seigneur', whom he repeatedly wishes to kill in *Le Passé simple*, finally succumbs to death in *Succession ouverte*.

Though much is known of Chraïbi's experience and suffering as a

---

1. Charles Mauron (1986), *L'Inconscient dans l'oeuvre et la vie de Racine*, Paris: Stalkine Reprints, p.33.

protest writer in exile, a psychoanalytical reading of his work enlightens us about his disturbed personality such as we encounter it in the depiction of his characters. His work exposes to us a central character around whom other characters form a kind of rotating constellation and through whom they communicate. These constellations form what Roland Barthes, after Freud in *Totem and Taboo*, defines as the 'primal horde' in his book *Sur Racine* (1963). This 'primal horde' as explored by Barthes is constituted by: (a) the father who, like 'le Seigneur' in *Le Passé simple*, has the power of life and death over his sons; (b) women whom Barthes describes as 'toujours convoitées, rarement obtenues'[2] but rather asexual and submissive in Chraïbi's work; and (c) the brothers–enemies, divided over the father's wealth, this same father who haunts them and comes back from the dead to punish them for his murder. The hatred between brothers is more noticeable in *Le Passé simple* than elsewhere in Chraïbi's work, except probably between Driss and Hamid. But, if Hamid is to be viewed (as is going to be discussed later) as Driss's double, then he also falls into this category of brother–enemy. And the final element necessary to complete the 'primal horde' is the son. Barthes defines the latter as being split between the terror of the father and the necessity to destroy him, a definition which applies well to Driss Ferdi.

To illustrate best this analogy between the Racinian tragedy, as seen by Barthes, and the work of Chraïbi one has to read the latter's novel in terms of psychic structures. The core element in such a study will be the ego because of its unstable and conflictual situation. If confronted with such a situation, then, as Laplanche and Pontalis explain:

> [The] ego, conceived of as a field of consciousness, defends itself by evading this situation, by systematically ignoring it; in which case, the ego is the area which has to be protected from the conflict by means of defensive activity.[3]

Accordingly, Driss Ferdi could represent the ego, which is the kernel of the story, and the other characters (the father, the mother, the brothers), who gravitate around him like satellites, are essential to the whole structure. Their study would enable us to pin down the ego and understand its trajectory. Through the technique of distancing mentioned earlier, the ego is in constant displacement, and its relation

2. Roland Barthes (1963), *Sur Racine,* Paris: Seuil, p.14.
3. J. Laplanche and J.B. Pontalis (1988), *The Language of Psychoanalysis,* London: Karnac Books, p.133.

to other characters, according to its position, leads us to different understandings of the story. Consequently, the characters can have different significations in the text. Charles Mauron's explanation as to the ego's position is that if it moves from an inferior position to a superior one then the other characters are images from the past and the future of the narrator. However, if the ego is in a stagnant position, i.e. that of the repressed, the other characters are images of the superego or the repressed desire or the id.

In the first instance, one could rightly say that the work of Chraïbi is directed towards the past. Many elements of a sociohistorical analysis of Morocco are inherent in his works. The authoritarian bourgeois father of *Le Passé simple* is reflective of the powerful mercantile society Chraïbi grew up in until his departure for France after his baccalaureate in 1945. The depiction of such a society goes hand in hand with an observation of the period of French colonization of Morocco. This is a theme which is explicit in *La Civilisation, ma Mère!. . .* But, in addition to being images from the past, Chraïbi's novels are also a vision of the future. And, for this, one has to look at the metamorphosed mother in *La Civilisation ma Mère!. . .*, because from a state of total submission in *Le Passé simple* she is presented with all the assets of an emancipated woman.

In the second instance, where the ego is inhibited, the other characters appear as figures by which the repressed desire is expressed. This desire is then displaced and projected on to a double. This double, as defined by Otto Rank, is 'a predilection of the author to depict traits of himself or desire for another existence'.[4]

In Chraïbi's work one can detect more than just one double. The narrator endures different frustrations which are projected on to different characters, which, in turn, appear to us as different doubles. These doubles are, to borrow Mauron's words, 'des métamorphoses d'un personnage – voire de l'auteur'.[5] As the narrator and the author are unmistakably the same person, we recognize in the doubles the variety of inhibitions to which Chraïbi is prone.

The most manifest doubles in Chraïbi's novel are the father, the mother and his brother. In a strong power relation, 'le Seigneur' and Driss are inseparable. 'Le Seigneur' is a double who is necessary to Driss's self-awareness. On the contrary, the mother and Hamid as doubles are haunting figures from Driss's past as an abused child and adult. Unlike 'le Seigneur', they are doubles Driss has to get rid of if

4. Otto Rank (1971), *The Double: A Psychoanalytic Study,* trans. H. Tucker, Chapel Hill, N.C: North Carolina University Press, p.xiii.
5. Mauron, *L'Inconscient*, p.110.

he is to find his own self. In short, what follows will be an attempt to discuss the father as a positive double and the mother and Hamid as negative ones. The first has a salutary effect while the role of the others is detrimental.

The conflict between father and son in *Le Passé simple* is that between master and subject or tyrant and captive. Such a conflict is inevitably violent. Violence is present, both in the narrator's account of his childhood and in the language he uses to convey his message. So, as the relationship between father and son is based on authority, it is unavoidable, due to the fact that they are both confined in what Barthes calls the 'tragic space'. It is from their coexistence in the same space that the crisis stems. In considering 'le Seigneur' as the double of Driss, the emphasis should be placed on the fact that he is an inverted double. As in the Lacanian mirror-stage, if the subject identifies itself with the image reflected in the mirror the self is not completed, but rather becomes object or other. Driss encounters the law of his father and his castrating power. He identifies with him, not in terms of similarities but of opposites. For Barthes, 'être, c'est non seulement être divisé, mais c'est être retourné'.[6] Accordingly, 'le Seigneur' is an inverted double of Driss, a relation that enables them to complement each other without reaching a total rupture.

The complementarity between Driss and 'le Seigneur' depends on their position *vis-à-vis* each other. 'Le Seigneur', with the religious connotations the generic entails, is an omnipresent godlike figure; his presence, be it physically, as in *Le Passé simple,* or spiritually, as in *Succession ouverte,* annihilates all others:

[La] présence du Seigneur assis buste droit et regard droit, si peu statue qu'il est dogme et si peu dogme que, sitôt devant lui, toute autre vie que la sienne, même le brouhaha de la rue vagi par la fenêtre ouverte, tout est annihilé.[7]

In relation to the godlike father, Driss's position is that of a subdued creature. His own experience depends on 'le Seigneur' and he is conscious of his inferior status before him:

Sa loi est indiscutable. J'en vis. . . [A] la seule évocation du Seigneur assis en tailleur sur son carré de feutre pieux, je suis redevenu un simple piéton du Chemin Droit.[8]

6. Barthes, *Sur Racine,* p.46.
7. Driss Chraïbi (1954), *Le Passé simple,* Paris: Denoël, p.17.
8. Ibid., p.14.

This God–creature relationship is based on authority and power, concepts which lose their meaning if either of the characters is absent from the scene. If one were to consider the mother as the double of Driss, one would realize that her absence parallels the father's loss of power.

This complementarity is also vital for Driss. Though he constantly wishes and plans the death of his father, he never achieves his purpose and keeps bringing him back to life, as in *Succession ouverte*. The father's presence as an other is essential for Driss to be his own self. The narrator is somehow unable to free himself from his oppressive father. He is stuck in his past and in his antagonism with the father. This 'predilection' for the past reveals some masochistic tendencies in the narrator, which can only be justified by his feelings of guilt towards his father. It is his father, whom he paints as a monstrous despot, who after all enabled him to have access to education at a time when very few Moroccans would go beyond the primary school level. It is this same father who paid for him to go and study in France. He is ungrateful and conscious of his ingratitude. No matter what opportunities his father's wealth offered him, Driss's prime preoccupation is to free himself, even if his freedom is translated in terms of ingratitude. This is a notion Barthes defines as 'la forme obligée de la liberté'.[9]

As mentioned above, Driss's guilt towards his father is what keeps him in his oppressed position. His tormented mind prevents him from resting. Like the Racinian hero as studied by Barthes, he never sleeps; a fact mentioned at different stages of his narrative: 'Je ne sais pas si j'ai rêvé ou simplement somnolé';[10] later again he refers to himself as 'enfant insomniaque'.[11] This pathological sign is obviously preoccupying for the narrator as he repeats three times in the lapse of a short scene the same sentence, 'Derrière mes paupières closes désespérément dans ma tension de trouver le sommeil.'[12] These torments and anxieties could be ended if his mind could break the barrier symbolized by 'la ligne mince'. However, 'la ligne mince' keeps projecting him back to his past, from which he draws his pleasure by retelling and rewriting it.

In his desperate attempt to break with his father, Driss tries different methods. The most violent rupture is to murder the father. The idea of killing him painstakingly grows in his mind:

9. Barthes, *Sur Racine*, p.31.
10. Chraïbi, *Le Passé simple*, p.42.
11. Ibid., p.63.
12. Ibid., pp.64–5.

> Ce couteau avait tout coupé. . . et, un jour parmi les jours créés par Dieu, avec un peu d'adresse, un peu de sang-froid, le lancer vers le Seigneur, quelque part vers le corps du Seigneur, vers sa nuque par exemple, où il se planterait jusqu'au manche, comme une aiguille.[13]

However, this phallic and oedipal scene diverges from the original myth. Driss is prevented by the mother from carrying out the act. The father does not die but rather outlives the mother, who commits suicide. Consequently, the son does not fulfil his desire by killing the father he hates, but by destroying the mother he loves. Not being a real double, the father cannot be destroyed by death as a double would be.

Unable to escape the father through death, Driss opts for other alternatives, namely his imagination and writing. The only action the father has no power to master, since it is out of visible reach, is the son's imagination. As a way of disobeying his father and refusing to listen to his account of his tea business, Driss lets his mind go free; as he says, '[Je] vous échappe. Par mon imagination.'[14]

To surpass the authority of the pursuer father, Driss projects his pursued ego on to his doubles, namely his brother and mother. As mentioned earlier, the cohabitation of both father and son in the same 'tragic space' is what provokes the tension in their relationship. As a way of annihilating his antagonistic son, 'le Seigneur' locates him outside the 'tragic space' (this being Casablanca) by sending him to Fes as a companion to his mother. According to Barthes, 'sortir de la scène, c'est pour le héros, d'une manière ou d'une autre, mourir'.[15] Not in the case of Driss, though. His location outside the 'tragic space' is what enables him to free himself from his pursuer by destroying his pursued double, identified with his brother Hamid. The death of Hamid becomes a necessity and a reason for the protagonist to live. Hamid as a double bears all the weaknesses which Driss needs to eliminate if he is to be equal to 'le Seigneur'. The fragility of Hamid is described by Driss in the following words:

> Il est chétif et doux. Il a neuf ans et je lui en donne deux. . . chien écrasé, détresse des ghettos, clochard, rêve d'Icare, si intensément que j'estime que ma mère aurait mieux fait d'exécuter une pression utérine au moment d'accoucher de ce gosse-là.[16]

13. Ibid., p.43.
14. Ibid., p.50.
15. Barthes, *Sur Racine*, p.12.
16. Chraïbi, *Le Passé simple*, p.25.

This wish for Hamid's death at an early stage of the novel is an ominous preview of his real death two chapters later.

The narrator's execution of this double is almost inevitable for he is a constant reminder of the former's oppressed and frustrated condition. At the news of Hamid's death, it is therefore predictable that the narrator's feelings are not those of grief but of joy:

> J'ouvris le télégramme. Le lus. Le relus. Chose étrange, ce n'était ni la stupeur ni la douleur qui me vrillait, mais la joie. Je me rappelle encore comment, la moitié gauche du crâne, la moitié gauche de la face, la moitié gauche du buste, la jambe gauche; de cette derrière montait un faisceau de frissons à propagation ondulatoire. L'action était née.[17]

The narrator's rejoicing at his double's disappearance implies the possibility of fulfilling himself. His last sentence in the above quotation, 'L'action était née', signifies his deliverance from the castrating father. With the death of the brother as a double, the relationship between 'le Seigneur' and Driss as that of a tyrant and captive ceases to exist and gives way to a new relationship, in which Driss is able to rebel against his oppressor.

However, considering the variety of inhibitions to which the narrator is subject, other doubles on to whom frustrations are projected are to be dealt with if Driss is really to be free from the father's grip. The mother as another negative double is a frustrating image from the narrator's past, a past that haunts him and hinders his capacity to assert himself.

To attain and preserve his self, Driss has to draw a barrier between this image of his self, which he wants to keep and protect, and the image of his double, which is unconsciously conceived as incompatible.

Driss refuses to identify with the weak personality of the mother, and consequently she becomes the recipient of his projected feelings and disturbances. This act of projection, as defined by Laplanche and Pontalis, is:

> [A] mode of refusal to recognise (méconnaissance) which has as its counterpart the subject's ability to recognise in others precisely what he refuses to acknowledge in himself.[18]

---

17. Ibid., pp. 108–9.
18. Laplanche and Pontalis, *Language of Psychoanalysis,* p. 354.

In other words, the mother is, so to speak, the scapegoat who has to bear Driss's own failings. Driss strives to be as strong a person as 'le Seigneur', but what he refuses to recognize is that he is in reality just as vulnerable as the mother on to whom he projects his failings. He portrays her as submissive, afraid and oppressed by 'le Seigneur', but most importantly as a silent sufferer. The mother's silence is, in fact, rather eloquent. It is to be seen as a shield against the external aggression embodied by 'le Seigneur'. Her sensitive and silent character is somewhat descriptive of the attitude of an artist who, in this case, is nobody else but Driss Chraïbi himself. His sensitivity, seen through the depiction of his double, is translated by his inability to express his rebellion out loud and verbally. On the contrary, he takes refuge in writing as an expression of self-assertion. And it is also in writing that he dismisses his weaknesses by attributing them to his mother. In a similar way to Hamid, the mother is an image the narrator needs to expel from his self. To achieve this, the double has to meet the inescapable fate, i.e. death. Once again, like the Racinian drama, the tragic death which is most aggressive is suicide. In *Le Passé simple*, the reader is explicitly told that the mother commits suicide in order to end the suffering inflicted on her by 'le Seigneur'. However, the implicit meaning that we can impute on the basis of the above analysis is that it is the narrator who is behind this death. Though in the novel it is the father who blames the mother's suicide on Driss – 'Ma tâche consistait simplement à te signifier que tu as été cause de sa mort'[19] – it is after all the writer's voice which is behind both Driss and 'le Seigneur'. Consequently, this declaration could be understood as an indirect confession on the part of the narrator.

The death of both negative doubles symbolizes the ending of Driss's psychic division. It also enables him to affirm his identity and to approach his father, no longer oppressed by him but as an equal. In fact, in the last chapter of *Le Passé simple*, entitled 'Les Eléments de synthèse', the narrator assesses the situation as he gains awareness of his own self. As he succeeds in overcoming his inhibitions, he draws closer to his father with whom he begins to identify: 'Je le sentais soudain proche de moi, perméable à la souffrance et, dans cette souffrance, plus sincère, plus complet, plus humain.'[20] He also begins to regard his father as equal: 'Nous avions la même taille et, assis dans des fauteuils jumeaux, le buste vertical, nous étions au même niveau.'[21]

19. Chraïbi, *Le Passé simple*, p.262.
20. Ibid., p.235.
21. Ibid., p.243.

The removal of Hamid and the mother from the scene is for the narrator a way of getting out of the grip of his haunting past. By asking the following question 'Enterrer le passé? qui a dit cela, un romancier?'[22] the narrator and the writer merge to produce one voice, leaving no doubt that Driss Ferdi and Driss Chraïbi are the same person. Also, while devices such as metaphors and metonymies could be used to study the subject–author relationship, viewing this relationship as a 'game of doubles' can assist us greatly in comprehending the ambiguities which surround it.

22. Ibid., p.239.

– 5 –

Unmasking Women: The Female Persona in Algerian Fiction

Farida Abu-Haidar

Zohra, la femme du mineur (1925), by Abdelkader Hadj Hamou, *Myriem dans les palmes* (1936), by Mohamed Ould Cheikh, and *Hind à l'âme pure ou l'histoire d'une mère* (1942), by Aïssa Zehar, are the titles of three works drawn from a corpus of Algerian narrative pieces, published between the 1920s and 1940s. Written by male authors from within the indigenous community, they are among the earliest examples of Algerian francophone fiction where the central character is female. Yet the women, as indeed most of the characters depicted in these works, bear little resemblance to real-life people. Exotically portrayed in order to add local colour and to appeal to non-indigenous readers, they stand in marked contrast to the sensitively drawn characters in Algerian novels which began to appear from about the middle of the present century. This chapter, which focuses on a selection of novels published from the 1950s until the present, aims to show the different ways in which women are portrayed in Algerian fiction. The voices of the authors whose works are surveyed here tend to range from the quietly philosophical tone of the first generation, to the vociferous indignation of the 'angry young men' of the second generation, culminating in the disturbing cries of anguish of young women writers of the 1980s and 1990s.

In order to trace the beginnings of the earliest realistic depictions of women in Algerian fiction, the reader would have to turn to the first examples of Arabic narrative writing. It was in the pages of the periodicals founded by the Association of Algerian *Ulema*, or Muslim learned men, that the call for the emancipation of Algerian women was first voiced. Spurred on by the popularity and success of the reformist movement in Egypt, led by religious leaders like Muhammad

Abduh and Qasim Amin,[1] the first exponents of Arabic fiction in Algeria frequently made the inferior position of women the central theme of their short stories. In uncompromisingly bold language they drew disturbing pictures of Algerian society. Their aim was to jolt the nation out of its stupor and to call for a number of social reforms, including nationwide educational opportunities for Algerians of both sexes. Since they wrote specifically for an Arab readership and not for 'outsiders', they did not feel the need to tone down their critical approach.

Many writers of Arabic fiction, however, did not advocate women's emancipation *per se*. They merely saw it as an important step towards the nation's emancipation and eventual independence. This view, of course, has been shared by others, among whom was Flaubert, who, in *L'Education sentimentale*, stated: 'l'affranchissement du prolétaire... n'était possible que par l'affranchissement de la femme'. Feminist themes and a genuine interest in women's issues were to emerge later, in the francophone works that were to gain international acclaim and to place Algerian literature firmly on the international scene.

It is generally agreed that the year 1950, in which *Le Fils du pauvre* by Mouloud Feraoun (1913–62) was published, marks the emergence of the Maghrebian francophone novel. Taking this date as the starting-point of the Algerian novel, critics seem to overlook two first novels by women writers which appeared in 1947, three years before Feraoun's first fictional work. These are *Leïla, jeune fille d'Algérie* by Djamila Debèche (b. 1910) and *Jacinthe noire* by Taos Amrouche (1913–76). The central character of Debèche's novel is an educated young woman, from a traditional background, who overcomes family opposition to lead the kind of life she sees fit for an educated person, and strives to help others less fortunate than herself. Amrouche's novel sheds light on the author's student days at a Catholic establishment in Paris. Besides, it tackles a number of hitherto unexplored pressing issues, like marginality and exile, two themes which were to act as centrifugal forces in later Algerian novels.

Debèche's and Amrouche's novels have been eclipsed by the early works of 'the generation of 1952', that is to say, the triumvirate of Mouloud Feraoun, Mouloud Mammeri (1917–89) and Mohammed

1. Muhammad Abduh (1849–1905) and his younger contemporary Qasim Amin (1865–1908) were among the earliest and most important Muslim religious reformists and Arab nationalists who called for the emancipation of women. In his highly controversial works *Tahrir al-Mar'a* (The Emancipation of Women) (1899) and *Al-Mar'a al-Jadida* (The New Woman) (1901), Qasim Amin attacked the inferior position of women in Islamic societies.

Dib (b. 1920), and hence not given much importance in works of literary criticism. Whatever their weakness as literary works, *Leïla, jeune fille d'Algérie* and *Jacinthe noire* deserve special acclaim in their pioneering approach, both as novels by women, and as novels concerned with women, especially when one stops to think that in other parts of the Arabo-Islamic world at that time hardly any headway had been made by women writers and little importance given to women's issues in fictional works by male authors. There is no doubt that Amrouche's novel is superior to that of Debèche in both form and content. In her subsequent novels, *Rue des Tambourins* (1960) and *L'Amant imaginaire* (1975), Amrouche drew sensitive portrayals of Algerian educated women torn between two different cultures. The fact that she was a Christian in a Muslim environment made Amrouche's alienation even more intense. Debèche published one other novel, *Aziza* (1955), in which she showed the contradictions experienced by young women of her milieu who were encouraged to acquire a French-style education and then expected to endure the tyranny of a husband in a traditional marriage.

Amrouche and Debèche created a female space in their works. The depiction of a space given almost entirely to women occurs also in works by male authors where the father is invariably absent. He is either dead or away in France doing a menial job. This is the picture presented in some of the novels of Dib and Feraoun. In Mammeri's novels, on the other hand, the space is divided almost equally between men and women, and yet the female presence remains as predominant as it is in the works of his two contemporaries. Mammeri begins his first novel, *La Colline oubliée* (1952), by comparing spring in the Kabyle hills, where he grew up, to women's short-lived youth, saying that the two do not last long. He then goes on to describe how women's oppression does not stem from male dominance alone, but from harsh patriarchal values maintained by older women. Mammeri, for example, compares the different attitudes of a couple towards their childless daughter-in-law. The father-in-law does not blame the young woman for not bearing him grandchildren, and wonders what he has done to annoy the saints. The mother-in-law, on the other hand, lays the blame entirely on the young woman, putting pressure on her son to repudiate her. Far from condemning forceful matriarchal figures, like the mother in this novel, Mammeri seems to portray them with a great deal of compassion and understanding, making his readers realize that a harsh, monotonous life, an enforced marriage and years of endless childbearing are responsible for their seeming cruelty. A strong female character is also portrayed in Mammeri's third novel, *L'Opium et le bâton* (1965), in the person of the central character's widowed mother. In the absence of a father figure, the mother assumes the roles of both parents and rules over her three sons with determination.

In his Algerian trilogy, *La Grande maison* (1952), *L'Incendie* (1954) and *Le Métier à tisser* (1957), Dib shows that strength in women is not physical but moral. The central character, Omar, is a young boy who is surrounded by women, comprising his grandmother, mother and sisters. Yet, in spite of the fact that Aïni, his mother, is prematurely old and haggard, becoming increasingly emaciated and ashen-faced through hunger and hard work, her physical weakness is overshadowed by the moral power she acquires to enable her to stay alive to care for her fatherless children and bedridden mother.

In early francophone fiction by male authors women were usually portrayed as sisters, wives and mothers. According to the Algerian academic Naget Khadda, 'la littérature algérienne, jusqu'à ces dernières années, confinait la femme au rôle social de mère, accessoirement d'épouse' (p.219).[2] The figure of the mother in Algerian fiction invariably towers over the others. This is hardly surprising when one considers that, as children at Koranic school, Algerian authors would have been taught the verse from the Koran venerating mothers and claiming that Paradise lay at their feet. Algerian popular proverbs give mothers more importance than fathers.[3] Writers, moreover, were surrounded, throughout their childhood and youth, by images of an absent spiritual mother (France), as well as a physically present one (their own mother). At school it would have been instilled into them that France, *la mère patrie*, was their mother. This concept must have been a difficult one to grasp for some of them, as is shown by Dib in *La Grande maison*, where the boy Omar cannot understand how his mother, Aïni, can be on the other side of the Mediterranean, when she is in fact at home.

For Dib the symbolic representation of the mother occurs in his novel *Qui se souvient de la mer* (1962), in which the word *mer* of the title is seen as a generous, life-giving force whose homonym *mère* stands for *la mère Algérie*. In the third part of Dib's Nordic trilogy,

2. Naget Khadda (1984), 'Mohammed Dib: esquisse d'un itinéraire', *Itinéraire et Contacts de Cultures, Littérature du Maghreb*, Paris: L'Harmattan, pp.197–234.
3. Among some well-known Arabic proverbs are the following two: 'He who loses his father has his mother's knee for a pillow, but he who loses his mother has nothing but a doorstep on which to place his head.' 'The child who has lost his father has not lost much. The child who has lost his mother has lost everything.' Rabah Belamri (1986), *Proverbes et dictions algériens*, Paris: L'Harmattan, p.38.

Neiges de marbre (1991), published almost thirty years later, the narrator's own mother symbolizes Algeria. Her death not only represents a finality in the physical sense, but also a significant end to the link which had kept him tied to the country of his birth. Khadda goes on to say, 'dans l'oeuvre de Dib, la femme est non seulement présente, mais souvent célébrée comme étant "l'avenir de l'homme"' (p.219), the last phrase echoing Louis Aragon. One should perhaps add that in Dib's works the female persona can also be transmuted into a symbol of evil. In *Cours sur la rive sauvage* (1964), the shifting vision Iven Zohar has of the woman he is running after changes from good to evil and back again to good. When she is good she is called Radia, but when she is evil she is Helle. The principle of binary opposition in this novel bestows on woman the double nature of good and evil.

Keeping to his symbolic representation, Dib gives his readers in *La Danse du roi* (1968) the character of Arfia, a *moudjahida*, an Algerian woman who fought in the war of independence. Arfia, therefore, represents all those Algerian women who took part in the national struggle, and for whom independence was not the panacea they were expecting, since the social climate of the time decreed that they should return to their traditional role of wives and mothers.[4] The other central character in this novel is Radwan, a *moudjahid*, who, like Arfia, experiences disillusionment after independence. Yet, of the two, Arfia appears to be by far the stronger character.

The practice of elevating women to heights of excellence and idealizing them occurs in Kateb Yacine's highly acclaimed work, *Nedjma* (1956), in which the author seems to shatter the well-constructed plot of the sociorealist novel of his predecessors, scattering it into a thousand pieces. Written as part autobiography, part fragmented recollections, *Nedjma* the novel recounts the story of Nedjma the woman, who is, at one and the same time, mother, loved one and country, all, according to Kateb, female beings to be cherished. Although Nedjma's mythical, silent presence is essential to the thematic structure of the text, Kateb occasionally brings her down to the level of an ordinary woman when he gives her the power of speech.

Women characters in some Algerian works, and especially those by the first generation, are shown to be shaped by a patriarchal concept

4. This situation is not characteristic of Algeria alone. In Britain, during two world wars, women had job opportunities which were denied them in peacetime. After each war, however, they 'were shunted back into the home to "liberate" jobs for men and to rebuild the population', Michelene Wandor (1981), *Understudies*, London: Methuen, p.11.

of woman as loving and beyond reproach. It is a concept which insists on the female persona being purer than the male, since she is not party to patriarchal power structures. In early Algerian literature one had to look at the relatively few novels by women in order to find female characters portrayed objectively, and where the feminine world was not set against the masculine, but stood on its own merit. One of the first novels to present women as creatures of flesh and blood and not as selfless, saintly mother figures is Assia Djebar's *Les Enfants du nouveau monde* (1962). In this work Djebar (b. 1936) shows how women of different ages and social backgrounds came together to join the men fighting in the *maquis*, during the war of independence. Djebar had made her entry into fiction with two previous novels depicting young Algerian women who wanted much more from life than tradition dictated they should even think of. In *Les Enfants du nouveau monde* she moves away from her concentration on everyday concerns, in order to take a wider view of Algerian society, and women's role in it, at a time of national crisis.

Djebar shows how the war of independence gave women, who had previously been silent and dependent on others, the chance to take full charge of their own lives. Lila, one of the younger women in the novel, recalls how as a child she used to walk to school holding her father's hand. This is repeated in Djebar's novel, *L'Amour, la fantasia* (1985), a work based on some of her childhood memories, where the narrator remembers being accompanied to school by her father while he held her hand. These repeated fragments of the author's autobiographical recollections, occurring in the two works, make the distinction between author and character practically non-existent. If one were to accept the premise that literature is a 'reflection' of the real world, one would find, in a number of Algerian works, a close relationship between the experiences of writers and the characters they portray. It could be said that this is generally true of most literature, as Anita Brookner's words, 'One has to use one's own life: one has no other material,'[5] seem to stress.

Djebar, the writer, emerged at a time when Algerian women were emerging as individuals in their own right. It is not surprising, therefore, that she did not remain an isolated voice, as Debèche and Amrouche had been before her, but was soon joined by a whole chorus of contemporary and younger women. Djebar's insistence on female bonding as a way of achieving greater self-realization has been clearly demonstrated in her three latest novels, *L'Amour, la fantasia*,

5. John Haffenden (1985), *Novelists in Interview*, London: Methuen, pp.69–70.

Ombre sultane (1987)[6] and *Loin de Médine* (1991). The first of these, while chronicling the author's early years, gives at the same time an account of the colonial history of Algeria between the years 1830 and 1962. In the third and final part of *L'Amour, la fantasia* Djebar gives voice to countless women who took part in the national struggle and whose poignantly informative oral testaments would have been lost had she not translated them and included them in her text.

In *Ombre sultane*, the author explores the intimacy and conspiracy which develop among women confined to the same space. Here the two women, one an *évoluée* and the other from a traditional background, join forces to be stronger than the male who holds sway over them. Djebar gives them names and identities, while the man in the novel is not given a name, but simply referred to as 'he' throughout. In *Loin de Médine* she introduces a totally novel concept of time and space. Setting her work in Arabia in the seventh century, and using fictitious female characters, as well as women who lived in the first century of Islam, she shows how female bonding is important for the female psyche anywhere and at any time.

The importance of female bonding in women's lives has been stressed by other writers, among them Leïla Sebbar (b. 1941), who is more concerned with the here and now of Algerian immigrant experience in France. In her works of fiction, *Fatima, ou les Algériennes au square* (1981) and *Parle mon fils, parle à ta mère* (1984), Sebbar describes the silent world of Maghrebian immigrant women living on the margin of society. Unaccepted by the people among whom they find themselves, they reach a point of despair when their children drift away from them, lured by the glitter of a world they themselves cannot begin to understand. But it is their daughters, like Shérazade,[7] the eponymous heroine of three of Sebbar's works to date, who seem to claim more of the author's attention. Determined not to end up like their mothers, and wanting to emulate their French peers, they escape out of the stifling but safe cocoons of their homes into an alien, uncaring world, where they drift aimlessly. Those who cannot escape become resigned to the fate decreed for them by their parents, like Malika in Ferrudja Kessas's *Beur's Story* (1990), or end up by taking their own lives, like Farida, Malika's friend.

6. *L'Amour, la fantasia* and *Ombre sultane* were translated into English by Dorothy S. Blair and published by Quartet in London under the titles of *Fantasia, an Algerian Cavalcade* (1989) and *A Sister to Scheharazade* (1987).
7. The first of these, *Shérazade, 17 ans, brune, frisée, les yeux verts* (1982) has been translated into English by Dorothy S. Blair as *Sherazade, Aged 17, Dark, Curly Hair, Green Eyes, Missing* (London: Quartet, 1991).

In works by male authors, mothers and older women had continued to be portrayed as selfless beings, devoid of sexuality, until Rachid Boudjedra's first work of fiction, *La Répudiation* (1969) exploded on the literary scene. Defying all conventions, Boudjedra (b. 1941), through the narrator, who bears his name, speaks openly of his repudiated mother's repressed sexuality. He goes on to condemn taboo-laden patriarchal societies for demoralizing the young and debilitating women. Dependent on men from their birth until their dying day, women in societies described by Boudjedra remain minors. At one point in the novel, the narrator cries out in disgust: 'une femme n'est jamais adulte' (p.46). Enclosed within four walls, awaiting the orders of a father, a husband, a brother or a son, they never discover the outside world. And again the narrator calls out in despair and indignation that every sip of coffee the men drink in the coffee-houses is a denial of the existence of women. But no one seems to want to remedy the situation: 'Personne ne s'occupe de ce mal qui ravage les femmes de la cité' (p.44). Yet, in spite of being shunned and denied by her husband, the mother in *La Répudiation* appears as a strong character, while her husband is portrayed as morally weak, a victim of his sensuality. It is only the power of patriarchy which makes him tyrannical, and hence gives him physical strength.

Boudjedra continued his condemnatory exposés in subsequent novels, which deal with a variety of themes. Yet the portrayal of the oppressed woman is constantly woven into the narrative of each one of his works, either as a subplot or as a series of asides. In *Les 1001 Années de la nostalgie* (1979), in which he introduces powerful female characters, Boudjedra states, in an aside, that in Manama, the fictional setting of his novel, women continue to live under the patriarchal yoke, with no function except that of producing future generations of wretched human beings. His last francophone novel, *Le Vainqueur de coupe* (1981), centres on an incident in which a young Algerian kills a French collaborator in a French football stadium. It is 1957 and the war of independence was entering one of its most severe stages. In spite of the fact that the novel revolves around the actions surrounding the incident, the football game that was taking place at the time of the man's death, and the thoughts of the young man who carries out the killing, Boudjedra manages to include a brief reference to a young bride, who, terrified of her bridegroom's inconsiderate forcefulness, commits suicide on her wedding night: 'On la trouva morte. . . et personne n'osa brandir les draps de la virginité parce qu'on ne pouvait plus savoir entre le sang des veines et celui de l'hymen, lequel était le plus vrai.' He goes on to say: 'Le mari. . . n'eut rien à déplorer. Il écrivit vite au village. . . qu'il cherchait femme nouvelle' (pp.102–3).

The Moroccan sociologist Soumaya Naamane-Guessous refers to the wedding night as 'cette nuit atroce', which remains in the minds of countless young women as a night of violence.[8]

George Eliot often introduced the word 'passion' into her novels to describe those pent-up feelings which women could not freely express in the taboo-laden society of Victorian England. Yet, in contemporary Algerian literature, the expression, much favoured by George Eliot, can also be applied to the feelings expressed by male writers, like Boudjedra and some of his contemporaries. The angry retorts in the works of Rachid Mimouni (b. 1945), for example, cannot but be described as 'passionate'. In his novel *Une Paix à vivre* (1983),[9] set in the early years of Algerian independence, Mimouni introduces male characters who refuse to take women seriously. Some think of them only as childbearers whose role in life is less important than that of men, the providers: 'la femelle doit procréer, élever et protéger sa progéniture, tandis que le mâle est chargé de pouvoir à la subsistance quotidienne . . . Sa mortalité est par conséquent plus élevée que celle de la femme' (p.144).

In Mimouni's highly acclaimed novel, *Tombéza* (1984), the eponymous hero is the illegitimate son of a rape victim, deformed because of the blows his mother received when she was pregnant. In this work Mimouni, through his narrator, criticizes societies which, beneath a veneer of piety, oppress women and dehumanize anyone who does not meet with their approval. He calls out in anger: 'hypocrite société! Comme si je ne savais pas ce que cachent tes apparences de vertus, tes pudibonderies, tes tartufferies' (p.34). He then asks in desperation what makes a community penalize a rape victim and allow the perpetrator of the crime to go free. 'Pauvres filles! Pauvres femmes!' he exclaims.

In her hauntingly lyrical novel, *La Grotte éclatée* (1979), set during the war of independence, the author, Yamina Mechakra, calls out in supplication: 'Allah! qu'ai-je donc fait pour naître fille!' (p.82). Written as the recollections of the narrator, who is a nurse tending wounded *maquisards* in a cave not far from the Tunisian border, the novel presents the reader with a galaxy of moving portraits of men, some wounded, some whole, who drift in and out of the cave. It is a time of great flux in the history of Algeria and in the life of the narrator,

8. Soumaya Naamane-Guessous (1991), *Au-delà de toute pudeur*, Rabat: Eddif, p.258.
9. This was in fact Mimouni's second novel. It was published in Algeria a year after his award-winning third novel *Le Fleuve détourné* (Paris: Laffont) appeared in France.

who does not remain unscathed. *La Grotte éclatée* is a moving account of the suffering endured during the war of independence by both men and women. It is, in the words of Kateb Yacine, who wrote the preface, 'Un long poème en prose qui peut se lire comme un roman'. It is the painful account of one woman who took an active part in the war, 'en "regardant" l'Algérie "avec les yeux de sa mémoire". . . en fondant sa voix dans celles de toutes les autres femmes'.[10]

Perhaps the following words uttered by Hawa Djabali (b. 1949) in her novel *Agave* (1983) can best describe the central character of Mechakra's novel and those of her generation who put up with so much suffering: 'Femme-mémoire revenue des guerres et des joutes oratoires, civilisée et repoussée aux confins du désert des patriarches. . . femme vieillie pour crier: "Aujourd'hui!" Femme sécurité contre l'oubli. . . décivilisée, humanisée, recèle tous les âges' (p.137). Unlike most women writing in the first person, the *je* in Djabali's novel is a man. He is the husband of the female central character, who is a doctor. In spite of the fact that she is an educated woman, the man still seems to have the voice. But at one point the masculine *je* becomes feminine, and the 'muted', voiceless woman takes on the 'dominant'[11] role, declaring: 'Pour exister dans ton monde, je suis devenue semblable à l'homme' (p.110).

In spite of the pain and tragic experiences described by Mechakra and Djabali, their novels remain full of hope. From about the early 1980s a few novels appeared where the voice in them was that of utter despair, as in Djanet Lachmet's only novel to date, *Le Cow-Boy* (1983). The young central character bemoans the fact that she was rejected by her mother because she was born a girl. Fettouma Touati, in her fictional work, *Le Printemps désespéré* (1984), subtitled *Vie d'Algériennes*, conveys the despair felt by three generations of women from the same family. The work describes the world of Kabyle women in Algeria, while Ferrudja Kessas's *Beur's Story*, mentioned above, describes the everyday life of Kabyle girls in France. Set in Le Havre, Kessas's novel paints a moving picture of the alienation felt by two teenage schoolgirls, similar to that expressed by Taos Amrouche several decades earlier.

Perhaps one of the most heart-rending cries of anguish is that of

10. In Christiane Achour (1990), *Anthologie de la littérature algérienne de langue française*, Algiers, Bordas, p.245.
11. The terms 'dominant' and 'muted', referring to men and women respectively, were first used by the anthropologist Edwin Ardener (1975), 'Belief and the Problem of Women', in Shirley Ardener (ed.), *Perceiving Women*, London: Malaby Press.

Nina Bouraoui (b. 1967) in her two novels to date, *La Voyeuse interdite* (1991) and *Poing mort* (1992). Bouraoui's works can best be described as *littérature de l'étouffement*, where the cry emanating from within is a muffled one, uttered as a last resort because there is no one to listen and no escape. In her first novel, Bouraoui describes a cloistered young woman watching the world outside from behind heavily curtained windows. There is no bonding between the female inhabitants of the ancestral home, as there is in some other novels. Instead, a feeling of mutual suspicion and hostility permeates the household, while the young girls contained within it wither and age before their time. The word *cloîtrée*, frequently uttered by both men and women writers before Bouraoui, acquires a more sinister dimension in this novel. In her second novel, *Poing mort*, Bouraoui's narrator reaches even lower depths of despair. Set mostly in a cemetery, the novel reeks of death, as when the narrator says with resignation: 'Je vis avec la mort et je meurs d'ennui avec la vie' (p.14). The idea of being weary of living and ageing before one's time is also expressed by Leïla Rezzoug (b. 1956) in her novel *Apprivoiser l'insolence* (1988), where the narrator, Maïa, says that the vicissitudes of life have planted on her fourteen-year-old face 'des rides de vieille dame fatiguée de vivre' (p.15).

In spite of the fact that a number of men have helped in giving objectively truthful representations of women in their novels, the documents of women writers present a more comprehensive picture, which is both subjective and objective. In the words of Christiane Achour: 'les femmes écrivains introduisent une marque originale dans cette littérature, proposant des écritures nouvelles, des regards différents sur la réalité culturelle algérienne'.[12]

There are numerous and varied representations of women in the Algerian novel, ranging from the early images of the long-suffering mother and submissive daughter, to the active combatant, the European woman and the newly independent professional woman, all of which one cannot possibly include in a cursory survey. Yet the picture that emerges, whatever the age or social background of the woman, is of someone with a strong presence. The portrayal of women is one of the many facets of modern Algerian literature which continue to provide a valuable commentary on the cataclysms through which Algerians live. A close study of the works of Algerian authors gives an impression of their lives and times more vivid than any historical work can convey. According to Raymond Williams, 'society determines, much more than we realize and at deeper levels than we ordinarily admit, the writing of literature, but also. . . the society is

12. Achour, *Anthologie de la litteratuare algerienne*, p.233.

not completely, not fully and immediately present until the literature has been written'.[13] Most Algerian writers see the very act of writing itself as a sign of commitment to their community, and particularly to those still voiceless individuals within it. Assia Djebar puts it more eloquently when she writes: 'Ecrire ne tue pas la voix mais la réveille, surtout pour ressusciter tant de soeurs disparues' (*L'Amour, la fantasia*, p.229).

Bibliography

Amrouche, Taos (1947), *Jacinthe noire*, Paris: Charlot.
—— (1960), *Rue des Tambourins*, Paris: La Table Ronde.
—— (1975), *L'Amant imaginaire*, Paris: Nouvelle Société Morel.
Boudjedra, Rachid (1969), *La Répudiation*, Paris: Denoël.
—— (1979), *Les 1001 Années de la nostalgie*, Paris: Denoël.
—— (1981), *Le Vainqueur de coupe*, Paris: Denoël.
Bouraoui, Nina (1991), *La Voyeuse interdite*, Paris: Gallimard.
—— (1992), *Poing mort*, Paris: Gallimard.
Debèche, Djamila (1947), *Leïla, jeune fille d'Algérie*, Algiers: Charras.
—— (1955), *Aziza*, Algiers: Imbert.
Dib, Mohammed (1952), *La Grande maison*, Paris: Seuil.
—— (1954), *L'Incendie*, Paris: Seuil.
—— (1957), *Le Métier à tisser*, Paris: Seuil.
—— (1962), *Qui se souvient de la mer*, Paris: Seuil.
—— (1964), *Cours sur la rive sauvage*, Paris: Seuil.
—— (1968), *La Danse du roi*, Paris: Seuil.
—— (1991), *Neiges de marbre*, Paris: Publisud.
Djabali, Hawa (1983), *Agave*, Paris: Publisud.
Djebar, Assia (1962), *Les Enfants du nouveau monde*, Paris: Julliard.
—— (1985), *L'Amour, la fantasia*, Paris: Lattès.
—— (1987), *Ombre sultane*, Paris: Lattès.
—— (1991), *Loin de Médine*, Paris: Albin Michel.
Feraoun, Mouloud (1950), *Le Fils du pauvre*, Paris: Seuil.
Kateb, Yacine (1956), *Nedjma*, Paris: Seuil.
Kessas, Ferrudja (1990), *Beur's Story*, Paris: L'Harmattan.
Lachmet, Djanet (1983), *Le Cow-Boy*, Paris: Belfond.

13. Raymond Williams (n.d.), 'Notes on English Prose', in Raymond Williams, *Writing in Society*, London: Verso, p.72.

Mammeri, Mouloud (1952), *La Colline oubliée*, Paris: Plon.

—— (1965), *L'Opium et le bâton*, Paris: Plon.

Mechakra, Yamina (1979), *La Grotte éclatée*, Algiers: SNED.

Mimouni, Rachid (1983), *Une Paix à vivre*, Algiers: ENAL.

—— (1984), *Tombéza*, Paris: Laffont.

Rezzoug, Leïla (1988), *Apprivoiser l'insolence*, Paris: L'Harmattan.

Sebbar, Leïla (1981), *Fatima, ou les Algériennes au square*, Paris: Stock.

—— (1982), *Shérazade, 17 ans, brune, frisée, les yeux verts*, Paris: Stock.

—— (1984), *Parle, mon fils, parle à ta mère*, Paris: Stock.

—— (1985), *Les Carnets de Shérazade*, Paris: Stock.

—— (1991), *Le Fou de Shérazade*, Paris: Stock.

Touati, Fettouma (1984), *Le Printemps désespéré*, Paris: L'Harmattan.

– 6 –

Commuting the 'Sentences' of Malek Haddad

Sara Poole

Même en s'exprimant en français, les écrivains algériens d'origine arabo-
berbère *traduisent* une pensée *spécifiquement algérienne*, une pensée qui aurait
trouvé la plénitude de son expression *si elle avait été véhiculée par un langage
et une écriture arabes.*

Malek Haddad, 'Les Zéros tournent en rond'

How do you write about imperialist oppression in the language of the
oppressor? The poet and novelist Malek Haddad addressed the specific
problems facing the Algerian author writing – because his Arabic was
too poor – in French, particularly during the 1950s and 1960s, in a
number of theoretical writings, which have in turn been much
discussed by critics. An investigation of Haddad's novels, however,
shows that this particular concern has tended to distract attention from
a more general and fundamental question also raised, and in fact
explored more often, in his fiction: that of the very nature of
communication, and hence of the function of the artist.

'Les Zéros tournent en rond' (henceforth 'Les Zéros'), from which
the quotation above is drawn, is the essay in which Haddad seeks to
explain and explore the specific linguistic and cultural predicament of
francophone Algerian writers during the war of independence. And
the vexed question of how to express what is essentially not French
in French – the dilemma of the francophone Algerian writer – is never
absent from the novels. Thus in *La Dernière Impression* (henceforth
Impression),[1] Haddad's first novel, and the only one to be for the most
part set in Algeria, the importance of two highly significant episodes

---

1. Malek Haddad (1989), *La Dernière Impression*, Algiers: Editions Bouchène.
All references are to this edition, others being out of print.

is underlined by reference to nothing less than the grammar of the French language. When the protagonist Saïd journeys to Aix-en-Provence to offer his condolences to the parents of his French lover, killed by a stray bullet, he learns that this unexceptional couple, whom he compares to two corks bobbing along in a current, also have a son serving in Algeria:

> - Quel malheur, dit le père, lui aussi il est parti là-bas. 'On' l'a rappelé. 'On' l'a rappelé. 'On'. Magnifiques pudeur et discrétion d'un Français moyen pour désigner la fatalité ou l'Etat. Le mektoub des bouchons tient dans un pronom indéfini. (p.114)

Here, then, the impersonal pronoun *on* − 'they' − is highlighted as representing the anonymous military bureaucrats whose signature on a page has sent the young Aixois to war. Later, it is the fact that a verb must always take an object − that Saïd is returning home specifically 'to do something' − that is remarked upon:

> Il ne rentrerait pas en Algérie pour prendre un tram, pour acheter un journal, pour embrasser sa mère. Il rentrerait en Algérie pour faire quelque chose. C'est une des magies de la langue française d'avoir fait qu'un verbe ait besoin d'un complément d'objet. Et c'est un signe des temps qu'en Algérie, comme ailleurs, pour un Algérien, il y a toujours quelque chose à faire. (p.127)

Two of Haddad's novels appear to attack the problem even more directly in that they have an Algerian writing in French as main character. In *Je t'offrirai une gazelle* (henceforth *Gazelle*) the anonymous author–protagonist, at a loss for words when told that his novel has been 'understood', responds with 'Ah! bon?', and Haddad steps into the narrative to explain: 'Il dit "Ah! bon?" quand il n'a rien à dire. Il admire les Français parce qu'ils savent parler.'[2] While this explanatory aside does not raise that major issue of the use of the colonizer's language directly, it does link the French as a nation to an ability to express themselves verbally − the French, that is, as opposed to other peoples with their other languages. And Haddad continues: 'La langue est peut-être française.' The play on the senses of *langue* is an amusing but telling conceit whereby the organ of speech itself becomes French. A more direct reference to that central issue comes later, however, when the verb *aimer* is remarked upon, and we learn that 'En arabe,

2. Malek Haddad (1978), *Je t'offrirai une gazelle*, Paris: Union Générale d'Editions, p.54. All references to this edition. (First published 1959).

c'est un verbe qui dépasse l'idée' (p.97). We cannot but conclude that *aimer* has been found wanting.

Almost halfway through the next novel, *L'Elève et la leçon* (henceforth *L'Elève*), the Algerian doctor–narrator details his daughter's Europeanized characteristics, including in his list 'des mots français pour parler du monde arabe'.[3] And in Haddad's final novel, *Le Quai aux fleurs ne répond plus* (henceforth *Quai*), referred to by Charles Bonn as 'ce monument de l'ambiguïté',[4] and, by the same token, the language schism are brought to our attention by overt, not to say intrusive, symbolism in the form of word-play on the word 'liberté'. Khaled, the main character, has offered his friends' daughter a doll from Algiers, which he introduces as 'Houria'. The little French girl cannot pronounce the aspirate H:

> L'enfant essaya mais en vain.
> - Et ça veut dire quoi, Ouria?
> - Ça veut dire: liberté.
> . . .
> - C'est trop dur à dire, la liberté, en arabe.[5]

Haddad the poetic novelist thus appears, from these episodes, to bear out the theories of Haddad the philosopher–essayist–linguist, who maintains that only '*si elle avait été véhiculée par un langage et une écriture arabe*'[6] would his thought have attained its true expression, and whose characters and situations point up that inadequacy. However, such a view requires three major qualifications. Firstly, the theoretical arguments, although stated time and time again in articles and interviews, remain vague; as Christiane Achour has noted, *Les Zéros*, despite its plethora of 'sentences' (sententious pronouncements), lacks precision 'quant aux définitions de la langue, de la culture'[7] – although these latter are the two most vital concepts it is concerned to discuss. For evidence of this claim, one need look no further than the single elided term 'arabo-berbère'. Secondly, the arguments are vague

3. Malek Haddad (1982), *L'Elève et la leçon*, Paris: Union Générale d'Editions, p.65. All references to this edition. (First published 1960).

4. Charles Bonn (1985), *Le Roman algérien de langue française*, Paris: L'Harmattan, p.111.

5. Malek Haddad (1982), *Le Quai aux fleurs ne répond plus*, Paris: Union Générale d'Editions, pp.44–5. (First published 1961).

6. 'Les Zéros', p.34; italics in the original.

7. Christiane Achour (1990), *Anthologie de la littérature française*, Paris: ENAP Bordas, p.109.

because they are about inarticulateness in general as well as simply the inarticulateness of the colonized. French was not strictly a foreign language for Haddad. It was the only language he could write in. His mother tongue was the Kabyle variety of Berber, a language not transcribed.[8] His Arabic, especially his written Arabic, was rudimentary. But he was convinced that the French imposed on him, and on all those like him educated in French-run schools, could not affect some indefinable ethnic kernel that was his essential Algerianness. This is why he can speak of his own Arabic way of thinking, his French vocabulary, and the at best 'correspondence approximative'[9] between the two. He is therefore mooting the idea of thought existing independently of and indeed preceding verbalization, or language, and thus, as Jacqueline Leiner[10] has pointed out, comes close to echoing the surrealists, or at least Breton, by positing a language of the subconscious. And like Breton, like Freud, he does not think in terms of a Jungian collective or human unconscious built on the humus of primitive man's psyche (hence perhaps the affirmation that, 'L'attribut "homme" est loin d'être un dénominateur commun.'[11] He is thus led to propose an ethnic unconscious, that unconscious which he feels he cannot translate into French.

That same ethnic Arab unconscious could of course – could only – be expressed in Arabic. But not by the francophone Malek Haddad. The artist who declared in a 1958 interview that, 'Je veux communiquer mon rêve et mon regard'[12] was, according to his own definition, if not entirely aphonic, at least inarticulate. The language that he did have failed the self it could not express; in his experience, then, since he had only one language, language in general, language *per se* failed as a medium via which to convey that self and its essence. Like Artaud, he might have written, 'Il me manque une concordance des mots avec la minute de mes états.'[13]

Thirdly, and turning to the novels, the above few instances of

8. That it was not can, of course, be ascribed at least partly to the Arab imperium that North Africa experienced a millennium before the French variety.

9. 'Les Zéros', p.34.

10. Jacqueline Leiner (1974), 'Le Problème du langage chez Frantz Fanon, Malek Haddad et Albert Memmi', *Présence Francophone*, no. 8, pp.9–15.

11. 'Les Zéros', p.35.

12. Malek Haddad (1958), 'Interview', *Les Lettres françaises*, no. 751, 11–12 December.

13. Antonin Artaud (1925), in *OEuvres Complètes*, Paris: Gallimard, vol. I, p.98.

references to the problems associated with using French are not a selection, a handful out of many; they constitute the sum of such references. The main concern of the novels is a much more general frustration and despair. They bristle with examples of the playing with and the testing of language *per se*. Thus it is that, in the opening pages of *Impression*, Saïd, a young man unsure of his feelings about nationalism and designer of a bridge that is about to be blown up, avoids any explanation of the contemporary situation which might include loaded abstract words such as 'war' or 'peace' or 'right': 'Les ponts, les ponts, ça n'est pas avec des principes qu'on fait des ponts, c'est avec de la graisse et des boulons. Les mots, ça ne tient pas debout' (p.11). Words may not 'stand up', but they can wield the power of life and of death; writing against a context of warfare, Haddad evokes words as potential killers: 'Il y a des mots qui ne sont pas plus gros qu'une balle' (p.25). No bigger, but equally deadly, is of course the implication, a notion returned to towards the end of the novel, where the power of the word to save or slaughter is underlined:

> Ils n'ont l'air de rien ces mots, ces petits mots, elle n'a l'air de rien cette phrase, cette petite phrase: c'est une question de vie ou de mort.
> De vie ou de mort. (p.157)

Saïd exclaims against an 'infernale alchimie des mots' (p.88), but it is stressed in this novel, here by virtue of the repetition of the same sentence structure, that an imperfect understanding of words imposes a similar incomprehension of the human psyche: 'Il ne comprenait plus les mots. Il ne comprenait plus les gens' (p.115). Finally, Saïd has specific difficulties with the verb 'to love' – 'c'est un verbe qu'il ne comprenait pas, un verbe tout saupoudré de métaphysique' (p.106) – a problem to be compared with those of future protagonists he prefigures.

It is significant that the second novel *Gazelle*'s anonymous author initially lives with a German girl, with whom, since he speaks no German and she no French, communication must be non-verbal. 'Pas besoin de dictionnaire' (p.40), a phrase appearing twice, has a defiant ring. Later Gerda offers the author a harmonica, a gift of music which, we are reminded, 'parle toutes les langues' (p.64). She seems never to be concerned about their lack of a common language: significantly we are told that 'elle vivait malgré les mots. . . elle vivait parce qu'elle était faite pour vivre' (p.74). The author, 'qui ne savait pas vivre', needs to break off with her. This is where he needs the dictionary, 'livre fatal'. Because words or language fail, their deathly and ultimately destructive quality is put to use to kill the relationship:

> Alors l'auteur prit sur la table de nuit le petit dictionnaire rouge français–
> allemand. Il chercha le mot 'séparation'. Il montra du doigt le mot *séparation*
> à Gerda qui le répéta à haute voix en lui donnant la musique lourde de la
> langue originelle. Puis l'auteur chercha 'définitivement'. Il le chercha
> longuement, craignant presque de le trouver. Le petit dictionnaire rouge
> semblait un livre fatal, la clé des songes et des cauchemars, le manuel du
> malheur d'un alchimiste délirant. . .
> . . .*Défavorable*. . .*défaitiste*. . .*désastre*. . .
> Le mot dansa enfin comme l'objectif à la jumelle qu'on règle, comme la
> projection d'un générique qu'on met au point. Le mot s'installa, se fixa,
> s'immobilisa. *Définitivement*. . . (p.75; original italics)

Characteristic of this and indeed of all of these novels is a tendency
to personify the word. The first noteworthy instance of such a device
in *Gazelle* suggests that, where once the anonymous author felt
language sufficed to convey his ideas – perhaps because they were
themselves limited then – it no longer can. Words no longer transmit
or obey those inner promptings:

> L'auteur . . . laissait les sentiers rocailleux de sa majorité. L'âge adulte
> fondait autour de quelques bougies sur un chétif gâteau d'anniversaire. Il
> se gratta les genoux à l'endroit des graviers. Il mordillait un porte-plume
> en bois. En ce temps-là les mots étaient obéissants. Les idées ne dépassaient
> pas le regard des parents. (p.67)

Elsewhere the limitations of language are repeatedly stressed. Certain
events show them wanting, reveal that inadequacy: 'Les mots se
taisaient impressionnés par le langage des situations' (p.88). Music, it
is more than once stressed, is far superior:

> Avec la musique peut-être, avec la musique il aurait dit, il aurait pu dire. . .
> mais les mots, dès lors qu'ils font l'école buissonnière, dès lors qu'ils veulent
> voler de leurs propres ailes, c'est la catastrophe, tout est fichu.
> . . .
> - La musique, c'est du vrai, ce n'est pas de l'à-peu-près, de l'approchant.
> (p.122)

And again: 'Il faut passer par-dessus les mots' (p.96).

The impression is one of disillusionment – and one of conflict. On
the one side there is 'real life'; there is the vitality of Gerda; there is
the passion of the fictional lovers Yaminata and Moulay. On the other
there is that poor substitute, language, incapable of rendering the vital,
the sacred. And, because the author is by trade a wordsmith, life is

reduced to word-size. Thus we learn – noting the repetition and introduction of the negative – that 'pour l'auteur. . . la vie était, la vie n'était qu'un phénomène littéraire' (p.80).

Does the author finally refuse to have his book published because it is reductive of life? His remark in the closing pages that 'les mots, le langage, n'ont jamais rapproché personne' (p.121) would seem to suggest that, for this fictional author, language incapable of such *rapprochement* confounds usual definitions of itself by failing to communicate – and that it is therefore no longer of use.

L'Elève, the third novel, is less preoccupied with such questions; the examination of the range of conflicting emotions, rather than the (linguistically) adequate rendering of them, would seem its principal concern. But the opening pages of this novel contain some of Haddad's most vehement vituperations against language and its deficiencies. Here the doctor–protagonist must tell a friend he is dying:

> Il a essayé de sourire.
> - Foutu, hein!
> Foutu? Ce sont les mots qui sont foutus. Une idée, passe encore. (p.10)

This is page ten. On the next page, in front of his daughter:

> Je vais écouter, je vais beaucoup écouter. Je n'ai pas à raconter l'énormité de mon silence.
> Ce sont les mots qui sont foutus. (p.11)

Finally he adds to this obsession by means of that personification mentioned previously and which, as *Impression* had done, portrays language as potentially dangerous, threatening: 'Que les mots soient foutus je le conçois. Mais qu'ils deviennent méchants m'épouvante' (p.14).

In the final novel, *Quai,* that personification is maintained. The notion of life perceived as a literary phenomenon by those who do not know how to live is again evoked, presented here as a quotation from one of Khaled's previous novels (p.73). It is insisted upon: 'Maintenant, je crois plus que jamais que la vie est un phénomène littéraire, oui, plus que jamais' (p.74) and later repeated, with the negative 'nothing but' added for emphasis. The idea that to make anything into a literary phenomenon is to stifle it is similarly reinforced; this time, love provides a variant: 'L'amour est-il pour vous un phénomène littéraire? / Pourquoi pas!' (p.57). And this, in many ways darkest of the four novels, is also – or maybe therefore – the one which is paradoxically the most eloquent on the inadequacies of language. Thus a light-hearted conceit on words centred on their having 'got above themselves' masks that (by now familiar) feeling that they do not communicate as they should: 'Quand on me dit montagne, moi, je pense maquis. Les dictionnaires sont à refaire. Je me demande ce qu'attend Dieu pour remettre les mots et les chansons à leur place' (p.81). A reflective passage on the nature of love is transformed into a mini-exposé on how language is constantly found wanting:

> Est-il possible, vraiment, de savoir prouver son amour, de l'avouer, de l'expliquer? Car les mots sont encore plus nécessiteux que les oreilles mendiantes. Et puis l'amour a besoin de talent, et puis seul le silence a du talent. . .
> Comment dire: la nuit est petite et fraîche come toi? Comment dire: je viendrai t'embrasser quand les enfants dormiront? Comment dire ces cheveux qui façonnent une main, le moment qui sépare l'éternité, la gêne qui s'ensuit, la gratitude infinie de la brute qui a vu se réveiller en lui un ange coupable et heureux? Comment dire: je t'aime, tout simplement: je t'aime?
> Il faudrait ne jamais parler, il faudrait toujours prier. Il faudrait ne jamais écrire, respectueux devant le silence, intimidé devant le papier blanc. (p.49)

And, where the anonymous author in *Gazelle* limited himself to pointing out his view that 'les mots n'ont jamais rapproché personne', Khaled formulates a much more detailed view of the role of the creative artist:

> Il y a un tas de gens qui pensent qu'un écrivain est nécessaire à la vie et à la survie d'une communauté en lutte. La belle erreur, oui, la belle erreur, c'est une erreur, mais elle est très belle. Les écrivains n'ont jamais modifié le sens de l'Histoire, l'Histoire qui est assez grande dame pour savoir se diriger toute seule. Les écrivains, romanciers et poètes, artistes en général, ne sont que des témoins . . . des témoins et des épiphénomènes.

What he says can usefully be compared with something Louis Guilloux had written, on behalf of writers on the Left, in 1929: 'La révolution se fait sans nous et même contre nous. Elle ne tient pas compte de nos livres, de nos problèmes, de nos discours, et elle a raison. La vraie foi révolutionnaire ne bavarde pas.'[14] And, again, with an opinion W.H. Auden, who in the 1930s had tried to serve as an ambulance driver in the Spanish Civil War, was to voice in 1967: 'The

14. *Monde*, 2e année, no. 73, October 1929.

world about us is, as it always has been, full of gross evils and appalling misery, but it is a fatal delusion and a shocking overestimation of the importance of the artist in the world, to suppose that, by making works of art, we can do anything to eradicate the one or alleviate the other. . . Where social evils are concerned, the only effective weapons are two: political action and straight reportage of the facts, journalism . . . Art is impotent.'[15]

So artists are witnesses, reporters of facts. Here two poets seem both to have concluded that the notion of 'pen as sword' is fanciful romanticism. Auden can accept the limitations of his self-accorded role because the language he manipulates is both his own and that of the foreign culture he was to embrace – and because he presumably trusts it. But if Haddad shares this view of the artist lent to Khaled Ben Tobal – Haddad who was in France, writing in French, throughout a period of war between his own and his host country – then he cannot even be said to be a witness. He is witness only to the fact that he isn't witnessing events crucially important to him. And he is witnessing that state of absence, conveying it, imperfectly, because that negative presence, or void or lack, is by definition non-existent and therefore inexpressible, unsayable - incommunicable in language. The anonymous author in *Gazelle* withdraws his novel from the publisher. *Quai*'s poet Khaled jumps from a train when learning of the betrayal by his wife (of whom he had written that, 'Tous ces mots que tu savais, tu étais à la fois ma source et mon écho' (p.118). He will never reach his friend in Provence, a friend to whom he could always talk of his work; a friend who, as perhaps befits the friend of the author who cannot translate his thought into language, works 'dans le domaine de la traduction' (p.77).

There are, then, in these novels, many more explorations of the nature of language *per se* than there are references to the French–Arabic dichotomy. As is so often the case, the creative works of the artist here give the lie to the theoretical writings, the essays and interviews pinpointing one apparent source of anguish, the fiction revealing it as being rather, or at the very least in part, located elsewhere. 'Je sais que quand j'ai voulu écrire j'ai raté mes mots et c'est tout',[16] wrote that major proponent of the need to say the unsayable, Antonin Artaud, some twenty years after he had talked of that missing *concordance*. And it is with this paradox that Malek Haddad, writer, and his writer–protagonists struggle to come to terms.

15. W.H. Auden (1967), 'The Real World', *The New Republic*, 9 December, p.26.
16. A. Artaud, 'Préambule' (1946) to the *OEuvres Complètes*, vol. I, 1984, p.9.

'Don't Look Back': Albert Memmi's
La Statue de sel

Seán Hand

Je suis étonné de ne pas avoir peur; mais l'habitude dispense du courage et, en vérité, j'ai longtemps épié ma découverte: je meurs pour m'être retourné sur moi-même. Il est interdit de se voir et j'ai fini de me connaître. Comme la femme de Loth, que Dieu changea en statue, puis-je encore vivre au-delà de mon regard? (*Ss*, p.368)

Albert Memmi's closing meditation in the 1953 *La Statue de sel*[1] offers not merely a quasi-autobiographical explanation for the work's title. It alludes (retrospectively, of course; hence one aspect of its irony and complexity) to the subtle themes and dynamics of a work which, in terms of francophone writing, is both the testament of a particular consciousness which can never be satisfactorily defined by the established and endorsed sociopolitical units through which it comes into being, and the prophetic and exemplary self-reflection of a culture emerging from a colonial panopticon into postcolonial structures and identities. In both cases, there is a looking back as well as a looking forward: a looking back which in Sartrean as much as in Biblical terms can petrify an emerging subject (through fear, punishment, loss of nerve), but which, in spite of the abyss which such doubt opens up, is structurally necessary to the emergence of an unhappy consciousness; and a looking forward which represents the attempts of a 'progressive–regressive' consciousness to overcome its conditions of existence and act within its situations, but which carries within it all the while the ethical problem of living beyond its retrospective gaze, with all the exhausting weight of guilt, regret, loss and despair which such intelligence carries. *La Statue de sel* is doubly a *bilan*, then:

1. Albert Memmi (1953), *La Statue de sel*, Paris: Gallimard. Referred to in parentheses as *Ss*. All references to the Folio edition.

a personal assessment of the land left behind and the subject's uncertain future; and the necessarily personal contribution to an emerging colonial and postcolonial history or historiography, wherein one of *La Statue de sel*'s primary virtues is its refusal to endorse a dominant narrative, that is to petrify the emerging colonized consciousness. Hence the work's obligation to transcend the traditional generic limits of autobiography, whose game Albert Memmi has elsewhere called false and 'menteur',[2] and to strive instead for a more authentic 'ordonnance théâtrale', wherein 'une vie ne se raconte pas. On la rêve, on la réinvente à mesure qu'on la raconte, on la revit sans cesse d'une manière différente.' The looking back is doubly transgressive, then: the doubting backward gaze reveals things as they really are, and none the less sees and re-presents each time anew. No wonder such a look is generally banned: it not only strips power relations bare and exposes fear and hypocrisy; it equally assumes and exploits the full multiplicity and potentiality of the defining structures within which we are situated, including (importantly for emerging writing) on the level of genre. Such work can have a real truth value, in the phenomenological as in the political field, in that structurally its story unfolds as a series of revelations, as a constant act of surprising itself. Memmi has described it as 'une autobiographie plus vraie que nature';[3] and one is equally reminded here of a remark made by him with regard to the confessional literature of Gide or Montaigne to the effect that 'il est vrai que je me surprends constamment à raconter des histoires'.[4] The ambivalent gesture in *La Statue de sel* of looking back and not looking back can be explained, then, by Albert Memmi's general belief that the self remains ultimately strange to itself, that it already contains an other within it which is revealed in all the anguish of being. This vision of the self is then represented structurally as the endlessly transmogrifying search for an order, one which naturally tests generic definitions. To quote *Ce que je crois*: 'Je ne peux savoir *qui* je suis; par accumulations successives, je pourrais savoir *comment* je suis. Le portrait de l'artiste par lui-même ne saurait être qu'une composition de marqueterie.'[5]

2. See Albert Memmi (1976), *La Terre intérieure: entretiens avec Victor Malka*, Paris: Gallimard, p.11; Albert Memmi (1985), *Ce que je crois*, Paris: Grasset, pp.28–9.
3. Memmi, *La Terre intérieure*, p.109.
4. Ibid., p.81. For mention of Gide and Montaigne, see Memmi, *Ce que je crois*, pp.29, 44.
5. Memmi, *Ce que je crois*, p.32.

This mosaic structure and the artisanal work which 'marqueterie' suggests are laid forth fully in *La Statue de sel*. The story line, which parallels Albert Memmi's own childhood, presents the first-person passage to manhood of Alexander Mordekhai Benillouche, a poor Tunisian Jewish boy whose mother is Berber, whose father (a skilled *bourrelier*) is of Italian origins, who expresses himself in Tunisian dialect but is obviously defined by both Hebrew and French, and comes to define himself ultimately in the latter (since *La Statue de sel* is written in French). The course of the work is that of a traditional *Bildungsroman*, to which are attached the particular circumstances and universal structures of colonization, anti-Semitism and the Second World War. Within this chronological structure, the boy encounters the usual *rites de passage*: the move from a maternal to a paternal world, the discovery of rivalry, violence and hatred, birth, circumcision, bar mitzvah and death, school and sexual yearnings, pride and prejudice. The usual boyhood! But there is the particular phenomenological anguish of identity arising from his estrangement or exclusion from each or all of the cultural groups impinging upon him. These 'events' in turn are divided into three significant parts, constituting a more consciously worked *ordonnance théâtrale*: the first, 'L'Impasse', focuses on the boy's family upbringing in the blind alley of the title; the second, entitled 'Alexander Mordekhai Benillouche', sees the boy move to the *lycée* and begin to question more seriously the traditional structures of his upbringing; the third, 'Le Monde', depicts a full confrontation with the social other in its most depressing and violent forms. The evolution of these structures of circumstance into constructions of learning means, moreover, that, while these stages are never neatly chronological, they are represented via a consciousness which registers its embodiment by increasingly foregrounding the structurality of each stage, whether in the home, the classroom or the street; in a name, a function or a stereotype; in a confrontation, revelation or disappointment. Through their cumulative exposure, the conniving definitions of embodied consciousness are shown to be the primary condition within which the young man will struggle to reach self-definition by looking back at them intellectually in order not to look back existentially. Even this in itself places him from the beginning in an irreducible structure, one involving the other who must be overcome but who equally must be sustained, through the narrator's growing cultural and political *prises de conscience*, but also by simple virtue of his anguished attempts not to petrify those upon whom he casts his retrospective gaze.

As we are told in a fittingly ambiguous opening to the first chapter, the child's world is punctuated by the father's asthmatic breathing. This wheezing dispels the child's nocturnal fears even as it records the father's slow demise. From the initial series of childhood confrontations with a specific other (amusingly embodied in the first chapter by an encounter with an aggressive goat, 'la plus terrible et la plus maternelle', which charges rather than cries out in anguish when the boy pulls its coat), the narrative starts to supply its own sublating structural orders. Here the three parts – the 'Impasse', the name and the world – begin to bear more abstract re-visions of the subject's political and cultural condition. Beyond the mother's breast and the father's breathing, the 'Impasse' is shown to contain structures of ritual and play which call forth only the blind and muffled response of unthinking innocence, a state in which you do not look back critically. As we are told in the first chapter's first paragraph, in a statement whose tenses and intentions already break this enchantment: 'Je veux m'en souvenir: ma vie connut des jours d'innocence où il me suffisait de fermer les yeux pour ne pas voir' (*Ss*, p.17). The child's emergence from sleep and his subsequent innocent play in the 'Impasse' at the beginning of the work equally mark a more programmatic emergence of a growing consciousness and its determined if anguished gaze. As the book's closing pages admit: 'L'Impasse n'a jamais existé. Elle ne fut que le calme de mon coeur avant qu'il ne comprenne' (*Ss*, p.371). Already by the sixth chapter of Part I, then, in a transition which coincides with the family moving from the 'Impasse' to a new apartment 'au Passage', the narrator is rendering transparent how this communal crush, in which 'chacun restait transparent pour tous' (*Ss*, p.76), contains hypocrisy, stupidity, hysteria and pettiness. In reaction to this violation of his privacy, the boy simultaneously rejects the sickly sweet advice given him by Uncle Aroun and company, that is to say, he refuses to have his intellectual gaze directed uncritically back to an oral folk tradition, and projects his own image of himself out of the community, in a manner which employs that very tradition against itself: responding at one point, for example, to his newly-born brother who has muscled in on his bar mitzvah, he contests the charms designed to protect the baby from the evil eye by observing: 'Volontiers, j'aurais enfoncé mon doigt dans l'oeil de cette larve' (*Ss*, p.82).

As we can hear in that statement, it is through a growing linguistic mastery that the boy begins to construct a looking back that is a looking forward, and to transform the ritual and play, which would, if unchallenged, reduce him to a 'practico-inert' state of passivity, into the primary materials for his own marquetry. This is a lesson already realized as early as the fourth chapter, which ostensibly recalls how boys would buy sweets by the school gates, and how class difference was at once physically experienced in terms of hunger and the food one could or could not afford, in particular here a Nestlé chocolate bar, whose wrapping enclosed one of a collectable series of picture cards with which one could potentially win a bike. The rituals and play of the children here are in fact prefaced by transparent observations on how it is language which offers the real test and the real key to self-liberation. Only French is spoken officially in the school, and the linguistic abyss which this presents sets an existential test in which identity can only emerge through the shock of alienation:

> Il s'agissait peu de nuances mais de rupture totale . . . J'étais devant un gouffre, sans moyen de comunication avec l'autre bord. . . Ces angoisses enfantines peuvent paraître futiles; ma situation n'est assurément pas unique: des millions d'hommes ont perdu leur unité fondamentale, ils ne se reconnaissent plus et se cherchent en vain. Mais je me dis aussi que cette rencontre n'a rien de rassurant; que d'autres essayent de recoller leurs membres épars sans y parvenir jamais me confirme au contraire dans ce déchirement. Toute ma vie, mes amitiés, mes acquisitions furent soumises à une constante réadaptation de ce que j'étais. (*Ss*, pp.43–4)

This realization and the already operative intellectual programme of restructuring – of not looking back – are all the more powerful for their affective and material base. The boy adds on the next page how he began to demand that his mother bless him each morning before leaving for school. Occasionally, though, the exhausted and harassed woman would spit a curse at him instead, an event which filled him with dread and foreboding, since '[j]e n'ai jamais pu me débarrasser de cet envoûtement magique du langage. . . Comme si, loin d'être un outil transparent, le langage participait directement des choses, en avait la densité' (*Ss*, p.45). This same density, of course, allows the linguistically gifted boy to begin to make his own image, a looking back within oneself that is none the less devoted to the project of self-realization.

The clearest and most crucial instance of this *dépassement* of linguistic definition is that of the name itself, and the whole of the book's second part is placed under the highly symbolical proper noun of Alexander Mordekhai Benillouche. As the boy himself spells out, the name is a caricature of colonial structure, and a clear indication of the petrifying forces directed against him. Alexander: 'claironnant, glorieux, me fut donné par mes parents en hommage à l'Occident prestigieux. Il leur semblait traduire l'image qu'ils avaient de l'Europe' (*Ss*, p.107). Mordekhai 'est si obstinément révélateur, qu'il équivaut à clamer "je suis juif!" et plus précisément "j'habite le ghetto", "je suis

de statut indigène", "je suis de moeurs orientales", "je suis pauvre'"
(*Ss*, p.108). Benillouche: 'le fils de l'agneau en patois berbéro-arabe.
De quelle tribu montagnarde mes ancêtres sont-ils sortis? Qui suis-je
enfin?' (*Ss*, p.109). Put together, the ensemble signifies: 'indigène dans
un pays de colonisation, juif dans un univers antisémite, Africain dans
un monde où triomphe l'Europe' (*Ss*, p.109). Through looking back
at his own name, the narrator becomes aware of the structural
condition of his own city, his own community, his own core. Once
articulated, his own name is made subject to a keenly dissecting eye
(one which more than once recalls his father's professional skill in
assessing with a single look the number of usable pieces of leather
extractable from a skin). However, assumption of his name becomes
here projective rather than passive (in this, his alter ego is a cousin of
the same name who criticizes the narrator for failing to observe the
required ritual on the death of his Uncle Joseph, and who, in that
sense, we are told, is the real Alexander Benillouche). This deeply
personal *dépassement*, the narrator's critical inhabitation of his own
name, provides him with the bodily basis for looking back, for
reducing those who would petrify him to the status of object
themselves. One of the best examples of this process of spiralling
sublation comes near the end of the second part in a chapter
appropriately entitled 'L'Escalier'. This centres on a bourgeois party
held by a coterie of middle-class adolescents who are scout leaders,
and who invite the narrator since they wish to have an instructor for
the Jewish part of their educational programme. The narrator's
unflinching gaze (to which he himself is not immune) exposes their
childish and patronizing games and their imitation of their parents'
obnoxious rituals, and focuses especially on their ridiculous adoption
of animal names for themselves – Owl, Deer, Rhinoceros – and on
the slightly sinister moment when the invited National Commissioner
of the Scouts, known as Loup-Gris, shaking hands with each of the
troop in turn (and raising his right forearm in a quick gesture),
discovers that 'Alexander' is not yet initiated, is a stranger, does not
bear a totemic name, thereby exposing and embarrassing the whole
system of classification. He obviously disapproves of the narrator's
presence, but it is too late: through another caricatural set of names,
their true structure has been glimpsed and relentlessly spelled out. The
chapter concludes with the narrator silently contesting the scout cry:
'Éclaireurs, toujours prêts!' by asking: 'Ready for what?'. Not for the
ghetto, certainly, through which the narrator begins around this time
to take long walks, as a physical inhabitation of what the name
encapsulates. From this break with middle-class definitions, and a
companion break with his father's desire to hold him within the debts

created by his own names, given in the second part's final chapter, 'Le Choix', we move into the third part, 'Le Monde', in which the narrator's syntagmatic and moral development is confronted by much greater existential challenges: poverty and prostitution, war, work camps and eventual voluntary exile, the last of these following in the wake of an incident where he is dissuaded from signing up for the Free French, once the full significance of his name, as he begins to sign the register, becomes apparent to the authorities.

The project of *dépassement* and the ever larger structures of repression encountered therefore ultimately induce Alexander on a novelistic level to look forward to a non-European, non-Jewish, non-African name: Argentina. But much of *La Statue de sel*'s value as a work of art is derived from its 'double couture', that is from its repetition or preservation of what on the surface it seeks to go beyond in its move from the 'Impasse' to the 'Départ'. The first-person transcendence of domination–dependency, in the form of parents, customs and traditional identities, may act as a third-person objectification of their existence but is simultaneously a second-person fostering of their flickering presence, a loving invocation and a sorrowful call for expiation. One is reminded of the amusing paradoxical moment in *Ce que je crois* when Albert Memmi seemingly announces to God: 'Pardonne-moi: tu n'as plus aucune place dans ma philosophie.'[6] Even the childhood games of 'shop', which involve measuring and mixing, or of 'king of the castle', which, like the former, involve privilege and subordination, have been preserved as much within the narrator's formal self-realizations as in their presentation (as playful prediction) of what will be repeated again and again beyond the 'Impasse deux fois cachée'. Put another way, the experiential progress into the symbolic is never free from an affective relapse into the imaginary. This idea adds a new level of meaning to the interdiction on looking back, but, when this itself is looked at in the book, we encounter the text's most sophisticated formal moments. There are numerous examples, both concrete and pervasive: the bloodstained link between the end of Part III, Chapter 1, 'Le Quartier', where the narrator is about to leave a prostitute's room, and the beginning of the following chapter, 'Les Autres', where he in fact opens the barricaded door of their own house in the wake of the latest pogrom; or the constant and cyclical play of light and dark which generates a *fort/da* of a maternal space. The most immediately remarkable formal effect, however, is that the work in fact begins not with an 'Impasse' but with an 'Epreuve', a dramatic account of sitting

6. Memmi, *Ce que je crois*, p.175.

an exam (amusingly, on J.S. Mill and Condillac), and of suddenly seeing at the moment of its commencement that this kind of task no longer concerns him. What he does instead is write some fifty pages of the narrative we then read. He concludes: 'Peut-être, en ordonnant ce récit, arriverai-je à mieux voir dans mes ténèbres et découvrirai-je quelque issue' (*Ss*, p.14). What this provides from the beginning, then, is an alternative looking back and looking forward, one freed from academic blinkers, experienced as an authentic choice, and offering the possibility of seizing and transforming the structures of identity. This moment of realization is then itself formally exploited in a further instance of looking back/looking forward, for the same scene is repeated but transposed in the penultimate chapter, the one immediately preceding 'Le Départ'. A comparison of these two versions (which obliges the reader to look back and look forward) shows how the later one is both dramatically more concise ('C'est que ma vie toute entière me remontait à la gorge' (*Ss*, p.13) versus 'Voilà que ma vie me remonte à la gorge' (*Ss*, p.357)) and more politically adumbrated by clear views on Vichy, Western culture and academic and administrative hierarchies. The whole narrative has been structured, then, around the authorial transformation of a moment which transforms writing, a politicoethical *dépassement* which successfully sustains a double looking back and looking forward.

The conclusion to Memmi's later *Portrait du colonisé* rejects both metaphysical essence and psychological essence. One must struggle in the present for the emergence of a whole and free human. *La Statue de sel* is, among other things, a clear embodiment and enactment of this ethical struggle, a personal looking back which gains impetus and logic from its political looking forward. And, in the process, we can add that Albert Memmi produced on the authorial level an emancipatory approach to the inherited or imposed structures of thinking and expression, one which has influenced not only subsequent colonized writers but, crucially, the writers and intellectuals of the dominant culture. (By way of simple indication here, one might begin to examine this aspect by comparing *La Statue de sel*, published in 1953 and serialized in part in *Les Temps modernes*, with Sartre's 1954 *Réflexions sur la question juive*. And, of course, one thinks at once of the prefaces by Camus and Sartre to *La Statue de sel* and the *Portrait du colonisé* respectively.) Albert Memmi has said of his subsequent novel *Agar*: 'je reste très marqué par le modèle cartésien. J'ai voulu mon roman transparent mais complexe.'[7] Our own critical

---

7. In *Albert Memmi, écrivain et sociologue*, textes réunis par Jean-Yves Guérin, Paris: L'Harmattan, 1988, p.171.

look back at *La Statue de sel* tells us that he had already succeeded on many levels – phenomenologically, politically, formally – in this aim of producing a transparent yet complex look at the past that will transform the future.

– 8 –

To be a Poet in Morocco

Jacqueline Kaye

On ne peut pas écrire de grands romans lorsqu'on a peur.

Le Chemin des ordalies, Abdellatif Laâbi's account of his long journey through torture and imprisonment, uses this quote from Gorky at a crucial moment (p.21). As Laâbi reads these lines, the lights in the prison go out. When light is restored, the world has utterly changed:

> Le livre de ou sur Gorki était là, posé ouvert sur ta poitrine. Tu l'as repris. Mais tu lisais à côté. Tu pensais à la Sibérie des tsars puis aux goulags modernes. Tes yeux se promenaient de mur de ta cellule, balayaient les objets à la manière d'une caméra fellinienne.

> Mon pauvre Gorki! avais-tu fini par dire sans savoir pourquoi. Et tu t'étais abandonné au sommeil.
> Le lendemain. Tu as appris comme tout le monde la libération d'un certain nombre de détenus et l'exécution de sept autres.
> Tu n'as pas pu entendre les détonations. Tu dormais profondément. Ton rêve ailé te portait de camp en goulag. Tu finissais par débarquer quelque part en Amazonie parmi une tribu vivant dans une phase de transition du matriarcat à un autre stade. Et tu faisais acte de candidature.
> Passons vieux chameau, tu as déjà raconté cela. (*Le Chemin des ordalies*, p.22)

How are our expectations of literature formed? The reader of the above passage will find the transition from the gulag to the prison quite natural, for who better than the Russians to furnish us with a guide to the horrors of modern despotism? Yet no critic or literary scholar would have bet real money on Russian writers being one of the major influences on Moroccan literature 'd'expression française'.

Some years ago the late Chou En-lai was asked what he thought had been the impact of the French Revolution on world history. He said that he thought it was 'too soon to say'. Chinese elder statesmen may be inclined to take the long view but literary professionals, always on the lookout for new material, are apt to take a very short one. A mere twenty years or so after independence, Maghrebian literature has become an established category. My anecdote is not altogether facetious for in fact one of the results of the French Revolution has been the introduction of the French language to Africa, and thus the creation of the category 'd'expression française'.

Perhaps all readings are always double: they involve expectation which does not correspond with the experience of the text. It seems that *Le Chemin* is a peculiarly doubled text. Laâbi's fine handling of language is constantly before the reader, but that of which he speaks short-circuits literary response. Convention says the critic must aim for scholarly detachment, but some writing is powerful enough to appeal to the real self, that self so often artificially left at the door of the library.

Le Chemin is a great book about imprisonment. It is great because it is magnificently written and unerringly accurate. The magnificence of the language is available to all with the requisite linguistic knowledge; its accuracy can be vouchsafed by all who know about prisons. Laâbi finds a way to describe how prison works on the individual by forcing him or her to confront their deepest fears, the sense of impotence, the pain of inflicting pain on others and the need to construct a new prison identity while never letting go of the old self, the true self, discovered under the most extreme of conditions of torture and degradation.

- Déshabille-toi.

Tu ne comprends pas d'abord cet ordre. On ne t'a jamais demandé pareille chose. Si, le médecin. Mais il était plus précis. Il te demandait d'enlever ta chemise ou de baisser un peu ton pantalon. Même ton aimée ne t'a jamais demandé pareille chose. C'est toi qui en prenais l'initiative dans un geste de fureur impatiente lorsque la tendresse atteignait entre vous son paroxysme et que le don se faisait transe, infinitude du corps humain.
- Enlève tout. T'as compris? Les chaussures aussi.
C'est un géant noir qui parle. L'un des trois Epouvantails. Ils avaient commencé leurs préparatifs. Le banc a été tiré, placé au milieu du débarras. Les ficelles dénouées, les chiffons dépliés.
Tu obéis.

Depuis quand avais-tu cessé d'obéir? De cercle en cercle, tu remontes à ton enfance. Tu farfouilles dans ta mémoire et paradoxalement tu ne trouves rien. L'obéissance? Connais pas. Ton père n'était pas ce pater familias qui hante les récits du pourtour de la Méditerranée et du monde arabe. Le dictateur en chambre, noyau insécable de la cellule familiale et sociale autour duquel gravitent l'activité économique, l'idéologie dominante, les mariages arrangés, les divorces décrétés, le cérémonial du culte et des fêtes. Tronc de l'arbre généalogique, main de la Providence en toute chose. C'était un petit artisan doux qui partait tous les jours au travail à six heures du matin pour revenir à huit heures du soir. Sauf le vendredi. Une mécanique de haute précision dans une société prétendument léthargique et somnolente, tournant le dos au travail productif. Ce petit artisan doux avait tenu à envoyer tous ses enfants à l'école 'franco-musulmane' pour qu'ils apprennent la langue des puissants du jour, pour percer le mystère de leur puissance.

Non, tu ne te souviens pas de l'obéissance à ce niveau-là. Tu n'as donc pas connu la révolte contre le père, ce qui explique peur-être que tu n'aies jamais eu envie d'écrire une de ces autobiographies édifiantes qui étaient comme une sorte d'examen de passage dans la littérature des colonisés. (*Le Chemin des ordalies*, pp.41–2)

The worst aspect of prison life is that the burden of anguish can never be directly expressed because of the danger of collapse or confrontation. *Le Chemin* explores the devices and strategies used for survival. But more importantly it picks up the moral point of view which utterly distinguishes the political prisoner from the criminal.

The personal is unavoidable here. When I first read *Le Chemin* it had nothing to do with Morocco and, had I put it down, I would have been unable to say for sure what language it was written in. I responded to it as a work which spoke directly to someone who had many friends imprisoned for political offences. Yet it is a fair conclusion that it will never be discussed alongside works by Primo Levi or Ariel Dorfman, let alone Gorky and Dostoevsky, who have been major influences on Laâbi. Some of his own frustration at this was expressed in an informal paper he gave at the Institut Français in London in 1990, entitled 'Reflexions autour de la poésie maghrébine d'expression française'. In this paper he complained at the constant self-justification required of him:

Mais, somme toute, je préfère prendre ainsi les devants pour éviter à notre débat de tout à l'heure les dérives ou les fixations qui nous éloigneraient de notre sujet: la poésie et la poésie seule.

Pour en finir avec cette déjà trop longue introduction, je dirai que l'écrivain maghrébin d'expression française est peut-être le seul écrivain au monde qui se trouve dans cette situation paradoxale: il doit justifier son existence, son être là, avant de se présenter en tant qu'écrivain tout court, au lieu de rentrer normalement dans le vif du sujet, le corps du texte, les interrogations essentielles, spécifiques ou universelles que pose toute expérience de création littéraire, sous n'importe quelle latitude ou climat. (p.2)

Although the title of Laâbi's paper deliberately invokes the restricted category of literary demarcations, his remarks denounce the provocation of the constant interrogation 'pourquoi écrivez-vous en français?' In fact, the literary strait-jacket of scholarly classification serves the average and the mediocre very well but hinders the emergence of the truly great. It is indeed strange that, long after Frantz Fanon had denounced André Breton for describing Aimé Césaire as 'un grand poète noir', Laâbi could be described by a group of fellow writers as 'un des plus importants écrivains maghrébins de sa génération',[1] the modifiers in each case deftly suggesting that we are dealing with the slightly second rate.

What would happen if we abandoned the two terms in Laâbi's title which cause him such irritation, but which are alluring because of their pseudo-precision, and concentrate on the term 'poésie'? What kind of a poet is Laâbi and can one write poetry in a state of fear? For there is no doubt that for him the production of poetry is a superior attainment:

Cette fonction multidimensionnelle de la poésie est capitale pour la compréhension de son impact social exceptionnel. Il n'y avait pas de séparation de la poésie d'avec la vie de la cité, de la tribu et plus tard de la *ummah* (nation). La poésie n'était pas appelée à gérer seulement les états changeants de la subjectivité, mais également les contradictions inhérentes à la société. Aussi, même si l'on doit faire une distinction entre poésie de l'élite et poésie populaire, la circulation entre ces deux niveaux s'opérait normalement car la transmission de la poésie était essentiellement orale. Le poème déclamé dans la cour d'un prince parvenait jusqu'aux réunions des *Saâliks* (les brigands ou vagabonds) et les poèmes de ces derniers parvenaient jusqu'à l'oreille du prince.

Cette fonction multidimensionnelle, ce caractère *oecuménique* de la poésie arabe nous permettent de mieux comprendre d'où vient la poésie maghrébine d'aujourd'hui, les enjeux qui sont les siens, la spécificité et l'envergure de son projet.

Il s'agit pour elle de gérer un héritage exorbitant. Un héritage où la poésie n'était pas un genre littéraire parmi d'autres, mais le champ littéraire par excellence. ('Reflexions', p.7)

1. Ghislain Ripault (ed.) (1982), *Pour Abdellatif Laâbi*, Paris: La Table Rase, p.11.

In his interview with Jacques Alessandra in *La Brûlure des interrogations*, Laâbi argues:

> Je veux qu'il soit clair que je ne suis pas en train de développer une plaidoirie ou un réquisitoire. Personnellement, et dans la phase historique qu'il m'a été donné de vivre, je revendique autant l'arabe que le français. Je communique dans l'une ce que je ne peux communiquer dans l'autre. Quand je les additionne, je m'exprime intégralement. Je ne ressens plus ni exil ni drame. Je dois simplement faire le double du travail d'un écrivain monolingue. Mais le travail ne m'a jamais effrayé, ni mon époque d'ailleurs, ce règne de barbarie que j'assume parce que je crois que ce n'est qu'une chape qui recouvre le Continent réellement humain et fraternel que la poésie a pour charge de sauvegarder et de rappeler sans cesse à la conscience des hommes. (p.68)

In fact Laâbi's position on this has been consistent since the days of *Souffles*, when he deplored writing aimed at a metropolitan audience but defended the use of French as a language deliberately chosen to fulfil a specific function:

> Le tout est d'arriver à cette adéquation de la langue écrite au monde interieur de poète, à son langage émotionnel intime. Certains n'y arrivent pas. D'autres même en employant la langue écrite nationale restent à la surface d'eux-mêmes et de la réalité qu'ils veulent abstraire et mettre en cause. . . Malgré le dépaysement linguistique, les poètes de ce receuil parviennent à transmettre leurs profondeurs charnelles par l'intermédiaire d'une langue passée au crible de leur histoire, de leur mythologie, de leur colère, bref de leur personnalité propre.[2]

The language of the poet is his 'own language' and must be judged as such, not allocated to some pre-existing classification system. Marc Gontard argues in *Violence du texte*, 'En effet, si au Québec, par exemple, la langue française apparait comme un instrument de libération elle reste pour les Marocains un puissant moyen d'aliénation' (p.11). We can only feel relieved that Moroccan writers have so close at hand the perfect means of expressing alienation. Laâbi asks in 'Reflexions' why the Irish writer Samuel Beckett was never challenged for writing in French or Salman Rushdie for writing in English. Such questions should serve as a reminder that the expression of alienation through language is what modern writing is all about. The breakdown not only of English but of language itself is the point

2. *Souffles*, no. 5, 1967, p.5.

of *Finnegans Wake*, although I have never heard of Joyce's Irishness being used to argue that the whole massive book is an exercise in postcolonial aesthetics. Ezra Pound wrote much of his best poetry in prison and in an insane asylum. He lived all his adult life in exile. His poetry offends all the categories of the English language. At the opposite end of the political spectrum from Laâbi, Pound's work is also concerned with the desire to uncover the fragmented paradisal state which reality is intent on denying. This desire in Pound is never attributed to his position as a postcolonial. Pound's use of Chinese, Italian, Greek and musical notation has however been challenged as a monstrous hybrid. Monstrous hybridity is perhaps the term literary critics have recourse to when they are unwilling to put in the work. More interestingly, because Pound spent most of his creative life in France and Italy, he composed *The Cantos* in a language that he heard only inside his own head. A private language, the poet's own, projected on to the page to communicate but with no representational function.

Looked at in this way Laâbi's poetry belongs to the modern desire to find in language 'un puissant moyen d'aliénation'. Pablo Neruda and César Vallejo, for reasons politically closer to Laâbi than Pound, experimented with surrealism and myth to achieve the same effects. William Carlos Williams's poetry broke down English to its syllables, focusing the mind of the reader on a variable metrical pattern as if reading a foreign language. When we take these examples from other language areas, we are able to situate Laâbi's work in the context of modern poetics and spring him from the trap of the colonialist/ postcolonialist closed circle. Laâbi's desire to create 'le texte polyglotte' ('Reflexions', p.4) allies him firmly with these modernizers. For this reason also, he is a translator; he translates from Arabic into French and his own work into Arabic. 'Je peux même dire que je suis actuellement davantage lu en arabe qu'en français alors que mes oeuvres n'ont pas été encore toutes traduites' (*La Brûlure des interrogations*, p.47). Indeed, one of the salient features of modern poetry has been the transgression of linguistic boundaries: Pound working from Italian, Olson from Mayan and Persian, Bunting from Persian, Yeats from Japanese. Poets of the twentieth century have had the dream of a literature that like music and painting can create 'un langage universel qui transcende les frontières, bouscule les habitudes culturelles frileuses, élargit la vision des hommes à la vision de l'homme et de son monde' ('Reflexions', p.3). If we are to respect Laâbi's wish to be treated as a poet, we must not only review the question of his poetics but also examine the refusals inherent in such a title. Many of his works contain both verse and prose. The first of these was *L'Oeil et la nuit*, followed by *Le Chemin* and latterly *L'Ecorché vif*, which is subtitled 'prosoèmes'. This is a style to which Laâbi had given the name 'itinéraire', and it would equally describe *Paterson* and *Cahier d'un retour au pays natal*. In fact, Césaire's notebook method works with the same myth of return, as well as the archetypes of memory, loss and reinvention in a fragmented mosaic in constant motion which is sustained in *Le Chemin*. This indeed may be what Laâbi regards as his technical achievement in this book and he may prefer this reading of it to the kind of reading I offered at the beginning of this chapter. In interview he has suggested that the French text has been misread. 'Je savais que beaucoup de gens n'allaient pas me lire, mais me jauger et juger. L'aspect littéraire du livre allait être mis entre parenthèses pour que ne subsistent que l'autoportrait du revenant de la "maison des morts"' (*La Brûlure*, p.37).

If Laâbi prefers the technical accomplishment of this text, with its constantly self-revising memory structure, then he is placing himself firmly within a modern tradition which undermines narrative and privileges subjective consciousness and which can be traced back through *Light in August* to the *The Golden Bowl*. Looked at in this way, Marc Gontard's claim that 'c'est la traversée inscrite dans le langage et l'écriture d'un champ socio-culturel soumis à la violence'[3] is perfectly absurd unless one were to expand the field to include all modern life so that it becomes useless as a term of definition. Once again, we see the pointlessness of elevating social definitions above aesthetic, for such an exercise would force Laâbi back into the strait-jacket of national identity.

But if Laâbi uses prose he is careful to avoid its having any representational function and the reasons for this are quite clearly his often expressed suspicion about the dangers of 'realism': 'Une littérature de colonisés, victimes du complex du colonisés, aspirant tout au plus à être reconnus par le protecteur ou le maître colonisateur comme de bons, voire brillants élèves' ('Reflexions', p.5).

In fact, to break with the 'real' world one cannot take up the same arms as those which were used to create it. In his interview with Jacques Alessandra Laâbi's uses strikingly physical imagery to describe the process of creating poetry:

> La seule arme par laquelle nous pouvions rompre cet engrenage était celle de notre corps et de notre mémoire endorlois, de leur noeud irréductible d'atavismes, de leur pouvoir de parole. Rompre le cercle infernal de la domination, du silence et de l'anonymat, ne pouvait se faire que poitrine

---

3. Marc Gontard (1988), *Violence du texte*, Paris: L'Harmattan.

et gosier à découvert, que comme scalp public ou immolation par le feu de notre fureur d'être. L'émergence de cette parole neuve, irrédentiste opérait comme une extraordinaire libération d'énergie, une nouvelle genèse humaine. L'écriture est le signe donné aux organes de se remettre à battre, aux racines de repeupler le continent de l'histoire, aux mains de retrouver leur fonction guérisseuse aux yeux de recouvrer leur intensité visionnaire, à la parole de restructurer les éléments éparpillés du corps et de lui restituer sa mémoire propre. L'écriture est dans ce cas une grande épreuve physique, une véritable ordalie, en même temps qu'elle est un baume et un élixir de résurrection. (*La Brûlure des interrogations*, p.33)

This imagery of bodies and battles, of ruptures and uniforms, is a kind of vertebral column to Laâbi's poetry. His refusal to engage with narrative is a refusal to enter the charmed circle of 'reasonable' communication, a refusal which Aimé Césaire and Frantz Fanon had also identified as a necessary first step towards autonomy. The danger of refusing this refusal have been documented elsewhere, not least by Chraïbi in his account of the assimilation of *Le Passé simple* into the precolonialist posture when in an interview in *Souffles* in 1967 he described how he had found himself accused of playing 'le jeu des colonialistes'.[4]

However, the rupture of reasonableness and the completed narrative began long before the anticolonial struggle. It has been one of the great achievements of modernism. The earliest influence on Laâbi was Dostoevsky: 'Je découvrais avec Dostoievski que la vie est un appel intérieur et un regard d'impitoyable compassion jeté sur le monde des hommes' (*La Brûlure*, p.30). His succinct statement that 'la civilisation humaine s'est developpée au détriment de certaines facultés de l'homme' (*La Brûlure*, pp.28–9) is surely a perfect summary of the modern dilemma originating in the works of Marx. Laâbi's challenge as a poet who wishes to reconstitute the human is one very specific to this century. As a maker of poems he cannot be satisfied by slotting language back into predetermined structures, whether of verse or prose. He must therefore educate his readers while constantly denying their expectations. And this brings us to the question of his poetics. 'Race', published in *Le Règne de barbarie*, a collection of poems written between 1966 and 1967, is his first considerable achievement as a poet, where he confronts the problem of creating an organizing principle for free verse. The basic unit is the phrase, arranged in such a way that it appears as if the poet had struck the space-bar on the typewriter. This method creates unexpected juxtapositions. These

4. *Souffles*, no. 5, 1967, p.6.

phrases are interspersed with long lines reminiscent of Whitman's breath-shaped lines. Laâbi's use of capitalization has the same random quality. These capitalized words leap out of the page but their significance is arbitrary. Arbitrariness is in fact the point: 'nous sommes anachroniques' but 'vis-à-vis-d'un CERTAIN ORDRE':

Race

c'est que nous sommes seuls vidés contrebattus
au pied du Mur-murailles de lamentations véridiques nous encer-
clant dessus dessous AVEC LA MARQUE DU DESASTRE
maintenant décriés Notre réputation vampiriste   Face au
monde de la Raison du Droit et des Lois
tassés en paquets d'hommes-meurtrissures Dans des déserts
obstrués Au bord de la dépression de du suicide

et qu'au diapason de la solitude Nos yeux s'agrandissent
Vaste organe enregistrant les voix apocryphes canonisant la
jungle
et le SCALP

nos corps Ramassis de traumatismes De greffes suppu
rantes
DESORGANISES
notre marche téléguidée Rebuts de galaxies et de tertres
Nous ne sommes pas les humains auréolés du Livre de l'Art
et de l'Esprit
nous sommes anachroniques Certes nous le sommes
Mais vis-à-vis d'un CERTAIN ORDRE De violence
disons qu'instinctivement nous sommes allergiques aux manuels
  Aux sommes divinisant l'Intelligence
disons que nous ne suivons pas ceux qui réussissent Ceux
qui savent Ceux qui ordonnent baguette magique et robots
parlent Ejectent des cités équations Les surhommes
disons que notre peur est angoisse d'être Angoisse de mort
Mort de nous D'avec notre OEil tragique

(*Le Règne de barbarie*, p.71)

This dis-ordered verse relies powerfully on the force of negatives and on repetition.Given the inflexibility of accenting in French the unit of repetition cannot be rhythmic but is created by alternating certain sounds, constant contrast of 'S' and 'M' in the opening stanza for example. Both continuous sounds, but one open and one closed. The 'Mur-muraille' contraposed to 'dépression' and 'suicide' contrasts closed hardness with disintegration and this motif is picked up in 'Ramassis de traumatismes' and 'DESORGANISES.These effects are irrational as eventually they carry forward deeply atavistic feelings imitating the oral effects of language which exists before reason:

ne lisez pas
ECOUTEZ

This sound pattern is carried throughout the poem but it is not the only organizing device: repetition of initial words and imagery are both important. Poetry, according to Pound, was of three types: logopoeia, the play of the intellect among words; melopoeia, aspiring to the condition of music; and phanopoeia, the casting of images on the mind. Each of these kinds can combine with the others but each aims at a different effect. The first perhaps is the most obviously appealing to critics – wit, double meaning and the demand for interpretation create a private area of agreement between poet and reader and are most demanding of shared values and a sense of exclusiveness. Perhaps late nineteenth-century French poetry would fall into this category. Laâbi may have been 'taught' it in school. For obvious reasons it would be least attractive to a poet who wishes his verse to perform a revolutionary function.

Melopoeia is also problematic, though Laâbi often experiments with small-scale effects. He is writing, remember, in a language he is not hearing except in his own head and whose accentuation and stress are inflexible compared with Arabic. To create variety Laâbi has recourse to an enormous poetic diction. Pressing against the relative narrowness of the French lexicon, Laâbi's diction is vastly enriched by the inclusion of Maghrebian, words derived from the Arabic, 'Assaonas' 'Aicha Qandicha' (*Le Règne*, pp.77, 78) but more particularly his extremely esoteric use of French has the effect of alienating the French reader from his own language. Take the use of the words 'branchycéphales' and 'doliocéphales' (*Le Règne*, p.81). How many speakers of French could read these without recourse to the dictionary? An interesting parallel can be drawn here with the Scottish poet Hugh MacDiarmid, who was also a Communist. He wrote originally in Gaelic and synthetic 'Scots'. Both of these languages, he realized, although politically impeccable, severely restricted his audience. So he wrote in English – but what an English!

All is lithogenesis – or lochia,
Carpolite fruit of the forbidden tree,
Stones blacker than any in the Caaba,
Cream-coloured caen-stone, chatoyant pieces,
Celadon and corbeau, bistre and beige,
Glaucous, hoar, enfouldered, cyathiform,
Making mere faculae of the sun and moon
I study you glout and gloss, but have
No cadrans to adjust you with, and turn again
From optik to haptik and like a blind man run
My fingers over you, arris by arris, burr by burr,
Slickensides, truité, rugas, foveoles,
Bringing my aesthesis in vain to bear,
An angle-titch to all your corrugations and coigns,
Hatched foraminous cavo-relievo of the world,
Deictic, fiducial stones. Chiliad by chiliad
What bricole piled you here, stupendous cairn?
What artist poses the Earth écorché thus,
Pillar of creation engouled in me?
What eburnation augments you with men's bones,
Every energumen an Endymion yet?
All the other stones are in this haecceity it seems,
But where is the Christophanic rock that moved?
What Cabirian song from this catasta comes?[5]

MacDiarmid successfully alienates the English from their own tongue. They need a dictionary to understand it. But this is not really the point; it is not an anticolonial posture. The genius that lies behind these words is not motivated by hatred of colonial oppression but by love of language. The alliteration, the assonance, the beauty of the words as you hold them in your mouth like the pebbles they describe are what makes you read on. The love of language and the exuberance it causes are the only source of poetry. Nothing else – personal, political, social – will do it. Laâbi takes French and makes it perform amazing feats. He has great linguistic virtuosity but one cannot do this with a language unless one is in love with it. One cannot do it with a hated language or one which is imposed by force.

Laâbi's effects are, in the main, phanopoeic; they cast images on the mind of the reader:

5. Hugh Macdiarmid (1992), 'On a raised beach', in Douglas Dunn (ed.), *Faber Book of Twentieth-Century Scottish Poetry*, London: Faber.

cancéreux
tangue bannie brisure
                              tangue
sismographie du mythe
                              tangue tangue
à l'archi-pluriel de la Faute
nudité
je vous ai vus
                    nombril au nombril
à la queue leu leu
                    devant le monstre
il riait de plus laide   Une patte d'argile suvos nuques
L'autre aux confins de vos âmes   Le monstre baisait avec
sadisme   En regardant passer les étoiles filantes les Jets les
satellites artificiels les astronautes en tenue de sport en dehors
de leurs vaisseaux   Et vos yeux ne se détachaient pas de son
magnétisme dégoulinant

la catastrophe   la catastrophe
à deux pas de ma voix
                              vieux monde
                                   vieux monstre
entre toi et moi
                         de vieux comptes à régler
la catastrophe   la catastrophe
à deux pas
                  cancer détonant
vieux monde
                  vieille lèpre
                                   dérapant
sans fossile sans idiome la quadrature
                                   les sept têtes du mythe
sans boussoles sans axe
                         histoire acridienne
vieux monde vieille lèpre
                                   dévalant
c'est le moment c'est le mot
me dresse de quadrupèdes
                                   corps entier
                                        force congénitale
à l'archi-pluriel de la Faute
nommément

```
                halte
                       demi-tour
        le monstre vous salue bien
```

('Race', *Le Règne de barbarie*, pp.82–3)

Violent images are often delicately, almost tenuously, linked together by repetitions, such as the use of 'sans' and 'vieux' in the above passage or 'd'avance' and 'qui' in the one below:

```
        d'avance
                        traquenard indélébile
        d'avance
                        échauffourée hors-mémoire
        d'avance
                        main
        qui l'écrit l'aride vidé de ses supplices
        qui la racine resurgie du charnier
        qui météorite fasciné
                        l'oeil risqué
        main
                notre nuit parmi vous
        d'avance
                        la ruée qui nous dévore
        m o r t    m'apprenant
                                        épopée du risque
        quitte comme le cadavre miraculeux
        j'ai dit
                        mon incompatibilité de vous
        j'ai dit
                        l'orgasme du crime
        et mon incompatibilité
                                        de vous
        j'ai devant moi mon corps et l'armature du néant
        je gis sur cette pyramide du néant entre les serres de la civilisation
        de l'écrit
                        de l'acier
        du plomb entre les yeux
```

('Race', *Le Règne de barbarie*, p.84)

This reliance on imagery relates to Laâbi's constant privileging of the eye and the power of seeing which runs through all his writing.

This can further be explained in a number of ways. Sight is, in a sense, the most democratic of the senses, inclusive and indiscriminate. Sight is also the most modern of the senses as we tend to take in information by seeing rather than listening in a world dominated by electronic media and with our 400-year legacy of movable type. In a situation of extreme social oppression, where speech may be dangerous, to see and witness may be all that can be done. It is through the visualization of surreal effects that the over-rationalized surface of reality can be broken down. Laâbi's effects nearly always tend towards the violent and cataclysmic, often of a specifically sexual kind:

je gis
           paléolithique imberbe
tu le savais Fanon
dos à dos
                    chacun pour soi
ce fut trop bref
                         la guerre
                                    matière d'extinction
on nous a eus à l'usure
notre étoile se meurt
                             avant-avant terme
la catastrophe   la catastrophe
dans vos cases
                         dans vos palais
un peu plus nantis
                              un peu plus affamés
'civilisés'
                    carnivores à n'importe quelle échelle
je vous ai vus
                    nombril au nombril
à plat ventre
                    devant le monstre
il s'esclaffait imitant Zeus   Vous jetait graine par graine ses
pavots somnifères   Il bandait multi-sexes et vous violait lan-
goureusement pendant que votre progéniture récoltait son sperme
pour la fécondité abêtissante de vos femelles   Et vos corps
se rétrécissaient   S'amenuisaient   Se contractaient en varices
en cristaux de schiste

Nudité
           ma stature
le terrifiant scalpel des migrations

je suis de ce silex
me revient à la mémoire
poésie
    PAROLE DONNEE
        d'hommes à hommes

        ('Race', *Le Règne de barbarie*, p.85)

Often in such passages the effects may be Whitmanesque, but the vision of destruction is unlike the old transcendental belief that the visionary world may be glimpsed beneath the outworn shell of the old. First the old world has to be destroyed to allow the new to emerge:

L'acte poétique est un acte totalisant.
Il n'est pas méditation sur le réel; un ensemble de moments, d'instantanés, de faits volés au réel. C'est un réel nouveau qui se construit à partir d'une destruction et en fonction d'un projet.
Et cette reconstruction ne peut pas s'effectuer en dehors, audessus, à côté des réalités. Elle est au contraire un organe même de la réalité nouvelle en construction. Elle dépend impérieusement d'une plongée corps et âme dans le corps vivant du peuple. Elle dépend en fin de compte de l'option et de la pratique révolutionnaires. Aussi, la poésie aura pour tâche de redécouvrir, par ses moyens propres, la dialectique concrète de la pensée, de l'histoire et des forces sociales.
Et la poésie est certainement une des activités créatrices les plus proches et les plus capables de cette saisie et de cette démarche. Ceci, elle l'a prouvé non seulement dans notre propre histoire, mais dans l'histoire des luttes de bien des peuples. Il n'y a qu'à voir l'affirmation de plus en plus nette de la poésie palestinienne de combat pour s'en convaincre. ('Intervention à la rencontre des poètes arabes de Beyrouth, 8–12 December 1970', *Le Règne de barbarie*, p.104)

'Race' was written before Laâbi's imprisonment. This and other poems composed before his arrest are contemporaneous with his editorship of *Souffles* and the general Third-Worldism of the late 1960s and early 1970s. Specific references are to the war in Vietnam, the Black Panthers, Cuba and the *Tricontinental* and Palestine. A great deal of work has still to be done on cross-currents of influence here such as the influence of figures like Pablo Neruda and Leroi Baraka Jones on African writers. Their rhetorical devices legitimated rage as an accurate response to the world.
    Laâbi's arrest, torture and imprisonment coincided with the general disillusion of the early 1970s as well as with ferocious repression in

Morocco. Writing from prison, Laâbi starts to incorporate a kind of
narrative into his work. Like Pound in St Elizabeth's, he has now only
memory and his own autobiography out of which to write. There is
more prose in *Le Chemin des ordalies*; *Chroniques de la citadelle d'exil* uses
a chronological structure; *Histoire des sept crucifiés de l'espoir* depends on
a strong narrative thread of beginning, middle and end for its effect.
The point here is not representation but the getting across of hard
information, and this function is always best served by narrative devices.
Poetry here is no longer primarily concerned with the hallucinatory
deconstruction of the real but as a means of accumulating and pre-
serving evidence for the historical record. Laâbi now has a story to tell:

22 heures

    ils étaient sept
    dans le quartier des codamnés à mort
    âge moyen: celui du choix
    identité: combattante
    pour une nouvelle dignité
    pour le pain fécond de la fraternité
    On venait d'éteindre dans les cellules
    ceux qui fumaient
    allumèrent leur première cigarette de la veillée
    Tous se mirent à faire le bilan
    des menaces
    des augures favorables
    à tarabuster leur mémoire
    pour lui arracher l'image fuyante
    auréolée
    de l'aimée
            de l'enfant
                        de la mère
    des camarades morts ou en exil
    les souvenirs de paix et d'allégresse
    amis rieurs et turbulents
    terroir ou cité des racines
    La journée fut ensoleillée
    mais pas trop chaude
    la soupe était bonne
    les nouvelles de la semaine
    ont été plutôt encourageantes
    des rumeurs ont circulé comme quoi
    les 'politiciens'

avaient eu des pourparlers en haut lieu
pour obtenir des grâces
adoucir des peines
Le gardien
quand il a fermé les portes
avait le même air bourru
mais sans dureté

(*Histoire des sept crucifiés de l'espoir*, p.9)

Although some of the structuring devices are like those of his earlier poetry, for example, see how 'de' holds the balance of these lines, the main effect is achieved by the power of understatement. Circumstances are enough to carry the reader forward. The parataxis of the lines from 'La journée fut ensoleillée' onwards suggests a situation which cannot be directly addressed by language; that rage and despair must find a language of suggestion and analogy rather than direct emotional appeal. Emotion is conveyed by the almost bathetic effect of 'adoucir des peines' when contrasted with the unspoken nature of the unsweetened punishment. Hour by hour, with the inevitability of a Greek tragedy, Laâbi's lines record only. Commentary would be a distraction. Not for nothing did Laâbi discover early that Dostoevsky had much to teach him:

> J'ai commencé à écrire au sortir de l'adolescence, à une époque où j'avais déjà dévoré une bonne partie de la littérature classique française. Mais mon premier choc fut la découverte de l'oeuvre de Dostoïevski. *L'Idiot, Le Joueur, Crime et Châtiment, Les Frères Karamazov* et *Souvenirs de la maison des morts* m'ont littéralement insufflé 'le mal d'écrire', comme on peut parler du mal d'amour. Il y avait là une capacité à restituer la vie, à faire toucher du coeur les ressorts les plus subtils de la psychologie humaine et à faire accéder à la tragédie morale de l'homme qui m'avait bouleversé. Je découvrais avec Dostoïevski que la vie est un appel intérieur et un regard d'impitoyable compassion jeté sur le monde des hommes. (*La Brûlure des interrogations*, p.30)

In *Histoire* Laâbi showed that he too could find a language for the most dreadful corners of the human heart. And, like Pound in Pisa, he can also find paradise in the halls of hell. The solidarity and comradeship of his ideals become a living reality within the walls of the citadel of exile.

Now in exile in France, Laâbi's writing is continually experimental. *Sous le bâillon* is quite different from the prose and poetry assemblage of *L'Ecorché vif*. In fact, *L'Ecorché vif* experiments with an innovative juxtaposition of prose and poetry as a kind of memory work evoking scenes from the past as well as recording scenes and feelings of the present. The whole is structured towards an affirmation of lived ideals with no rejections of the past. In his final days, after being released from an insane asylum to die in exile, Pound wrote:

> M'amour, m'amour
> what do I love and
> where are you?
> That I lost my center
> fighting the world.
> The dreams clash
> and are shattered –
> and that I tried to make a paradiso
> terrestre.
>
> I have tried to write Paradise
> Do not move
> Let the wind speak
> that is paradise.
>
> Let the Gods forgive what I
> have made
> Let those I love try to forgive
> what I have made.

> (*The Cantos*, p.816)

In his poem *K. Marx*, Laâbi writes:

> Réveille-toi Marx
> et viens reprendre tes reliques
> ôte-nous cet opium de la bouche
> défends-toi bon sang
> dis-leur tes propres folies
> avoue les poèmes
> que tu écrivais en cachette
> et que tu jetais
> dans les marmites de l'avenir
> hurle ta détresse
> en juste déluge
> balayant la forêt carnassière des dogmes

puis fais-toi soleil
pour une nouvelle donne
magnifiant l'orchidée intacte
du Paradis terrestre

(*L'Ecorché vif*, p.113)

A coincidence? If so, it is a coincidence of a particularly striking nature. I began by castigating the inadequacy of allocating literatures to the confines of national identity. Writers are, after all, free to draw their influences from wherever they please. A moment's reflection will tell us how apt it is that a Moroccan poet in the 1960s and 1970s should have turned to Russia rather than France for his inspiration.

It may indeed be too soon to say what is the true literary status of Laâbi's poems. I would hazard a guess that he will be drawn more and more towards the Arabo-Islamic side of his inheritance and that, in exile in France and hearing French now all around him, the voices and rhythms in his head will become more and more insistently Arab.

Bibliography

Gontard, Marc (1988), *Violence du texte*, Paris: L'Harmattan.
Laâbi, Abdellatif (ed.) (1966–72), *Souffles*, Rabat.
——(1977), *Histoire des sept crucifiés de l'espoir*, Paris: La Table Rase.
——(1980), *Le Règne de barbarie*, Paris: Seuil.
——(1981), *Sous le bâillon, le poème*, Paris: L'Harmattan.
——(1982), *Le Chemin des ordalies*, Paris: Denoël (trans. Jacqueline Kaye, *Rue de Retour*, London: Readers International, 1989).
——(1982), *L'Oeil et la nuit*, Rabat: SMER.
——(1983), *Chroniques de la citadelle d'exil*, Paris: Denoël.
——(1985), *La Brûlure des interrogations*, Paris: L'Harmattan.
——(1986), *L'Ecorché vif*, Paris: L'Harmattan.
——(1990), 'Reflexions autour de la poésie maghrébine', London: unpublished.
Macdiarmid, Hugh (1992), 'On a raised beach', in Douglas Dunn (ed.), *Faber Book of Twentieth-Century Scottish Poetry*, London: Faber.
Pound, Ezra (1986), *The Cantos*, London: Faber.
Ripault, Ghislain (1982), *Pour Abdellatif Laâbi*, Paris: La Table Rase.

Part II

Sub-Saharan Africa

– 9 –

Linguistic and Cultural Heterogeneity and the Novel in Francophone Africa

Madeleine Borgomano

Linguistic as well as cultural heterogeneity is linked to the very origins of the novel in francophone Africa. The enormous cultural shock provoked by the massive and violent settlement of the Europeans in Africa generated an internal fission. School, as an institution which used both constraint and persuasion, has provided the means of introducing totally foreign cultural models. It has presented them as 'civilisation' while ignoring and despising African customs as 'manières de sauvages'.[1]

Thus a basic heterogeneity was established which was propitious for the birth of the novel, if we agree with the analysis of Bakhtin:

> Les embryons de la prose romanesque apparaissent dans le monde hétéroglotte et hétérologique de l'époque hellénistique. . . De même, à l'époque moderne, l'épanouissement du roman est toujours lié à la décomposition des systèmes verbaux et idéologiques stables, et, en contrepartie, au renforcement de l'hétérologie linguistique.[2]

This violently split state of cultural heterogeneity is extremely difficult to endure and the very choice by Cheikh Hamidou Kane of his title, *L'Aventure ambiguë*,[3] is evidence of that discomfort, as is the tragic story of Samba Diallo: 'Il n'y a pas une tête lucide entre deux termes d'un choix, il y a une nature étrange en détresse de n'être pas deux (p.164).' The first African novelists belong to 'cette génération forcément

1. Birago Diop (1961), *Sarzan*, in *Les Contes d'Amadou Koumba*, Paris: Présence Africaine.
2. 'Le discours dans le roman', quoted by Tzvetan Todorov (1981), *Mikhail Bakhtine: le principe dialogique*, Paris: Seuil, p.81.
3. Cheikh Hamidou Kane (1961), *L'Aventure ambiguë*, Paris: 10/18.

névrotique' (J.-M. Adiaffi). They were the ones who gave birth to the African novel. But the novel as a genre was unknown in African tradition. So authors were forced to adopt a foreign language, for reasons of publication and reception, but also because it was the language which they were taught to write; they were also forced to adopt foreign models to represent African realities, as no writing exists without models. So the African novel was born intrinsically heterogeneous on every level.

Linguistic and cultural heterogeneity involves the heterogeneity of the readers, which, in turn, involves the necessary heterogeneity of discourse. To quote Jean-Marie Adiaffi:

> Transporté dans un univers hétérogène de symboles, de mythes, comment arriver à décoder, à communiquer à nouveau dans un autre psychodrame. . . Comment la nouvelle littérature peut-elle investir une nouvelle cohérence, de nouveaux symboles, de nouveaux mythes, pour une nouvelle communication, une nouvelle représentation du monde, une nouvelle vision du monde?[4]

Cultural heterogeneity has in fact been perverted and corrupted by power relationships. 'Strength without justice is tyrannical', wrote Pascal. The same is true of the history of literatures and genres. Moreover, strength, mixed with scorn and misunderstanding, was masqueraded as justice by the means of a sly persuasion learned in school. The anecdote of the 'symbol', told by Bernard Dadié in *Climbié* comes to mind. Speaking 'in tongues' was punished and the guilty child was changed into a collaborator because of the need to get rid of the infamous 'symbol' by passing it on to another transgressor: a very perverse and cunning mechanism, indeed.

Many of the novels published at this first stage represented cultural heterogeneity as a heart-rending struggle. However, they saw themselves constrained to do this by adopting the best-known novelistic codes, those of the realist novel inherited from the nineteenth century.

Moreover, a kind of African doxa was established, prescribing that novels be protest novels, political novels. That choice was in keeping with the African tradition, in which art could never be gratuitous. But it was also enforced by the same violence which from the beginning had distorted the linguistic and cultural encounter.

Caught within this complex network of conflicting laws and

---

4. J.-M. Adiaffi (1983), 'Le maître de la parole', *Magazine littéraire, Afrique noire: l'autre littérature d'expression française* (Paris), May, p.19.

prohibitions, the African novel often short-circuited the currents which would have led to its renewal. In fact, quite like Djigui, in *Monnè*, it collaborated with the oppressor, condemning itself to the systematic monologism of a fixed and reductive 'roman à thèse', in opposition to the dialogical or even polylogical character of contemporary literature.

The Present State of the African Novel

However, the evolution of the novel is very fast in Africa. In this way, it follows the accelerated rhythm of history. Without ceasing to be 'contestatory texts', recent African novels now explore new paths, taking into account, in their very form as well as in their explicit discourse, their constitutive heterogeneity. This heterogeneity persists in Africa as a split. Various obligatory syntheses or syncretisms are always emerging, but oppositions and contradictions are still present, coexisting more or less harmoniously but nevertheless constantly threatened.

Stasis in the Linguistic Field

On the contrary, in the strictly linguistic field, it would seem that heterogeneity is no longer experienced in such a violent and polemical atmosphere as it appeared in Sartre's concise statement: 'Puisque l'oppresseur est présent jusque dans la langue qu'ils parlent, ils parleront cette langue pour la détruire' (*Orphée noir*). The oppressor, at this time, was still easy to identify. But nowadays it has been changed into an anonymous and scarcely recognizable mass of 'bastardies' issued from the 'Suns of Independence' (in the coarse style of Ahmadou Kourouma's first novel). The French language, unifying in its official capacity, is no longer perceived as totally foreign, inasmuch as it is promulgated by the school. It has been modified and adapted, even giving birth to genuine Creole languages such as Moussa French in Ivory Coast. Pierre Dumont gives his book the slightly provocative title *Le Français, langue africaine* and declares:

> Le temps des conflits est révolu, du moins au sens où l'on pouvait entendre 'conflit' au lendemain des Indépendances. . .[faisant place à] l'émergence d'une francophonie plurielle, multiple et conviviale, au sein de laquelle chaque utilisateur du Français devrait pouvoir se retrouver. (pp.7–8)

Such a discourse is proof of a certain optimism. But its very existence at least reveals the positive evolution of the linguistic situation. The novel, on the other hand, does not really take into account those developing languages: even if it makes some concessions, they always remain in the background, as a character's idiolect, as we see in Sembène Ousmane's novel, *O Pays, mon beau peuple*, in which Rokhaya's language is transcribed, and sometimes in Kourouma's works. But the language of the narrator, even if it is hybrid like Kourouma's, remains the language of a learned man.

Leaving aside the history of literature and linguistic perspectives, I would now like to consider the representation of heterogeneity nowadays, in the works of three contemporary novelists. I shall discuss the most recent text by the Ivory Coast novelist J.-M. Adiaffi, *Silence, on développe* (1982), the novels by Calixthe Beyala, of Cameroon, and the work of Ahmadou Kourouma, especially his last novel, *Monnè, outrages et défis* (1990), three very different and very new modes of representation.

Jean-Marie Adiaffi, *Silence, on développe*

J.-M. Adiaffi is both a poet, with *D'éclairs et de foudre,* and a novelist, with *La Carte d'identité* (1980) and *Silence, on développe* (1990). This book of 530 pages is presented as a challenge, whose very nature is a matter of heterogeneity. It has been often said among critics that African writers have short breath and that none of them have ever written a long novel. Notwithstanding the silliness of such a statement, Adiaffi wanted to prove otherwise.

Yet this oversized book cost him innumerable difficulties with publishers and its verbal excesses which defied the still watchful censorship of the Ivory Coast, aggravated the situation further. Its size may result in a lack of readers in Africa, where big books are not much appreciated, even by intellectuals, and where they are much too expensive.

An Aesthetic of the Hybrid

How can we name this hypertrophic text?

Ecoute la légende, l'épopée, le roman, la tragédie. . . dit le griot (p.71).

This book seems unable to choose between genres, styles, tones, languages: its option is to take everything into account, as a torrential flow, incorporating every genre and every voice. Many metaphors could be used for this, each putting into play the forces of the elements: did not Adiaffi himself entitle his epic *D'éclairs et de foudre*? But, by selecting the metaphor of the torrential river, I would like to juxtapose, rather boldly, Adiaffi and Marguerite Duras, applying Duras's comments on the Mekong to Adiaffi's writing:

> Le fleuve. . . il a ramassé tout ce qu'il a rencontré. . . il emmène tout ce qui vient, des paillotes, des forêts, des incendies éteints, des oiseaux morts, des chiens morts, des buffles noyés, des hommes noyés, des îles de jacinthes d'eau agglutinées. . . tout est emporté par la tempête profonde du courant intérieur. (*L'Amant*, p.30)

'Une gueulade', that is the word the text uses for itself. The overflowing current of that thunder-like voice violently contrasts with the title, *Silence, on développe*. This title itself, borrowed from a film shooting, but distorted, must be read ironically. Could it not mean that the novel itself 'fait son cinéma'? At the same time and quite seriously, it refers to the kind of muzzling done by the antagonistic forces in the sacred name of development. Against this desire to reduce Africa to silence rises the voice of a figure of malediction. Excesses spring from the situation of the enunciation, they are inscribed in a history and therefore become a claim for identity for those of whom it was said, not so long ago, that they had 'no history' (*L'Aventure ambiguë*).

Mingled Voices

It is very difficult, in a short time, to enumerate the voices which mingle in this text by means of an ever-changing dialogue. The unsteady narrator often adopts the tone of a griot, while transmitting in his own ways the many voices of African tradition, legends and myths. This plural voice sets the rhythm, articulates anger and expresses the desire for Utopia. Many variations on the names of musical instruments appear at the end of every chapter: sanza, ngoni, musical bow, Kokwa, flute, fawn oliphant. In the French text, words and formulae in the Agni language are scattered throughout. Following a well-established tradition of African literature, the narrator changes from the role of griot to that of interpreter and sometimes of guide; he translates and comments on African words between brackets, thus using a double enunciation which acknowledges the inevitable target of a double audience.

The narrator/griot/poet/historian/guide/interpreter sometimes also becomes a philosopher, as is the author himself, using then a learned language, even quoting Hegel or Kant. As imprecator, he willingly uses the violent rhetoric of political and militant speeches, thus becoming very assertive.

Sometimes, on the other hand, he is a lyrical poet, celebrating 'une jeune fille aux seins rêveurs' or the beauty of women (women play an important part in this drama). He also likes to sing the delights of love. He becomes an epic cantor to tell the adventures of his hero and the interventions of natural forces. But he may also use a deliberately coarse language and *ubuesque* excesses in accordance with the rude feastings and orgies of his monsters.

The multiple dialogues in the text allow the author to insert other languages, such as the political speeches of militants, the official discourse filled with clichés, the whispering of lovers or popular everyday language. But the narrator only occasionally uses such colloquial language, which he keeps at a distance by using inverted commas. Even though the discourse of the narrator can be colloquial and slangy, it is always well mastered. He distances himself less from African proverbs, frequently quoted and often mixed with his own discourse: 'Quand la chèvre est là, on ne bêle pas à sa place (p.125).'

Thus, the discourse of the narrator–griot is disrupted to make room for many heterogeneous discourses. And it appears increasingly contaminated by a discursive heterogeneity that it does not strive to homogenize. Far from blurring differences between modes and genres, it juxtaposes them without any suture. He yells, growls like thunder, and then becomes peaceful with tender words. He plays relentlessly with words.

Intertextuality

The devices are similar when we consider intertextuality. Though Adiaffi bases his narrative on the strongest legends of his tribe, he very often quotes, and not in a parodic way, fundamental texts of white culture: the Bible, the Gospel, various Greek myths, La Fontaine's fables and philosophical writings. In his first novel, *La Carte d'identité*, he made the journey of Meledouman look like the Way of the Cross, as well as a descent to hell.

The myth of twins, one of the most prevalent myths in Africa, gives his plot a unifying theme and generates an allegorical reading of the history of independence: 'Sa Majesté orduriale. . . Sage–Roi–Empereur–Pharaon–Prophète–Messie–Président à vie', who retains power after independence, is portrayed as a criminal usurper - the twin

N'da Fangan, who, greedy for money and power and sold out to foreign people, murdered his twin brother N'da Sounam, an honest and fair militant, whom the people wanted as president after independence. The perfect resemblance of the twin brothers allows one to be substituted for the other. And the secret is not revealed until the completion of the ritual cycle of fourteen years:

> N'Da, 'jumeau' en agni. . . nom porté par les jumeaux. . . nom distinctif qui s'enracine dans toute une mythologie. . . remplace souvent leur vrai nom. Les jumeaux sont considérés comme doués d'un pouvoir surnaturel, le pouvoir des Génies. . . par ailleurs, ils constituent un couple terrifiant. . . l'un incarne le Bien, l'autre le Mal. (p.24)

Heterogeneity (or, at least, duality) is understood in the novel as a constituent of the human being, in keeping with Agni and, more generally, African thought. Twinship is then perceived as a split and disquieting figure of that essential heterogeneity. The twin brothers, 'enfants terribles, enfants à rites, enfants dangereux' (p.149), must be exorcized. In Adiaffi's novel, the myth of the twins creates the figure of an alienating heterogeneity. By killing his twin brother, N'da Fangan 's'est mutilé de sa moitié rituelle' (p.132). Thus, worse than a murderer, he becomes a freak, a new Cain.

This kind of symbolic figuration, rooted as much in African philosophy as in intercultural mythology, seems very modern. It implies that an intrinsic heterogeneity, a splitting of the subject itself, has been taken into account. Such a perspective is very new in African literature. Yet, at the same time, this original use of myth would seem quite expedient. It offers a very simple justification for the failures of independence and, in some chapters, particularly the outcome when the good twin rises from the dead, it turns in the direction of Utopia. This tale appears to be a reassuring and restructuring representation, very like denial (in the Freudian sense) or like the intercultural figure of the scapegoat.

Heterogeneity, in this book, becomes hyperbolic and almost ready to explode, even if it remains controlled. In spite of his immoderate imprecations, the narrator, following tradition, maintains his position as 'le maître de la parole'. He leads and constructs the story according to his own will, transforming it into a violent pamphlet. He respects the African tradition of an art which is never gratuitous, and also complies with the tradition of the politically engaged African novel. The very excesses of the novel and the extent of its heterogeneity, instead of producing a monodic and unequivocal text, compensate for the implications of his political engagement.

Calixthe Beyala

Calixthe Beyala's work (four novels to date) gives a structural place to African linguistic and cultural heterogeneity in a completely different way. She has chosen, as did the main character in the last novel by Lopes, to migrate 'sur l'autre rive' and to situate her novel, *Le Petit Prince de Belleville*, among African people living in Paris. Yet her first three novels took place in Africa, even if they portrayed an unmerciful world, very different from usual African stereotypes.

Her first novel, *C'est le soleil qui m'a brûlée*, includes heterogeneity in its very title, a quotation of the biblical *Song of Songs*, which is more extensively quoted in the epigraph:

> Je suis noire et pourtant belle, filles de Jérusalem. . . Ne prenez pas garde à mon teint basané, c'est le soleil qui m'a brûlée.

In the Bible, *The Song of Songs* is already a very composite and mysterious book. The Roman Catholic Church has fixed its canonical allegorical interpretation, but it still remains rich in possibilities for other readings. Aimé Césaire used that same text in his well-known poem *Cahier d'un retour au pays natal* (1939), though he put it in the mouths of those who do not assume their Negritude:

> Ceux qui se drapent de pseudomorphose fière; ceux qui disent à l'Europe: 'Voyez, je sais. . . comme vous présenter mes hommages, en somme, je ne suis pas différent de vous; ne faites pas attention à ma peau noire: c'est le soleil qui m'a brûlé.' (p.59)

A quotation of a quotation, subjected to changes in gender and meanings, this polysemic title appears as the assertion of an assumed heterogeneity.

The four novels by Calixthe Beyala seem dialogical, or even polylogical. In the first one, a strange voice without any defined origin mingles with the narrative, disturbing and dissociating it. This voice has no other name but 'Moi'. Yet that insisting and repeating 'Moi' appears as an invisible and elusive witness to Ateba's laughable and tragic life. Could it be understood as a figure for the narrator: 'Moi qui vous raconte cette histoire', as is stated at the end of the novel? That would be a very modern hypothesis. Or else as a spirit? This traditional hypothesis would introject an old African perspective into the damaged world of the cursed QG. Or could it be a guardian angel? Or the soul of the missing and probably dead mother of Ateba? Could it be the young girl's own soul: 'Moi qui suis ton âme.'

Uncertainty is at the very heart of this novel, linked to that divided voice.

A device of the same kind, though less mysterious, appears in *Le Petit Prince de Belleville*, the title of which is also a modified intercultural quotation. It tells the story of a young boy called Mamadou Traore, recounted by the boy himself. Yet his narrative, written in an eclectic and naïve language, is frequently interrupted by his father Abdou Traore's discourses. They appear either as a diary, or as letters to an absent friend, and they are written in a flowery and poetic style. There, too, appear a double point of view and a double language, figures of a divided world.

Her second novel, *Tu t'appelleras Tanga*, tells of an encounter and dialogue between two women, black Tanga, victim of the ferociousness of Africa, and white Anna-Claude, a Jewish girl who had dreamed of Africa as Utopia. Their world is a prison where they are both incarcerated and the meeting is very awkward. However a kind of dialogue is established at the end, in which the white woman has her name changed and finds herself burdened with the responsibility of making her dead friend survive. Thus, heterogeneity becomes inscribed in the very heart of the subject itself.

Seul le Diable le savait is a more complex novel, torn between multiple voices. The world it represents becomes delirious and crazed, on the borders of the fantastic, inside disturbing and unsteady boundaries where the forces of Evil are very strong. The main character, a girl, carries in her own body the signs of her heterogeneity: her skin is ebony, her hair red and her eyes grey (the Devil alone knows why). She is torn between two false fathers, a pygmy and a 'good white man', neither of them being her true father, who is missing and about whom she knows little. The world of Calixthe Beyala's novels displays a paroxysmic and painful heterogeneity. She finds original devices to make it evident, but never suggests any possible harmonization.

Ahmadou Kourouma, *Monnè, outrages et défis*

Although filled with his own 'sound and fury', Ahmadou Kourouma's novel seems measured in comparison with the unbridled verbal tornado of Adiaffi. Compared with the heart-rending pessimism of Calixthe Beyala (slightly attenuated in her last novel), Kourouma's irony appears tonic. Heterogeneity and the representation of its forms and history are also at the heart of this book. Yet his own genius is to place the issue essentially on the linguistic level.

Linguistic heterogeneity is at the very origin of Ahmadou Kourouma's writing, as he himself admits. He asserts that his novel, *Les Soleils des Indépendances*, was first conceived in Malinke and then translated into French. Such a mediation could explain the strange and bewildering charm of his style.

Monnè tells of the contact between Africa and the West, through the story of a very small Malinke kingdom and its king, Djigui (whose name means 'vieux mâle solitaire et destitué dans un troupeau de fauves'). The old king is more than 100 years old. His exceptional and fantastic longevity has allowed him to survive from the epoch of Samory to the times of independence. The narrative of *Monnè* ends where *Les Soleils* begins and where *Silence, on développe* starts. Kourouma has regressed to a previous stage in African history, in search of its origins. But every reader is aware that the figure of this collaborating old man looks very like many well-known characters in the governments of post-independence Africa. The novel seems to show that history often repeats itself and that an excessive longevity can be a gift of power in Africa.

Although the perspectives of Kourouma about historical events are very impressive, the originality of his text is first to figure their resonance in language. When the first military column of 'nazaras' crossed, without them noticing, the hill 'truffée de sortilèges' that was supposed to protect Soba, it had already shaken the foundations of an old social and linguistic system.

An Unmerciful Picture of 'un Monde Achevé'

However, unlike many African writings which celebrate the marvels of old traditional times, *Monnè* draws an unmerciful picture of the society of Soba, picturing it as:

> un monde clos, à l'abri de toute idée et croyance nouvelle. . . une société arrêtée. . . castée et esclavagiste. . . un monde suranné que des griots archaïques disaient avec des mots obsolètes. (pp.20; 16)

But the novel also describes this society as organized and coherent:

> La communauté entière croyait à ses mensonges. . . Chacun croyait comprendre, savait attribuer un nom à chaque chose, croyait donc posséder le monde, le maîtriser. (p.20)

Inside language, words were not divided from things, as very often they were used as things and had the magic power to act upon things.

In this past world, to speak was literally 'to do things with words', at least for the king and the griot, who 'crée l'histoire officielle. . . en affirmant les vérités historiques qui s'imposaient' (p.190). This is the description of a homogeneous society, homogeneous because it remained insulated, protected from any contact: a 'realized' world, as the griots said, here using a very ambiguous expression (in French 'un monde achevé').

This society had known factors capable of producing heterogeneity, when it was conquered by Islam which imposed a foreign religion. But this event was buried in the very distant past because the griots tended to retell history, smoothing over any cracks in the telling: 'La religion était un syncrétisme du fétichisme malinké et de l'Islam' (p.20). Islam, remodelled, had been integrated and nothing else interfered with homogeneity: the Arabic language was adapted, too, and reserved for religious expression. (Kourouma transcribes into French the Malinke's transcription, writing, for example, 'l'alphatia', an adaptation from 'el fatiha', a surah from the Koran which begins the prayers.)

These vestiges of homogeneity were extremely fragile, at the end of the nineteenth century. They could only survive in very distant areas and were a factor which led to degeneration. But they were considered so reassuring that Djigui and the griot Diabate would struggle very hard to maintain them at all cost. Yet the absorption of heterogeneity would have been a question of survival. But then language itself must have been questioned and reconstructed. The title of the fourth chapter is:

> Chaque fois que les mots changent de sens et les choses de symboles, les Diabate retournent réapprendre l'histoire et les nouveaux noms des hommes, des animaux et des choses. (p.40)

Yet King Djigui has too great a need of compensating and exorcizing praises of his favourite griot to let him go away to complete such an immense task. Thus, he becomes highly responsible for the problems carried by a savage heterogeneity. He prefers improvization, which he invents day by day, abdication and collaboration, which he cannot avoid, but which he masks under deceptive names:

> C'est vraiment malheureux qu'Allah nous ait mal fabriqués, nous, nègres: Il nous a créés menteurs', 'Les noirs naissent mensongers. Il est impossible d'écrire une vraie histoire du Mandingue. (p.85)

Thus begins the history of a missed encounter, a failed dialogue. Far from giving this homogeneous but blocked society a chance to renew itself, the heterogeneous contribution deeply ruins it. The unsteady narrator of the novel, sometimes a learned man, sometimes mingled with the people of Soba or with Djigui himself, practises an 'irony tinged with scepticism', allowing him to show a distant and critical solidarity and to constantly play with multiple meanings – another form of heterogeneity.

The novel shows how the positive possibilities of heterogeneity are spoiled. The power relationship is evidently the first cause of failure: the two cultures and languages were not equal; it was a cultural rape. French words and encyclopedia were violently forced into Malinke, without any kind of reciprocity. Far from giving birth to a harmonious crossbreeding, they produced a freak.

The original misunderstanding is first a question of translation. It is maintained by the interpreter, master of the game, as the only one who possesses both codes. Yet his interventions are always deeply perverse: though he superficially knows the French language, he knows nothing of French culture. Moreover, he is forever playing a duplicitous game: not willing to completely betray the black people to whom he belongs (thus he saves Soba from being destroyed by changing Djigui's boastful speech ('les rodomontades de Djigui') into a claim for allegiance), yet, in an opportunistic way, he takes the white people's side. His translations are clever, but approximate adaptations: 'De même que le mil ne se sert jamais sans assaisonnement, il ne faut jamais traduire les paroles sans commentaires' (p.66). The novel plays such games with the signifier as are generated by Malinke pronunciation of French words: the 'shameful' sounds ('la consonance déhontée') thus produced are used by the old king as a pretext to decline learning the language of the winner. Yet the true reason for this refusal is very different; the ruse of the conquered is a reply to the symbolic violence of the conqueror:

> Maintenir un interprète entre le blanc et lui, c'était se réserver une distance, quelque liberté et un temps de réflexion, des possibilités de réticences et de commentaires: entretenir une certaine incompréhension. (p.232)

As a result of all these breaches and trickeries, an actual misunderstanding occurs and the language that used to be reliable becomes strained and laced with suspicion: Soba discovers a 'langue de bois'.

The word 'civilisation' is solemnly introduced: yet the interpreter does not find an equivalent Malinke word for it:

Le grand dessein de la colonisation. . . s'appelait la civilisation, que, faute de mot correspondant, l'interprète traduisit par 'devenir toubab'. Le mot fit sursauter Djigui. L'interprète rassura tout le monde en expliquant que civiliser ne signifie pas christianiser. La civilisation, c'est gagner l'argent des blancs. . . l'ère qui commence sera celle de l'argent. (p.57)

Yet, to earn the money of the white men, it is first necessary to pay taxes, which are called 'prestations', as there is not any money. To become 'civilized' will mean buying the products of the white men, but how will it be possible to buy them when unceasing extortions have bled you dry? The aim of 'civilization' will be also to trace the road ('tirer la route') (thereby allowing more white people to penetrate the virgin land); it will be also to map out the railway' ('tirer le train'), which Djigui thought unwittingly to be a promised magic toy, the supreme honour which quickly appears as an abyss, a monster eating up every living force.

Civilization solemnly abolished slavery, and yet established hard labour ('les travaux forcés'). Peacemaking was heavily armed. The notion of freedom was impossible to translate as it was full of contradictions. Not to mention the reversals of French history, with the two wars and their after effects, which the people of Soba endured with perplexity. Happily, there was one positive point, when the people of Soba discovered that 'civilization is able to cure'. But civilization can only cure bodies and it contaminates language.

Words no longer mean anything and, when you think you understand them, they just twist themselves perversely. In such a world where 'everything is upside down' (p.270), the people of Soba begin to search for 'hypothetical shelters and means of escape' (p.96). And they find some, inventing quickly the work inside work ('le travail dans le travail'), which allows the cleverest of them to restore artfully, for their own sake, an order inside disorder. The era of suspicion and cunning brings the era of devastating heterogeneity.

The novel ends with a sarcastic declaration in a huge verbal display:

Nous attendaient le long de notre dur chemin: les indépendances politiques, le parti unique, l'homme charismatique, le père de la nation, les pronunciamentos dérisoires, la révolution; puis les autres mythes: la lutte pour l'unité nationale, pour le développement, le socialisme, la paix, l'autosuffisance alimentaire. . . et aussi le combat contre la sécheresse et la famine, la guerre à la corruption, au népotisme, à la délinquance, à l'exploitation de l'homme par l'homme, salmigondis de slogans qui, à force d'être galvaudés nous ont rendus sceptiques, pelés, demi-sourds, demi-aveugles, aphones, bref plus nègres que nous ne l'étions avant. (p.287)

This representation of the perverse process of cultural and linguistic heterogeneity could be read, like the novels of Adiaffi and Calixthe Beyala, as 'a negotiation with the forces of disintegration', a way of defending oneself. Yet it seems to contribute as a lucid effort to develop an active awareness of the effects of the system. It does not suggest any Utopian reconstruction of an outmoded or mythical homogeneity. Rather, it appears as a dynamic. Although the contents and conclusions of Kourouma's novels are very pessimistic (a healthy and stoical pessimism), the very act of writing, by its own existence, denies that pessimism. The text shows how to survive and create with an irremediably disparate identity.

– 10 –

'Confidently Feminine'? Sexual Role-Play in the Novels of Mariama Bâ

Nicki Hitchcott

Barbara Harrell-Bond: One thing which seems to set African women apart from many women in Western society is their confidence in their femininity.

Mariama Bâ: Yes, that is true. We do not imitate men. Yes, African women are fulfilled *as women*.[1]

The above remarks, taken from a 1980 interview recorded in Dakar, provide an interesting point of departure for a discussion of sexual politics in the novels of Mariama Bâ.[2] 'Femininity', a social construct, is embraced by Bâ as the essential property of womankind, a property with which black African women apparently feel more confident than their 'male-imitating' Western sisters.[3] Later, Bâ's advocacy of the 'confidently feminine' reappears in Femi Ojo-Ade's pro-traditionalist criticism of Bâ's first novel, *Une si longue lettre*, in which he claims that 'Ramatoulaye's feminism as an expression of freedom constitutes only a partial aspect of the totality of African life. Femininity is the virtue of the traditionalist; feminism, the veneer of the progressive striving

1. Barbara Harrell-Bond (1980), 'Mariama Bâ, Winner of the First Noma Award for Publishing in Africa: an Interview', *African Book Publishing Record*, vol. 6, p.209. This interview was published in English translation (emphasis in the text).
2. Mariama Bâ (1979), *Une si longue lettre*, Dakar: Les Nouvelles Editions Africaines, and (1982), *Un chant écarlate*, Dakar: Les Nouvelles Editions Africaines.
3. This anti-feminist stance is also adopted by a number of anglophone African women writers such as Buchi Emecheta and Ama Ata Aidoo. See Jane Bryce (1992), 'West Africa', in Claire Buck (ed.), *Bloomsbury Guide to Women's Literature*, London: Bloomsbury, p.202.

to become a man.'[4] What becomes immediately apparent is that Bâ's reading of feminism relies on a negative semic core. Feminism here connotes superficiality and gender alienation. A feminist therefore rejects her womanhood in the quest for an inauthentic cultural identity.

In this chapter I examine the semic contents of feminism and femininity/masculinity in the texts of Mariama Bâ; I consider to what extent the politics of her writings can be reconciled with the personal politics expressed in the interview with Barbara Harrell-Bond; and I discuss critical responses – both African and European – to these precursory examples of black African women's writing in French.

In each of Bâ's texts, the narrative is generated by the formation and subsequent breakdown of the heterosexual couple: Ramatoulaye/ Modou and Aïssatou/Mawdo in *Une si longue lettre*,[5] and Mireille/ Ousmane in *Un chant écarlate*.[6] Significantly, it is the transformation from a monogamous unit (the Western model) to a polygamous family structure which destabilizes – and eventually destroys – the original happy couple.[7] One reading might, therefore, identify a certain degree of pessimism in the treatment of heterosexual monogamy and an unstated resignation to the polygamous desire of men. This, it would seem, comes close to Mariama Bâ's own reading of her texts:

> It has been thought that man, not because he is black or white, has a different physiology from that of women. A woman is always more easily satisfied. She is different. There is this polygamous desire which is not specific to the Black race, which inhabits all men – black or white. . . All men are basically polygamous.[8]

According to Bâ's personal politics, sex and gender are one in the same: it is a man's 'physiology', not his socialization, which explains his sexual infidelity. Polygamy is, then, to some extent, excused as the natural conclusion of men's uncontrollable instincts. On a textual level, even the politically 'progressive' Mawdo is presented as a slave to his 'natural' desires:

---

4. Femi Ojo-Ade (1982), 'Still a Victim? Mariama Bâ's *Une si longue lettre*', *African Literature Today*, vol. 12, p.84.
5. Hereafter abbreviated as *Lettre* (page references in parentheses).
6. Hereafter referred to as *Chant* (page references in parentheses).
7. J.O.J. Nwachukwu-Agbanda (1991) argues that 'Mariama Bâ and/or her protagonist has a deep respect for the marriage institution founded on Western and modern notions of matrimony' ('"One Wife be for One Man": Mariama Bâ's Doctrine for Matrimony', *Modern Fiction Studies*, vol. 37, p.565).
8. Harrell-Bond, 'Mariama Bâ', p.211.

On ne résiste pas aux lois impérieuses qui exigent de l'homme nourriture et vêtements. Ces mêmes lois poussent le 'mâle' ailleurs. Je dis bien 'mâle' pour marquer la bestialité des instincts. . . Tu comprends. . . Une femme doit comprendre une fois pour toutes et pardonner; elle ne doit pas souffrir en se souciant des 'trahisons' charnelles. (*Lettre*, pp.52–3)

This biological apology for polygamy is restated in Ramatoulaye's references to the gap between Modou's front teeth, 'signe de la primauté de l'amour en l'individu' (*Lettre*, p.57).[9] However, the text proceeds to undermine itself as it reveals Modou's actions to be motivated rather by 'amour propre' than by unsatiated sexual desire:

Modou teignait mensuellement ses cheveux. . . Modou s'essouflait à emprisonner une jeunesse déclinante qui le fuyait de partout. . . Il avait peur de décevoir et pour qu'on n'eût pas le temps de l'observer, il créait tous les jours des fêtes. (*Lettre*, p.72)

It is for social, not biological, reasons that the three male protagonists – Mawdo, Modou and Ousmane – choose to take a second wife. These men have internalized the image of the bourgeois African man modelled for them by a self-perpetuating phallocentric society. In Awa Thiam's study of polygamy, 80 per cent of the men she interviewed claimed to have taken a second wife for sexual reasons. While, as she explains, African women often regulate childbirth with periods of sexual abstinence, the availability of contraception would provide a solution to such problems:

Du fait que la femme arrive à s'absentir de relation sexuelle, on ne voit pas pourquoi il n'en serait pas de même pour l'homme. . . Les hommes font et 'c'est naturel'! Mais les femmes n'ont aucun droit de désirer ce que font les hommes. A ce niveau, c'est à une révolution des structures familiales et, par-delà celles-ci, des structures sociales qu'il faut parvenir.[10]

As a set of culturally determined characteristics, 'masculinity' is venerated by both sexes in these texts. In *Un chant écarlate*, Ousmane is sent to the 'Toubab' (i.e. white) school in an attempt by his father to 'save' his son's 'masculinity'. In the atypical role of mother's helper and confidant, the young Ousmane is rejected by Ouleymatou, who 'ne veut pas d'un garçon qui balaie, porte des seaux d'eau et sent le

9. Hence her mother's preference for Daouda Dieng (*Lettre*, p.89) and her own relief when faced with the teeth of her daughter's lover (p.123).
10. Awa Thiam (1977), *La Parole aux Négresses*, Paris: Denoël, p.121.

poisson sec' (*Chant*, p.18). Likewise, Djibril Gueye is concerned that his son is in danger of becoming 'une femmelette' (*Chant*, p.16), a notion that is echoed later in the text in Djibril's condemnation of a local boy who spends his time in the company of girls: 'Sauf miracle, ce garçonnet deviendrait un "gôr djiguène" destiné à passer sa vie, accroupi aux pieds d'une courtisane dont il demeurerait l'homme de main' (*Chant*, p.107). 'Gôr djiguène' is explained in the author's footnote to page 107 as 'littéralement homme–femme; homosexuel'. Thus, in the Wolof language, a homosexual man who resists his traditional gender role is biologically indeterminate: a 'man–woman' or androgyne.[11]

Although indisputably heterosexual, the content of the young Ousmane's character, when submitted to a semic analysis, reveals a number of semes traditionally associated with the typically 'feminine' gender role: when rejected by Ouleymatou, Ousmane cries and is tortured by jealousy (*Chant*, p.18); later, day-dreams of Mireille, 'sa princesse' (p.25), abound in the formulae and conventions of the romantic novel. Following the proairetic code of the romantic heroine, Ousmane begins to lose interest in the people and things around him: 'Ousmane se surprit à préférer la solitude aux discussions fracassantes. . . Tout lui paraissait dépourvu d'intérêt en dehors de Mireille!' (p.25). Reason and common sense are replaced by the indices of falling in love: 'rêve', 'folie', 'songes' and 'désir' (p.26); and even Ousmane's body behaves appropriately: 'Ses jambes hésitaient, son coeur dansait' (p.27). It is therefore slightly ironic when the text appears to criticize its own construction, commenting that 'des amoureux plus imaginatifs que Mireille et Ousmane inventeront peut-être un jour un vocabulaire et des gestes neufs' (p.28).

While, as this narratorial intervention suggests, the stock phrases and proairetic formulae are neither 'new' nor 'imaginative', what is innovative about this text is, firstly, the biological sex of the subject – to my knowledge, this is the only example of a male romantic subject in African women's writing – and, secondly, the attribution of a number of traditionally 'feminine' characteristics to this subject.

11. In a discussion of the work of Yambo Ouologuem, the celebrated author, Cheikh Hamidou Kane, denounces homosexuality, claiming that 'Ouologuem has a concept of love which is atrocious; homosexuality which does not exist in our culture; all that is vice, incest, animality, and so many things that belong to white people or exist in white man's mind. He gives all these traits to African characters. This is false.' See Phanuel Akubueze Egejuru (1980), *Towards African Literary Independence: a Dialogue with Contemporary African Writers*, Westport, Connecticut: Greenwood Press, p.118.

It is interesting, then, that when the narrative axis becomes destabilized (i.e. when the actantial roles of subject–object begin to shift back and forth between Ousmane and Mireille), Ousmane appears to shed these 'feminine' attributes and adopt a more conventionally 'masculine' gender role. Significantly, it is after Ousmane's desire has been sated, through sexual intercourse with Mireille, that his role shifts from romantic subject to Cornelian hero. The object of his quest is no longer focused on Mireille, but on the resolution of his dilemma:

> D'un côté, mon coeur épris d'une Blanche. . . de l'autre, 'ma société'. Entre les deux, ma raison oscillante, comme le fléau d'une balance qui ne peut trouver un point d'équilibre entre deux plateaux aux contenus également chers. (*Chant*, p.56)

Inevitably, Ousmane is unable to resist the pressures of society and conforms to traditional patterns of 'masculine' behaviour. Just as, historically, a black man who slept with a white woman was (literally) castrated and forced into sociocultural exile, so Ousmane begins to feel culturally castrated by Mireille:[12]

> Mireille ne le suivrait donc jamais. Amer, il mesurait l'incompréhension qui les séparait: un océan. Plongeant vif dans sa race, il vivait, accordé aux valeurs nègres et au tam-tam vibrant. Sa nature, passionnément, se chargeait de l'héritage culturel drainé par son passé. (*Chant*, p.141)

In spite of Mireille's decision to marry Ousmane, thereby renouncing her own culture and religion, there is no evidence in the text (apart from the marriage itself) that Ousmane is prepared to compromise any aspect of his Senegalese sociocultural traditions. The narrator comments that 'en épousant un homme, on épouse aussi sa manière de vivre' (*Chant*, p.133). It would seem that, before his marriage with Mireille, Ousmane had internalized those myths about white women which Fanon deconstructs in *Peau noire, masques blancs*, and which Bâ's text itself exposes through the racist clichés of Yaye Khady.[13]

According to the mythology of racism, if a white woman loves a black man then he is loved and recognized as white, that is, as superior to other blacks. Fanon describes the way in which some black men

---

12. For a limited discussion of Ousmane's motives as '"reverse" exoticism', see Elinor S. Miller (1986), 'Two Faces of the Exotic: Mariama Bâ's *Un chant écarlate*', *French Literature Series*, vol. 13, pp.144–7.

13. Frantz Fanon (1952), *Peau noire, masques blancs*, Paris: Seuil, p.58.

have embraced this inauthentic self-image and internalized the myth that a white woman's body represents the whole of white culture, civilization and pride.[14] Sex with a white woman is subsequently mystified as 'ce rite d'initiation à l'authentique virilité'.[15] This explains Yaye Khady's warning of the insatiable nature of a white woman's sexual appetite. She informs Ousmane, 'si tu suis ta Blanche insatiable, ton intestin unique rompra' (*Chant*, p.130).[16]

Having been educated by whites, Ousmane initially aspires to what he falsely assumes to be a superior role model. As he begins to reimmerse himself in his own black culture, it becomes apparent that Mireille is no longer useful to him. He therefore chooses to exchange her for a more appropriate status symbol. Ousmane's desire for Ouleymatou is generated not by a voracious sexual appetite but by his quest for a socially acceptable identity. Indeed, only one of Bâ's male protagonists manages to break out of the social mould of the Senegalese bourgeois male and the fact that he has done so by detaching himself from the Senegalese community is not without significance. Lamine defies the scorn of friends and family who, like Ousmane, condemn his way of life as a rejection of his roots in favour of the traditions of the colonizer, stating that, 'Eh bien, si respecter ma femme et la laisser s'épanouir selon ses options signifie être colonisé, alors, je suis colonisé et l'accepte' (*Chant*, p.153).

For the traditionalist, Lamine's non-sexist philosophy is the equivalent of assimilation, as Ousmane explains: 'Tu vis "Toubab", tu penses "Toubab". Du nègre tu n'as plus que la peau. . . Ce que tu perds est énorme. C'est ton âme d'Africain, ton essence d'Africain. Et c'est grave, grave!' (*Chant*, pp.152–3). This essentialist condemnation of sexual equality demonstrates what Katherine Frank has referred to as 'the historically established and culturally sanctioned sexism of African society'.[17] The sexual hierarchy, like the polygamous exchange of women, is both perpetuated and endorsed by the myths of 'tradition'. Feminism represents the threat of change to traditional patriarchal structures, therefore anyone who sympathizes with the feminist cause is branded a 'Toubab' and immediately cast into sociocultural exile.

Daouda Dieng, although 'taxé de "féministe"' at the Assemblée

14. Ibid., p.51.
15. Ibid., p.58.
16. It is interesting that blacks are objectified by whites with an identical mythology via very different routes.
17. Katherine Frank (1987), 'Women without Men: the Feminist Novel in Africa', *African Literature Today*, vol. 15, p.15.

Nationale (*Lettre*, p.90), is presented as the epitome of bourgeois 'masculinity' in every aspect of his personal life. The reader can only conclude that marriage to Ramatoulaye would have simply provided the finishing touch to his luxury villa filled with the icons of bourgeois materialism. Material acquisitions are a desirable 'white-minded' phenomenon; sympathy with the feminist cause is not.[18]

Although the reader can disentangle strands of Mariama Bâ's personal theory that men are physically incapable of sexual fidelity, the structures of her texts undermine this scientifically inaccurate hypothesis and reinforce the feminist view that 'sex is a biological term: gender a psychological and cultural one'.[19] Men behave differently because society requires them to and because this maintains the assymmetry between women and men.

Having declared that she is not a feminist and resigned herself to the 'essential' differences between the sexes, Mariama Bâ's personal credo would seem to have evolved from an internalization of patriarchal mythologies. However, her active participation in several women's organizations, including 'Soeurs Optimistes [not féministes] Internationales',[20] and her decision to write about women – black and white – suggest a political awareness of both the importance of solidarity among women and the possibility and need for change. This apparent conflict of interests is restated in the publisher's blurb for *Une si longue lettre*:

> Mariama Bâ, membre de plusieurs associations féminines ayant des activités sociales et culturelles, se veut cependant 'Sénégalaise moyenne' et femme au foyer. C'est avoir trop longtemps choisi d'ignorer qu'elle était, peut-être avant tout, porteuse de 'Parole'.[21]

To what extent, then, does the dichotomous nature of Bâ's personal relationship with feminism interact with the female characterization of her novels? Femi Ojo-Ade condemns *Une si longue lettre* as a text which 'smacks of Beauvoirism'.[22] He defines Beauvoirism as 'preach[ing] a fake freedom, a liberty that is no less a lie than the

---

18. Although the accumulation of treasures already existed in Africa, the status of these new acquisitions is strictly 'bourgeois' and therefore associated with colonialism.
19. Ann Oakley (1972), *Sex, Gender and Society*, London: Temple Smith, p.158.
20. Harrell-Bond, 'Mariama Bâ', p.212.
21. *Lettre*, publisher's blurb, back cover.
22. Ojo-Ade, 'Still a Victim?', p.84.

cataleptic civilization passed on to the colonized by the colonizer'.[23] Ojo-Ade's remarks represent Bâ's heroines as examples of what Beatrice Stegeman has described as the 'New Woman' typology.[24] The 'New Woman' challenges the 'value of submergence' implicit in the communal tradition of African society and adopts the individualist ideology generally associated with Western feminism.

While the heroines of Bâ's first novel are atypical in so far as both are educated working women, capable of supporting themselves financially, only Aïssatou is attributed with the qualities of the 'New Woman'. Her decision to divorce Mawdo demonstrates a rejection of the polygamous tradition and an awareness of the self as an individual, rather than as a component in a family or social grouping. Ramatoulaye, however, resigns herself to the role of co-wife, thus allowing the perpetuation of polygamy and reinforcing her object status as an exchangeable commodity.

As 'New Woman', the character of Aïssatou necessarily combines certain semes of 'femininity' with those of a more typically 'masculine' gender role. 'Quiétude' and 'tendresse' (p.51) combine with 'dignité' and 'courage' (p.50) in a character who, in the style of 'Superwoman', transforms from 'bijoutière' (one of the lowest members of the Senegalese caste system) to 'pionnière'. Ramatoulaye tells her:

> Comme j'enviais ta tranquillité lors de ton dernier séjour! Tu étais là, débarrassée du masque de la souffrance. . . Oui, tu étais bien là, le passé écrasé sous ton talon. Tu étais là, victime innocente d'une injuste cause et pionnière hardie d'une nouvelle vie. (*Lettre*, p.53)

Just as, for the traditionalist, feminism is inexorably bound up with the philosophy of the colonizer, so Aïssatou becomes associated with symbols of Westernization: 'Ainsi, demain, je te reverrai en tailleur ou en robe-maxi? Je parie avec Daba: le tailleur. Habituée à vivre loin d'ici, tu voudras – je parie encore avec Daba – table, assiette, chaise, fourchette' (*Lettre*, p.130). Aïssatou's assimilation into Western life implies a condemnation of her decision as the renunciation of her Africanity.[25] The clumsy rhythm of 'table, assiette, chaise, fourchette'

23. Ibid., p.85.
24. Beatrice Stegeman (1974), 'The Divorce Dilemma: the New Woman in Contemporary African Novels', *Critique: Studies in Modern Fiction*, vol. 15, no.3, pp.81–93.
25. Aïssatou's move to the USA is, of course, the final index of her assimilation.

contrasts with the communal warmth of Ramatoulaye's traditional meal: 'Plus commode, diras-tu. Mais, je ne te suivrai pas. Je t'étalerai une natte. Dessus, le grand bol fumant où tu supporteras que d'autres mains puisent' (*Lettre*, p.130).

To a certain extent, then, the character of Aïssatou appears to represent the kind of feminist which Bâ and Ojo-Ade denounce as a woman who 'imitates men', a 'progressive striving to become a man'.[26] Ultimately exiled from her African roots – both socially and geographically – Aïssatou evolves within the text as a figure of what traditionalists believe to be the essential incompatibility of feminism and Africa.

That is not to say that Bâ's texts are simply structured by the binary opposition of feminism/tradition. While Ramatoulaye does not follow in the 'Western' footsteps of Aïssatou, her relationship with feminism is as complex as that of Mariama Bâ herself. Although Ramatoulaye, the narrator, exposes the dehumanizing nature of marriage as an amputation of the self (*Lettre*, p.11), Ramatoulaye, the protagonist, endorses Bâ's own theory of the essential unity of women and men.[27] Indeed, the words of Mariama Bâ are recited almost verbatim in the text of her first novel. Compare:

Mariama Bâ: Although I am divorced, I wish I were married. Men and women are complementary.[28]

with:

Je reste persuadée de l'inévitable et nécessaire complémentarité de l'homme et de la femme. (*Lettre*, p.129)

The 'necessary complementarity' of women and men is a pro-traditionalist formula which constitutes a panacea to contain the 'plague' of feminism: whereas feminists promote solidarity of gender rather than race, traditionalists, like Femi Ojo-Ade, contend that Africanness is 'foreign' to those women writers who have 'let the questions of male domination blind them to the necessary solidarity

26. Ojo-Ade, 'Still a Victim?', p.84.
27. Florence Stratton (1988) oversimplifies the issue when she concludes that Bâ herself identifies with Aïssatou because both author and character are divorced, and because Aïssatou's family name is also Bâ ('The Shallow Grave: Archetypes of Female Experience in African Fiction', *Research in African Literatures*, vol. 19, p.159).
28. Harrell-Bond, 'Mariama Bâ', p.209.

between man and woman'.[29] It is interesting, then, that in spite of all these statements, the textual examples of solidarity/complementarity are between woman and woman, not woman and man.[30] Friendship between two women is presented as a source of stability and strength, and is diametrically opposed to the fleeting and fickle nature of heterosexual love:

> L'amitié a un code de comportement plus constant que celui de l'amour. L'amitié peut, dans un coeur, dominer l'affection née des liens de sang. (*Chant*, p.228)

> L'amitié a des grandeurs inconnues de l'amour. Elle se fortifie dans les difficultés, alors que les contraintes massacrent l'amour. Elle résiste au temps qui lasse et désunit les couples. Elle a des élévations inconnues de l'amour. (*Lettre*, p.79)

Both texts establish a semantic axis with the positive and negative poles assigned to 'amitié' and 'amour' respectively. Not surprising, then, is Mariama Bâ's conviction that Ramatoulaye's relationship with Modou was 'an ideal marriage',[31] if 'amour' is inferior to 'amitié' in the emotional – and semantic – hierarchy.

While, on the semiotic level, Ramatoulaye's friendship with Aïssatou follows the code of platonic love, syntactically the text suggests 'amour' and not 'amitié':

> Je t'invoque. Le passé renaît avec son cortège d'émotions. Je ferme les yeux. Flux et reflux de sensations: chaleur et éblouissement, les feux de bois; délice dans notre bouche gourmande, la mangue verte pimentée, mordue à tour de rôle. (*Lettre*, p.7)

The sensuality of this passage relies on the indices of eroticism: 'chaleur', 'éblouissement', 'feux', 'délice', 'bouche' and 'mordue' are charged with connotations of sexual love. Later, the text recreates Ramatoulaye as the romantic heroine who, upon receipt of a lavender-perfumed letter, is excited and relieved at the prospect of reunion with Aïssatou:

29. Femi Ojo-Ade (1983), 'Female Writers, Male Critics', *African Literature Today*, vol. 13, p.176.
30. With the exception of the Lamine/Pierrette relationship discussed earlier. The text also hints that Ramatoulaye's daughter, Daba, will have a 'complementary' marriage.
31. Harrell-Bond, 'Mariama Bâ', p.210.

Ces mots caressants qui me décrispent sont bien de toi. Et tu m'apprends la 'fin'. Je calcule. Demain, c'est bien la fin de ma réclusion. Et tu seras là, à portée de ma main, de ma voix, de mon regard. (*Lettre*, p.104)

Like a 'heroic warrior', Aïssatou will return to rescue Ramatoulaye from her recluse's cell. This fairy-tale scenario highlights the opposing gender roles of the two women: Ramatoulaye's passive 'femininity' contrasts with the active 'masculinity' of Aïssatou. Unlike the proposals of Tamsir and Daouda, Aïssatou's return will constitute a positive turning point for Ramatoulaye: 'Réunies, ferons-nous le décompte de nos floraisons fanées ou enfouirons-nous de nouvelles graines pour de nouvelles moissons?' (*Lettre*, p.105). So the text dismisses Mariama Bâ's complementarily heterosexual couples as 'floraisons fanées' and promotes the 'nouvelles moissons' to be reaped from friendships between women. While Mortimer presents 'female bonding' as 'an important subtext in the work',[32] my own reading will identify female solidarity as the key to a more positive cultural identity.

The concept of solidarity acquires an interesting new dimension in *Un chant écarlate*, in which the African text empathizes with its European subject, Mireille. Against the international, transcultural nature of student solidarity, Bâ contrasts the sexual rivalry and inverted racism of the women in her texts. Unlike *Une si longue lettre*, Mariama Bâ's second novel contains little textual evidence of female solidarity. With the exception of Soukeyna's friendship with Mireille – which receives relatively little narrative space – relationships between women are motivated by bourgeois materialism and 'arrivisme'.

Yaye Khady gives her support to Ouleymatou's sexual advances on Ousmane as she would prefer 'n'importe quelle Négresse plutôt que cette Blanche' (*Chant*, p.190). For the women in this text, race and class take precedence over sex, not for reasons of black pride or anticolonialism; rather because, within the traditional hierarchy of the Senegalese caste system, marriage outside one's class (with a white woman or with a 'bijoutière') fails to generate the vast amounts of wealth and social recognition generally associated with a traditional marriage. Unlike Ramatoulaye and Aïssatou, Yaye Khady fails to challenge existing social structures, developing, instead, a narcissistic relationship with the social role of 'belle-mère':

---

32. Mildred Mortimer (1990), 'Enclosure/Disclosure in Mariama Bâ's *Une si longue lettre*', *French Review*, vol. 64, p.71.

Moi qui rêvait d'une bru qui habiterait ici et me remplacerait aux tâches ménagères en prenant la maison en mains, voilà que je tombe sur une femme qui va emporter mon fils. Je crèverai, debout dans la cuisine. (*Chant*, p.102)

Subsequently, Yaye Khady's distress over the conservative nature of Gorgui's baptism is generated by the lack of the traditional exchange of material goods and by her preoccupation with her social status:

Yaye Khady savait que le seuil de sa maison franchi, les moqueries se libéreraient. On s'exclamerait dans les rires fous:
– Quoi? C'est un baptême ou un deuil?
– Où les jeunes vont-ils pêcher leurs femmes?
– Un baptême sans échange rituel de pagnes et de cadeaux? Chez Yaye Khady, une grande consternation! (*Chant*, p.189)

The exclamation mark suggests both 'style indirect libre' and a degree of disapproval of the absurd nature of Yaye Khady's anxieties. Further irony is invoked when the reader discovers that the unassuming ceremony is not the idea of 'une Blanche [qui] n'amène rien dans une maison', but of Ousmane himself (p.188). Like Tante Nabou in *Une si longue lettre*, Ousmane's mother's solidarity lies only with the society she inhabits: a consumer-orientated society which Mireille – and the text itself – condemns:

Ignorant les possibilités financières de Mireille, elle [Yaye Khady] avertissait, haineuse:
– Tu es assise sur l'argent de mon fils. Par n'importe quel moyen, je te délogerai un jour. Mireille rougissait. Elle n'acceptait pas les exigences d'une société tournée entièrement vers l'apparence, à la recherche du prestige, et dans laquelle son mari se mouvait avec une aisance surprenante. (*Chant*, p.150)

It is within this 'société tournée entièrement vers l'apparence' that women such as Yaye Khady and Tante Nabou have found their niche. Like the 'bad mothers-in-law' of romantic novels, the potential power of these women has been negatively channelled into collusion with the patriarchs. It is interesting, then, to consider Femi Ojo-Ade's conclusion that it is Ramatoulaye's motives which are motivated by bourgeois bitterness and materialism. For him, 'Ramatoulaye's middle-class origins are to her a source of pride and her commitment as a pioneer is, first and foremost, to that class.'[33]

If that were the case – and my own reading suggests the contrary – then why does Ramatoulaye defy the aspirations of her class by '[choosing] her moments of perspicacity and paucity of knowledge rather dexterously, and always to the detriment of Man [*sic!*] and mother-in-law'?[34] Surely, if Ramatoulaye were the archetypal bourgeois pioneer, then her solidarity would lie with the men and mothers-in-law who maintain it? The capital 'M' in 'Man' – by no means an innocent mistake – suggests that Ojo-Ade's male traditionalist socialization has blinded him to a generous reading of Bâ's text. Ironically, the grouping of 'Man and mother-in-law', would seem to substantiate my own conclusion: Ramatoulaye's personal conflict is generated by a resistance to the mould of the 'confidently feminine' (prepared by mothers-in-law and men) combined with a fear of the unknown (i.e. her authentic female self).

In the face of female solidarity with patriarchal values, Mariama Bâ's heroines demonstrate three different kinds of response: Aïssatou chooses temporary exile as a means for rediscovering her self; Ramatoulaye selects the balancing act discussed by Davies and Graves in *Ngambika*,[35] and Mireille, the 'Other's Other', unable to resist the traditional power structures of African society, resorts to the antisocial acts of murdering her child and attacking her unfaithful husband. What these women have in common is not their colour, their class or their 'femininity', but the mutual experience of man's infidelity. Or, as Mbye Boubacar Cham puts it: 'Abandonment in the novels of Mariama Bâ is predominantly a female condition. It is both physical and psychological, and it transcends race, class, ethnicity and class.'[36] However, sexual abandonment is presented as a cultural rather than an emotional defeat, for it is the existing social structure which allows it to occur.

33. Ojo-Ade, 'Still a Victim?', p.83. In an equally anti-feminist article, Charles Ponnuthurai Sarvan (1988) extends this criticism of Ramatoulaye to that of feminism in general, arguing that 'in the novels of Mariama Bâ we see that feminism may at times overlook that economic inequality that affects the majority of women, children and men' ('Feminism and African Fiction: the Novels of Mariama Bâ', *Modern Fiction Studies*, vol. 34, p.464).
34. Ojo-Ade 'Still a Victim?', p.83.
35. Carole Boyce Davies and Anne Adams Graves (1986), *Ngambika*, Trenton, NJ: Africa World Press, p.12.
36. Mbye Boubacar Cham (1984–5), 'The Female Condition in Africa: a Literary Exploration by Mariama Bâ', *Current Bibliography on African Affairs*, vol. 17, p.30.

Whereas many of the women characters in Bâ's novels constitute their identity in terms of first class/caste, then race, and then gender, the ideology which emerges from a close reading of her texts posits a new female identity, rewriting the traditional African concept of the collective in terms of solidarity among women. Like Mireille, Bâ's texts suggest that a woman alone cannot resist the historically sanctioned practices of patriarchy, for such strength comes from the collective memory of the shared experiences of women. The friendship between Ramatoulaye and Aïssatou stands as a model of such solidarity, which seems to provide a positive first step in overcoming the constraints of the poles of modernism and tradition and a move towards a reorganization of cultural identity in which gender no longer plays second fiddle to issues of race, class, ethnicity and caste.

– 11 –

Tradition and Continuity: The Quest for Synthesis in Francis Bebey's *Le Fils d'Agatha Moudio*

Abimne D. Njinjoh

The profound attachment to the historical traditional past in order to best perceive the future and construct the present for healthy human existence is the central preoccupation of anglophone and francophone contemporary African authors alike. For instance, Alan Paton, the South African novelist, in *Cry, the Beloved Country*, sees the wholesale departure of his characters from the traditional sanctioned environment of Ndotsheni into the fragmented and turbulent urban world of Johannesburg, with disastrous consequences. Joseph Toundi, Ferdinand Oyono's young and naïve protagonist in *Une vie de boy*, who departs completely from his local traditional milieu and black father in quest of a new white father in the modern sophisticated French colonial world, is mercilessly destroyed.

The repercussions emanating from the contact of traditional African values (on top of an exacting cyclical order) with modern Western civilization following the advent of Europeans, especially missionaries, in Africa cannot be overemphasized. They were multiple, alienating and often tragic. Chinua Achebe alerts us of this looming disaster in a timely manner in *Things Fall Apart* when he points out that:

> the white man is very clever. He came quietly and peaceably with his religion. We were amused at his foolishness and allowed him to stay. Now he has won our brothers and our clan can no longer act as one. He has put a knife on the things that held us together and we have fallen apart.[1]

This awareness of things falling apart has inspired and motivated the other African writers to gird up their loins towards reconstructing the

1. Chinua Achebe (1958), *Things Fall Apart*, London: Heinemann, p.160.

'fallen bits'. Thus, Léopold Sédar Senghor's 'retour aux sources' (return to roots) concept is intended to be seen in terms of an effort to blend the past with the present in order to best conceive and project the future. Alex Haley, in his famous work, *Roots*, provides a tangible link between the West Atlantic blacks and their African past.

The constant search for 'roots', or 'birth-cord', as evoked by the Ghanaian novelist, Kofi Awoonor in *This Earth, My Brother. . .*, is a leading theme in African literature in general and Cameroonian literature in particular.

The particular experiences of Francis Bebey's characters in general and those in *Le Fils d'Agatha Moudio* in particular, suggest that Bebey is preoccupied with the celebration of traditional African values. They also indicate that Bebey is concerned with the ultimate achievement of balance and harmony in human relationships. It is in this light, therefore, that Bebey is preoccupied with the celebration of the African traditional experience and is involved in depicting the spiritual essence of the cyclical continuity of the African cosmology.

On the other hand, Bebey also appears to sympathize with the characters in his fiction who have fallen out of harmony with the spiritual essence of their culture. Although they have fallen out of balance and have been alienated by temporary exile into the world of Western values, he makes them return to their original roots to regain a semblance of spiritual and cultural balance.

A close look at *Le Fils d'Agatha Moudio* indicates that the particular experiences of the characters in the novel tie up with the recurrent paradigm in African literature which states that a return to one's starting point after having left one's home to enter a world of fragmentation and chaos is an essential component of the individual's wholesome return to his roots. This is why the authenticity of the characters in *Le Fils d'Agatha Moudio* is strongly anchored and deeply rooted in the indigenous African context of 'civilisation d'équilibre' (balanced civilization) within the strict confines of the cyclical structure of African life.

Tradition within the context of this chapter refers to the time-honoured beliefs and customs deeply rooted in the natural African physical environment as opposed to the bare and insipid Western materialistic milieu. The African physical cosmic world is considered as an integral part of tradition. Synthesis on the other hand, implies the fusion of the apparently conflicting Western and African values. It involves the harmonious integration of the perception of two world views and two cosmologies – the African and the European.

Set in the small rural village of Bonakwan, *Le Fils d'Agatha Moudio* provides the ideal setting for the portrayal of the twin aspects of traditional integrity and cyclical continuity. These dual aspects of tradition and continuity in the novel are appropriately explored through Bebey's subtle handling of plot, setting and characterization. Bebey initially explores the natural environmental setting of Bonakwan to show how the traditions of man are inherently related to his natural environment, through Mbenda, the fisherman protagonist. At first, one gets the impression of a life built on the principle of 'survival of the fittest', through the Bonakwans' permanent contact with the sea and its monstrous waves. But the reality is that the regular fishing expeditions of the village fishermen situate the Bonakwan villagers as a people in an enduring and immutable rapport with nature. Nature here is obviously a giver as well as a destroyer of life, but only along the lines of synthesis and continuity, in conformity with the concept that death feeds life, making renewal possible. It is in this light that Bebey describes the natural life of the fishermen of Bonakwan:

> Soleil splendide de l'été, mer tour à tour calme et agitée, horizon, réel des jours qui naissent et meurent, mince fumée lointaine sortant du bateau gros comme un grain de sable. . . village de pêche. . . poissons de toute sorte. . . veillées autour du feu après la dure journée et la mer rude, contes, chants, devinettes, proverbes, danses, rêve souriant à la belle étoile, nattes de raphia à même le sol. . . fraternité, solidarité, le ciel, la mer, les hommes, des hommes perdus dans une nature écrasante, les hommes simples vivant au rythme de la mer, sous l'oeil vigilant de millions d'étoiles, des hommes pour Dieu et pour Satan, brassant leurs efforts pour la vie d'autres hommes. . . C'est là, la pêche en haute mer. . . la pêche n'est pas un combat, mais une vie. Vie heureuse, combien devrais-je donner pour te retrouver?[2]

Given his fishing career at the early age of fifteen, Mbenda, the protagonist, is at the very heart of nature. His attachment to his natural environment is even more evident in his confession that:

> tous les miens ne savaient même pas voir combien l'idée de quitter ma condition heureuse de pêcheur, pour un pantalon, une chemise, et une cravate [en ville] m'était désagréable. . . J'aime à me promener par les jours de grand soleil, mon pagne immense [comme la mer immense] autour de mes reins, en remerciant le ciel de m'avoir créé grand et fort. Je n'aimerais pas devenir fonctionnaire . . . J'aime ce que je fais dans la vie et je crois que le grand air me réussit bien. (*FAM*, pp.16, 30)

2. Francis Bebey (1967), *Le Fils d'Agatha Moudio*, Yaoundé: Editions CLE, pp.202–3. Hereafter cited as *FAM* with page numbers indicated in the body of the chapter.

Nature stands at the centre of the thoughts, activities, and occupations of the Bonakwan traditional universe. It is accorded pride of place in daily conversations, especially during traditional visits involving marital arrangements, like Fanny's engagement to Mbenda:

> On frappe à la porte, on entre, et l'on parle de toute sortes de choses avec le maître des lieux: la saison se porte bien, les pluies vont bientôt revenir, les femmes, poursuivent leurs travaux des champs, malgré les chaleurs torrides, les enfants sont sages. (*FAM*, p.63)

Here, nature sets the ground and prepares the way for important negotiations and requests. Indeed, nature is inherent in, and forms an essential component of tradition. Conceived as an integral part of nature, the traditional village man must remain deeply rooted in Mother Earth because as François Sengat-Kuo aptly points out:

> L'arbre ne s'élance à la conquête du soleil
> qu'en s'agrippant ferme à la terre nourricière
> les pieds mouillés au lac des tombeaux.[3]

Like the tree which needs the sun as well as the soil or Mother Earth for the purpose of survival and continuity, the Bonakwan fishermen are condemned to maintain a permanent liaison with the sea and its ruthless waves in keeping with the going and coming of the seasons.

The traditional universe of *Le Fils d'Agatha Moudio* is complemented by the spiritual cyclical conception of the Bonakwan cosmology in which the gods of the forest and dead ancestors have a firm hold on the activities of the living. Hence, the traditional world in the novel is essentially a spirit-orientated cosmos, in which the dead, the living and the unborn hold each other in an embrace of cyclical continuity. This is why death can only be explained and comprehended through witchcraft. It is in this same light that Mother Mauvais Regard is portrayed as the regulator of human lives. She is the village ancestral spirit who sees and watches over everybody, but, at the same time, is also capable of inflicting punishment (when necessary) on those who depart from the traditional cyclical order. Her role as the ancestral representative is clearly expressed in her untiring care over Fanny, the (unborn) ancestral chosen fiancée/wife of Mbenda:

---

3. François Segat-Kuo (1971), *Collier de cauris*, Paris: Présence Africaine, p.20.

> La mère Mauvais Regard ramassa un gros caillou rond et lisse et le lança dans la direction de Fanny. C'était tout. Les esprits vus en songe ne pourraient plus rien contre ma femme à présent. (*FAM*, p.130)

We are not surprised by the special motherly care Mauvais Regard accords to Fanny in preference to Agatha and the other village women. Fanny as had earlier been stated, is the ancestral 'enfant chéri', that is, Edimo's chosen metaphysical child, who is deeply rooted in the circular structure of life and who stands for and defends rebirth and continuity. It is evident, therefore, that Bebey portrays Maa Médi, (the protagonist's mother), Mauvais Regard and the other old Bonakwan village women as the ordained supervisors of the cyclical structure of life in the novel.[4] It is their responsibility to see to its continuity through births, deaths and rebirths.

Mbenda, the central protagonist, symbolizes the search for balance and the semblance of synthesis in *Le Fils d'Agatha Moudio*. He is more than the strong mediating force that is obliged to unify the traditional and modern worlds. This dual role is symbolized by his polygamous marriage to Fanny, his parents' choice on the one hand, and Agatha, his personal choice on the other hand.

King Solomon's mediating and reconciliatory advice to Mbenda on the problematic situation in which Mbenda finds himself with two illegitimate children from his two wives mirrors Bebey's pre-occupation with the semblance of synthesis and balance in the novel:

> Ce n'est pas le premier enfant 'sans père' qui te vienne au monde, que je sache? Qu'as-tu donc fait du premier?. . . Tu n'as pas le droit de te laisser abattre ainsi, toi, La Loi, le plus fort des jeunes gens de chez nous. Et puis, tu sais, qu'il vienne du ciel ou de l'enfer, un enfant, c'est toujours un enfant. (*FAM*, p.204)

This comforting philosophical counsel from King Solomon, the Bonakwan village sage, is well registered in Mbenda's mind. It calls for the acceptance of his fate for the purpose of survival and continuity because the child stands at the centre of procreation and is the indispensable component of continuity in the Bonakwan cosmology.

---

4. Emmanuel Obiechina (1975) also expresses this view when he points out that 'man is at the centre of the traditional universe, not because he is most powerful but because he is able to regulate his relationships with the gods and the ancestors and to manipulate the immanent occult vitality of nature' (*Culture, Tradition and Society in the West African Novel*, London: Cambridge University Press, p.38).

Through King Solomon's philosophical counsel, Mbenda is able to affix for himself a practical code of conduct for the purpose of survival and continuity. Mbenda himself admits that:

Il a raison [le roi Salomon]. Tout compte fait, le fils d'Agatha attend de moi, non le ricanement méchant et idiot de l'homme trompé par le sort, mais le conseil paternel qui rendra heureuse l'étrange aventure de sa vie d'homme. (*FAM*, p.206)

The desperate quest for cultural harmony does not only reflect Mbenda's fate. It is also the plight of the contemporary African who, for the purpose of survival, is compelled to subscribe painfully and, indeed, endlessly to the balance between tradition and modernity, between collectivism and individualism. This is why Mbenda himself admits that:

Je compris: j'étais au carrefour des temps anciens et modernes. Je devais choisir en toute liberté ce que je voulais faire, ou laisser faire. Liberté toute théorique, d'ailleurs, car les anciens savaient que je ne pouvais pas choisir de me passer d'eux, à moins de décider *ipso facto* d'aller vivre ailleurs hors de ce village où tout marchait selon des règles séculaires, ... Dire à tout le monde présent que je refusais leur médiation, c'était presque signer mon arrêt de mort. (*FAM*, p.60)

Mbenda is not only at the centre of nature, tradition and continuity in the novel, he stands as Bebey's mouthpiece and epitomizes his philosophy of balance and reconciliation. His Herculean responsibility as the torch-bearer of tradition and continuity is well spelt out:

Pour Maa Médi [ma mère], j'étais le fils unique d'un mari décédé en ne laissant à sa femme que ce fils unique, et aucune autre richesse. . . j'étais le beau temps de la vie, qui devait se conserver beau et pur toute la vie. (*FAM*, p.23)

In the novel, the main character who symbolizes the incursion of Western values in Bonakwan is Agatha, because she is in permanent contact with the white hunters and the European quarters in the city. She is portrayed as having a superiority complex over everyone else in the village through her acquisition of Western manufactured goods. The birth of her halfcaste child with the head white hunter eventually completes her alienation. The birth of the mulatto child implies a betrayal on her part of traditional norms and a departure from the ancestral spiritual roots.

Unlike Agatha, who is alienated from the tradition of her people by her choice of Western values and lifestyle, Fanny is portrayed as the woman who is anchored to the Bonakwan tradition. Although like Agatha she too has an illegitimate child (with Toko, a Bonakwan 'indigène' who goes into self-exile), Fanny opts to remain tied to her traditional roots, perhaps because of the spiritual preservers of the Bonakwan cosmology, who had preordained her before her birth as the spiritual fiancée/wife of Mbenda.

Bebey's characterization and portrayal of these two women appears to suggest and symbolize the dichotomy of the traditional African universe and the alienating Western culture. Strangely enough, it is Mbenda who appears to strike a semblance of synthesis between these two cultures by opting to marry both women. On the one hand, Mbenda and Agatha, who tend to perceive life from opposite points of view (that is, Mbenda, the devoted village fisherman, and Agatha the sophisticated city goer), are reconciled in matrimony. Agatha's regular homecoming to 'roots' from her city exploits compares favourably with Mbenda's going and coming from the fishing expeditions in a way similar to the going and coming of the seasons. Paradoxically, Agatha remains essentially the cultural hybrid who synthesizes the traditional and Western worlds for reconciliation, harmony and survival:

> Agatha rentra, plus intelligente que lors de son départ fracassant de l'autre soir. Elle vint me faire des excuses et m'étonna parce qu'elle alla également en faire à Fanny. (*FAM*, p.179)

Temporary exile appears to be an important aspect that provides the quest for equilibrium in the novel. For example, Fanny and Agatha run away to their relatives in the village and city respectively as if to purge their sins of adultery with Toko (Mbenda's friend and go-between) and the head white hunter. Toko willingly accepts self-exile from the village as punishment for committing adultery with Fanny, Mbenda is jailed for fifteen days in Douala New-Bell prison for daring to ask 'salt-money' as compensation from the white hunters and Dooh is jailed for making money by dishonest means. The village elders are jailed and exiled to Mokolo prison in the far north of the country because of their active role in the 'Gros Coeur magic frog affair'.

Apart from Toko, who does not return from his self exile because adultery is considered an abominable act in the Bonakwan cosmology, most of the other characters in *Le Fils d'Agatha Moudio* return home to their starting-point, maturer and wiser than before, ready to contribute to the achievement of balance and to accommodate change. The prison here is used as a means to purge and render the traditional society more open to assimilate new values: 'En prison, Dooh avait appris un métier honnête. Dès sa sortie, il s'établit à son compte. Il était coiffeur pour le bonheur du village et des environs' (*FAM*, p.160). Dooh's eventual release from prison, his return to society and the transformation of his character represent the departure from society's roots to an eventual return and awareness of self.

Homecoming, as this chapter has indicated, remains the inevitable culminating point that completes the circular tradition. It is often manifested in the form of a trilogy, involving a departure, an arrival and a return to the starting point. The funeral song at the departure of some of the Bonakwan village elders to the Mokolo prison in the novel illustrates Bebey's preoccupation with the return to roots:

> Tu marches, tu marches sans arrêt, tu ne reviens pas, ô mon frère, tu ne reviens pas. Tu t'en va sans regarder derrière, et tu ne reviens pas, ô mon frère, je vois que tu ne reviens pas. Qui t'a menti en disant que c'est ainsi qu'il faut partir? Qui t'a donc appris à marcher ainsi? Quand l'homme marche, de temps en temps, il se retourne pour voir ceux qu'il a laissés derrière lui, ceux qui lui sont chers. Toi tu marches sans cesse, tu ne retournes pas. Qui t'a donc menti en disant que c'est ainsi qu'on quitte ses amis? Dis-moi: qui t'a donc menti en disant que c'est ainsi qu'on quitte ses frères? (*FAM*, p.194)

It is in the same vein that Agatha's homecoming glorifies and validates the authentic essence of the Bonakwan traditional values:

> je cherchais peut-être un homme qui me rendrait heureuse comme jamais cela ne m'est arrivée, mais je le voulais avant tout riche, et habillé d'un pantalon, d'une chemise, d'une cravate, d'une veste, et avec de beaux souliers aux pieds. . . Et puis ça n'a plus d'importance, puisque j'ai trouvé mon homme à présent. Il fera ce qu'il voudra faire dans la vie, mais moi, je veux rester auprès de lui. (*FAM*, p.35)

Agatha's final homecoming is the result of a decision involving a departure from traditional village ways into the sophisticated Westernized city ways and the final return to roots. This is how Francis Bebey's synthesis is reflected in the novel. Agatha appears to have discovered her true self and nature by returning to her roots.

Synthesis and the semblance of balance in *Le Fils d'Agatha Moudio* appear to remain the principle on which all events in the novel take their root along the lines of circularity and continuity. Although the traditional circular structure (which is built on the cyclical conception of life, wherein death feeds life and makes renewal possible) stands in opposition to the new world of modern science and material values, the two perceptions of life seem to gravitate towards each other for complementary coexistence and harmony.

Bebey's search for balance and cultural continuity is not only restricted within the fictional confines of *Le Fils d'Agatha Moudio*. By some remarkable coincidence, the departure from one's roots, the quest for self in foreign lands and values, is remarkably reflected in Francis Bebey's actual creative life. It is interesting to note that his first three novels – *Le Fils d'Agatha Moudio* (1967), *La Poupée ashanti* (1973) and *Le Roi Albert d'Effidi* (1976) – constitute a trilogy that conforms with the circular tradition in *Le Fils d'Agatha Moudio*. From the Cameroonian setting of the first novel, Bebey journeys to the Ghanaian urban setting of *La Poupée ashanti*. This second novel is followed by the return to the more familiar setting of Bebey's Cameroonian village environment in *Le Roi Albert d'Effidi*.

This search for balance and continuity is not only restricted to the fictional world of his novels. It also corresponds to a personal search in the life of the author himself. The fictional hybridity of *Le Fils d'Agatha Moudio* is reflected in the actual hybridity of Bebey in his domestic life. Like Spio in *La Poupee ashanti*, who is seeking fulfilment in the urban environment of Accra, Bebey is also still drifting in search of balance in the Western context of Paris. Like his novels, his music is an attempt to blend modern European and traditional African impulses. However, this is doomed to failure because man does not feed on universalism alone. He has to belong somewhere. This belonging, which Bebey has not been able to achieve, explains why his fictional characters militate for a 'retour aux sources'.

This 'retour aux sources' is very significant. It more than fulfils the circular tradition which is deeply rooted in continuity. The departure from 'roots' in the second novel can be attributed to the disillusionment of Mbenda and Agatha at the end of the first novel, which, perhaps, explains the necessity of a quest for success and continuity elsewhere – this time in the urban world of Accra. This apparent success, the monogamous marriage of Spio and Edna in *La Poupée ashanti*, which Mbenda could not realize with Agatha in the traditional village world of Bonakwan in *Le Fils d'Agatha Moudio*, is effectively achieved in the Western urban context of *La Poupée ashanti*. If Mbenda and Agatha identify with Spio and Edna in *La Poupée ashanti* in the light of the cyclical traditional continuity, it could be revealing to identify Edimo, Mbenda's dead father in *Le Fils d'Agatha Moudio* with 'le roi Albert d'Effidi', who, now reborn in Bebey's third novel of that name, is more mature and more open to change and continuity.

Bebey's final return to complete his trilogy in the Cameroonian village setting of *Le Roi Albert d'Effidi* more than proves and validates the idea that outside success holds no significance unless it is tightly laced with the African's home experience and in close harmony with the cyclical structure of the African cosmology.

12

Marxist Intertext, Islamic Reinscription? Some Common Themes in the Novels of Sembène Ousmane and Aminata Sow Fall

Peter Hawkins

There are some striking similarities to be observed between two of the four novels so far published by the more recent Senegalese author Aminata Sow Fall and two earlier texts by her famous compatriot Sembène Ousmane, an oppositional novelist and film-maker of broadly Marxist inspiration. The two pairs of texts that invite comparison, however invidious, are Sembène's *Xala* of 1973[1] (also a well-known film) and *La Grève des bàttu* by Aminata Sow Fall of 1979,[2] and *Le Dernier de l'empire* of 1981 by Sembène[3] and *Ex-père de la nation* of 1987 by Aminata Sow Fall.[4]

The similarities of form and subject-matter between these two pairs of novels are immediately obvious. To take the first pair, *Xala* and *La Grève des bàttu*, both are short, satirical novellas about the excessive pretentions and Western-style materialism of a corrupt African bourgeois figure, whose downfall is provoked by those outcasts of the bourgeois world, the beggars of Dakar. Even the secondary characters and subplots are similar: both main characters embark on an ill-advised polygamous marriage, to the chagrin of their first wives; both are the object of fierce criticism by student radical daughters with feminist

1. Ousmane Sembène (1973), *Xala*, Paris: Présence Africaine.
2. Aminata Sow Fall (1979), *La Grève des bàttu*, Dakar: Les Nouvelles Editions Africaines.
3. Ousmane Sembène (1981), *Le Dernier de l'empire*, Paris: L'Harmattan (henceforward referred to as *DE*).
4. Aminata Sow Fall (1987), *Ex-père de la nation*, Paris: L'Harmattan (henceforward referred to as *EPN*).

sympathies; both place excessive faith and financial investment in the magical powers of the marabouts, the Islamic holy men, in an attempt to resolve their problems; and both are served with excessive zeal by their subordinates.

The similarities are only slightly less marked in the second pair of novels, Sembène's *Le Dernier de l'empire* and Aminata Sow Fall's *Ex-père de la nation*. Both are longer, more ambitious political novels which use the convention of the memoir by a fallen politician to expose the manipulation of power, the corruption and the ruthlessness of a self-seeking political élite: both protagonists are idealistic but more or less naïve figures who are exploited and manipulated by their unscrupulous peers. Again, the secondary characters and subplots have common features: the psychological interest of the main character's long career experience and his sometimes difficult family relations, particularly with wives and grown-up children; and in both cases the presence of an antihero in the form of an oppositional political journalist.

Ostensibly the comparison is unfavourable to Aminata Sow Fall, who appears from this point of view as the epigone, the imitator. Why should she lay herself open to such an accusation? Her other two novels, *Le Revenant* of 1976 and *L'Appel des arènes* of 1982 bear witness to her creative imagination and her ability to present original and provocative social comment in novelistic form, and support her claim to be among the first women fiction writers to emerge from francophone Africa. Why should she deliberately choose, twice over, to cover the same ground as her more famous compatriot Sembène? A possible explanation is the one suggested by my title: the desire to reinterpret the material presented by Sembène from a Marxist perspective in terms of a different ideological position. Certainly there are considerable differences in the nuances of their novels, even if they seem to agree on the targets appropriate for their satirical attack.

Sembène's Marxism is well known and fairly explicit in his writings, although usually tempered by a love and respect for particular forms of African history and tradition. More recently he has shown some signs of disenchantment, although not losing his satirical edge, as in his recent film *Guelwaar*, an attack on the divisiveness of religious bigotry, which serves to mask the real economic servitude of dependency on aid. Aminata Sow Fall, on the other hand, is a practising Muslim, and an influential figure in the political and cultural establishment of Senegal, if not explicitly aligned with the ruling party, through her role as Directrice des Lettres et de la Propriété intellectuelle. In an interview with the author of this chapter,[5] she

5. Interview published in English in *African Affairs*, 1988, pp.429–30.

makes her position clear as a moderate Muslim critical of the abuses of power and religious authority conducted in the name of Islam or in the name of democracy, both of which are distorted and devalued in the process:

> I think people have given an unfair image of Islam, an image that is not true. . . No, I'm not progressive; but I do think that, in itself, the Muslim religion is not as backward, not as narrow as people think. I told myself that in fact the voice of the people was. . . being usurped, and that, in any case, men in power were not like other men, inasmuch as they are isolated. Is that kind of power a real power? They are people who end up losing sight of the reality of things; and they are praised; they are flattered. So it was the hypocrisy of people towards men in power that I wanted to analyse in my novel.

Let us examine the proposition, then, that her aim in these two novels is to present a different interpretation of the themes that she shares with Sembène, from the point of view of her moderate Muslim faith and her apparent belief in the values of liberal democracy.

In Sembène's *Xala*, the downfall of the hero El Hadj Abdou Kader Beye is his impotence, brought on by the curse alluded to in the title, and which we can probably assume to be economic as well as sexual: he is as much a social parasite as the beggar he persecutes outside the office of his import–export warehouse. In *La Grève des bàttu*, on the other hand, the downfall of the politician Mour N'Diaye is caused by his failure to respect the Islamic precept of giving alms to the poor. As Director of Public Health he banishes the beggars from the streets for the sake of Western tourist appeal, but in doing so he is going against a fundamental principle of the organization of Islamic society, that of help for the needy.[6] Since the beggars then counter with another Western invention, the strike, Mour cannot even practise the ritual atonement for his sin prescribed by the marabout Kifi Bokoul, that of distributing sacrificial meat to the beggars. The motifs may be similar in the two novels, but the underlying motivations attributed to the characters are clearly very different.

A similar pattern emerges in the conjugal relations of the two protagonists. In *Xala*, El Hadj simply over-reaches himself economically by taking a third wife: his ostentatious cupidity is not

6. 'In its social doctrine and legislation, the Koran makes a general effort to ameliorate the condition of the weak and often abused segments of society' (Fazlur Rahman (1987), 'Islam: an overview', in M. Eliade (ed.), *The Encyclopaedia of Religion*, New York: Macmillan, vol.7, p.308).

matched by his ability to create wealth, and he cannot sustain the expense of three households, and as a consequence is ruined. In *La Grève des bàttu*, Mour's offence can be seen to be not economic, but moral: he does not respect the Islamic injunction to treat his two wives fairly and equally, which Aminata Sow Fall highlights in her interview. By way of retribution he is humiliated by his second wife's refusal to respect and obey him.

In general terms, then, the downfall of the two protagonists, although superficially similar, illustrates two very different theses: El Hadj is ruined because he belongs to a parasitic and exploitative class, but Mour is unfit to become Vice-President for moral reasons, because of 'persistent moral failures, which are due to narrowmindedness, lack of vision, weakness and smallness of self', to quote the Koran.[7] We have to assume, however, that Mour remains a member of the administration. His humiliation is benign in comparison with the one that is inflicted on El Hadj, who has to submit to a horrific shower of spittle from the beggars who invade his last remaining home. The satire of Aminata Sow Fall is drily ironic, that of Sembène bitter and contemptuous; the fault of Aminata's hero is a lack of moral coherence, that of Sembène's of belonging to an exploitative class. The general thrust of Aminata's reworking of the same themes as Sembène, however witty and effective, is to redirect and reinterpret the reader's indignation in the direction of moral and religious preoccupations, and away from social and political ones.

The comparison of the later pair of novels is a more complex, more subtle affair. Both *Le Dernier de l'empire* and *Ex-père de la nation* tell the story of a *coup d'état* and the apparently self-inflicted fall from power of an African president, but in detail the resemblances are less obvious. Sembène's work, purporting to be a memoir by a recently retired elder statesman, Cheik Tidiane, is in fact a thinly disguised piece of satirical political fiction, a *roman-à-clef* in which most of the main characters are recognizable, beginning with Léon Mignane (Senghor) and Daouda (Abdou Diouf). The general thrust of the polemic is that the Senegalese political establishment is so corrupt and hypocritical in its pretentions to pseudo-democratic power, so much more self-serving than beneficial to its electorate, that a Marxist military régime might even be preferable. The context is clearly contemporary Senegal, even though no such coup has yet occurred there; but this proposition itself gives the attack a sharp political bite.

Aminata Sow Fall's novel is ostensibly set in Senegal, recognizable by the coastal geography and the Sahelian climate. None of the

7. Ibid., p.308.

characters or situations are identifiable, however, and the proper names appear vaguely African rather than Senegalese – Madiama, Yandé, Yoro, Séni, etc. The novel purports to be set in the 1960s, the years immediately after independence, but the precise scenario – of a well-meaning but weak, democratically elected president who turns into a tyrant before being overthrown – does not correspond to the post-independence period in any one obvious African country, although bearing some resemblance to several: Togo? Nigeria? Ghana? Mali? Aminata Sow Fall seems perhaps concerned to deflect the precise attack of Sembène's novel into a general meditation on the problems of post-independence African politics.

Despite the similarity of the main satirical target – a manipulative, corrupt, self-serving political élite – the implied analysis is very different. Sembène's approach seems to be to demonstrate the political and economic bankruptcy of the nationalist bourgeoisie and its ideology of Negritude – here called 'authénegrafricanitus' – which is totally out of touch with the real needs of the Senegalese people. This is the thrust of Cheik Tidiane's 'resignation speech' on the president's seventieth birthday:

> Une grappe d'individus, légalisée dans la rapine de l'économie nationale, et qui constitue un groupe de privilégiés. Ces mêmes individus bâtissent leur fortune sur la sécheresse; se voulant authentiques, leurs laïus se drapent des lambeaux de l'ancienne culture agonisante.[8]

Sembène is also keen to expose the complicity of the French government in maintaining this regime in neocolonial dependency through figures such as the presidential adviser Adolphe (probably Jacques Collin) and the machinations of the ambassador Jean de Savognard.

While many of these features are referred to in Aminata Sow Fall's novel – economic bankruptcy, interference by 'la puissance du Nord' – responsibility for them is minimized: the first is blamed on the persistent drought and 'uncontrollable' export of capital by unnamed individuals,[9] and the second is limited to demands for reimbursement of debts and the benign championing of human rights by a former French trade-unionist, Baudrain.[10] Sow Fall certainly attacks the self-interested, self-perpetuating political group who flatter and manipulate the president, who is presented at the outset as an idealistic trade-union campaigner, a man of the people; but equal blame seems to lie

8. *DE*, p.75.
9. *EPN*, pp.70–1.
10. *EPN*, p.164.

with the gullibility of the electorate, who are prepared to swallow the excessive personality cult which is built up around him.[11]

What of the presence of Islamic values in the two novels? Both protagonists are shown briefly as inheriting an Islamic faith from their fathers.[12] Curiously, it is Sembène who gives more prominence to Muslim devotion by mocking it – his hero Cheik Tidiane sees little point in practising his faith,[13] attendance at the mosque is presented as a way of avoiding sunstroke[14] and the Friday prayer is accompanied by the effluvia rising from the rubbish tips, urinals and open sewers.[15] The absence of any reference by Aminata Sow Fall's narrator-protagonist to the practice of his father's Muslim faith is, on the other hand, highly significant: it can be read as the reason for his moral decline and his inability to see clearly and act justly, in much the same way as Mour in *La Grève des bàttu*. He is unable to treat his two wives even-handedly; he is unable to find peace of mind after the tragic death of his daughter in a political demonstration; he oscillates between the desire to escape the responsibility of his presidential office and complicity in the most brutal repression of his opponents. The final straw is when he attempts to police gatherings in places of worship for fear of seditious activities, and succeeds in turning the whole population against him; significantly his doubts in this situation turn on the memory of his own father's devout Muslim faith:

> son chapelet noir aux perles luisantes, patinées; l'espèce de papillon noir que les prosternations avaient imprimé sur son front.[16]

It is as if Aminata Sow Fall is giving us a lesson in the disastrous moral consequences of the lack of a firm religious belief. To quote the Prophet again, 'Be not like those who forgot God, and God caused them to forget themselves.'[17] This reading of the novel in terms of spiritual vacuum can remain no more than a hypothesis, however, as the author does not make the message explicit. In the absence of any other obvious explanation for the moral decline of her once idealistic hero, the reader is obliged to fall back on an almost theological conception of the weakness of human nature: 'Power corrupts, and

11. Ibid.
12. *DE*, p.48; *EPN*, p.157.
13. *DE*, p.88.
14. Ibid.
15. *DE*, pp. 108–9.
16. *EPN*, p.157.
17. Rahman, 'Islam', p.303 (Surah 59:19).

absolute power corrupts absolutely.' But also, by deflecting attention towards the general political problems of emergent African states, the author is perhaps implying a valorization of Senegal, where such problems have not been experienced so dramatically, and the process of democracy, however unsatisfactory, has not yet been derailed. In this way *Ex-père de la nation* can be seen as offering a rival interpretation of the themes of Sembène's earlier novel, which serves to deflect the direct criticism of the Senegalese political scene by resituating the debate in a general, non-identifiable context and re-posing the problem in moral terms rather than social, economic or political ones. We are once again dealing with a reinscription of the themes of Sembène's earlier novel, albeit in a less explicit way, which broadens their general resonance but blunts their direct satirical impact, interprets them in a moral context rather than a political or economic one and suggests the relevance of Muslim religious values rather than revolutionary ones.

Despite their differences of approach, however, the two writers do concur on a wide range of issues concerned with the problem of creating stable and just political and social structures in African countries: the need for genuine economic independence, for freedom from foreign political interference, for a responsible and honest political class; respect for human rights and social justice, even for the poorest members of society, the importance of a freely expressed opposition, the elimination of corruption and the materialist pressures that fuel it. In this way they both, in their different ways, provide food for thought in the present context of more-or-less successful attempts to establish democratic and accountable regimes in places such as Cameroon, Togo, Benin, Nigeria and Ivory Coast, not to mention Senegal. If these novels are anything to go by, such action is urgently needed, but the pitfalls are many.

13

Amadou Hampaté Bâ's *Amkullel*: A Malian Memoir and its Contexts

Andrew Manley

Amadou Hampaté Bâ was born in Bandiagara, Mali, around 1900. By the time he died in 1991, he was revered as an <u>emblematic cultural</u> <u>figure</u>, the embodiment of African 'oral tradition', a (highly problematic) concept whose emergence he did much to stimulate. It was Hampaté Bâ, for example, who either originated or popularized the phrase 'In Africa, when an old man dies, it is as if a library burns down.' This chapter will, among other things, look at *Amkullel: l'enfant peul* in relation to the oral tradition. It will also examine the book in relation to other themes which ran through the author's life: Malian Islam, and the sociology of the colonial state in what was then called Soudan Français.

The Book

Amkullel opens with lengthy descriptions of Hampaté Bâ's antecedents on both sides, and of the circumstances that bring them together. All his forebears are Fulbé (Peul in French). His paternal ancestors arrive in Maasina (north-central Mali) during the fifteenth century, part of a wave of nomadic pastoralists from the Fuuta Tooro region of what is now Senegal. They become hereditary chiefs of their district, Fakala, and, when Shehu Ahmad Lobbo defeats the armies of the Segu empire and establishes a Muslim theocracy – the *Diina* – in the early nineteenth century, the Bâ and Hamsalah clans rapidly swear allegiance, becoming regional commanders in the new state. The arrival of al hajj 'Umar's jihad (yet another eastward movement of Fuuta Tooro Fulfuldé-speakers) results in war and the destruction of the *Diina* in the early 1860s. After reverses and the death of al hajj 'Umar, the Futanké invaders, now led by 'Umar's son, Tijani, carry out reprisals, including the massacre of all Bâ/Hamsalah males, except one young escapee, Hampaté, who goes into hiding under Tijani's nose in Bandiagara, the 'Umarian capital.[1]

Meanwhile, Hampaté Bâ's maternal grandfather, Paté Poullo, is a *woodaabé* Fulbé pastoralist from Fuuta Tooro who had accompanied the jihad from the start. During the counter-attack which leads to the death of 'Umar, he becomes close to Tijani, aiding the latter greatly with his mastery of the bush. Hampaté Bâ's grandmother, Anta N'Diobdi, is captured at the fall of Tenenkou, is brought to Bandiangara and marries Paté Poullo. Her discovery that Hampaté, her nephew and the sole surviving Bâ male, is clandestinely working in a butcher's shop, outrages her: as a Fulbé, such a low-caste occupation is an offence to the lineage's nobility. The ensuing confrontation leads to Paté Poullo interceding (successfully) with Tijani to allow Hampaté his life and freedom. Hampaté, however, insists on remaining loyal to the butcher who has taken care of him since childhood. Hampaté marries Kadidja, Anta N'Diobdi's daughter by Paté Poullo, and the author's 'double heritage' is complete.

He is the elder of two sons, born, he says, despite much *maraboutage* on the part of the Futanké notables, unhappy that Kadidja has gone to a Maasinanké Bâ. This hostility proves too much for the marriage: Kadidja is divorced at her request and remarries, to Tijani Thiam, member of one of the great Futanké religious lineages and commander of the Louta region (now in Burkina Faso), under Aqib (Aguibu) Tall. Aqib has been created 'king' of the Bandiagara region at the French conquest in the 1890s. Following an incident engineered against him by Aqib, Tijani is imprisoned in Bougouni, south of the colonial capital, Bamako. Kadidja and – for a time – Amadou journey there to be close to him, and Kadidja becomes a hotelier to passing *juula* (traders), revealing great business acumen. Finally, thanks to the persistence of a sympathetic French official, Tijani is released from his unjust imprisonment and Amadou returns to the extended family group in Bandiagara. There he meets his first white, and is simultaneously both terrified and intrigued. Later, against the family's will, he is forced to attend the *toubab* (white) school.

After an exemplary school career in Bandiagara and later Djenné,

---

1. The standard work on the 'Umarian movement in English is David Robinson (1985), *The Holy War of 'Umar Tall*, Oxford: OUP. This was translated into French in 1988. For the Maasina *Diina*, see both Amadou Hampaté Bâ and Jacques Daget (1981), *L'Empire peul du Macina*, Paris: Editions EHESS (first published in 1961), and Bintou Sanankoua (1989): *Un Empire peul du XIXe siècle: la Diina du Macina*, Paris: L'Harmattan.

he absconds to Kati, a military town near Bamako, to rejoin his mother and stepfather, who are now establishing themselves in a growing, bustling community. The French appoint Tijani *chef de quartier* of Kadobougou, a district composed of Kado (Dogon), who have fled the 1914 famine in the east of Soudan and settled around him, thanks to his continuing reputation from his days as chief of the Louta region. Tijani continues his work as a tailor, which, unlike butchering, is perfectly respectable among Maasinanké Fulbé. Kadidja has embarked on a new career as a fashion designer, selling her creations to a French trading house to be mass-produced for the new urban markets created by colonial towns like Kita. With the help of his parents, Amadou forms a youth association (*waaldé*) and makes friends with children from Kita's Catholic community. He has already been exposed to animism, both here and in Bougouni. He goes to Bamako to have himself circumcised in secret: the family do not have the means to support the celebrations that would be *de rigueur* for the descendant of princes, and Amadou must act in order to keep the headship of his *waaldé*. Returning to Kati, he is forgiven and, unknown to his parents, starts an informal job in the Commandant's residence. He also starts writing letters on behalf of the wives of soldiers away at the European front and gradually becomes an indispensable part of the military camp in time of war, making a good living in the process. Returning to school in Kati, to make up lost time, he is in 1918 selected for the élite Ecole régionale de Bamako, after having been rejected for military service on grounds of frailty.

His parents move to Bamako, saving Amadou a daily journey on foot of 24 km, and continue to prosper in the new colonial urban economy. Passing his exams, though only just, Amadou is returning to Bandiagara for a holiday when he makes the acquaintance of Ben Daoud Mademba, the son of Mademba Sy, the brutal and deeply eccentric French-installed king of Sansanding near Ségou, whose anomalous position continued until his death at the end of the First World War. Returning to Sansanding many years later, the middle-aged Hampaté Bâ discovers his old friend living in poverty in the ruins of the former palace. Coming shortly after the lonely death of his spiritual master, Cerno Bokar Salif Tal, this causes Hampaté Bâ to reflect on the passing nature of earthly glory.

Back in Bamako, Amadou goes to the Ecole professionnelle, the training ground for the colony's African *fonctionnariat*. He finds himself among a small group of students, many of whom will later be members of the Malian francophone intellectual élite. Passing his exams to be admitted to the Gorée (Senegal) Ecole Professionnelle – the pinnacle of a promising student's career at the time – he runs into the categorical refusal of his mother, who has never been happy with his French education, to countenance such a move. He obeys her wish and is punished accordingly for insubordination by the governor. The book ends with the young Amadou *en route* to Ouagadougou (in modern Burkina Faso), having been assigned to the colonial staff in this remote locality as a temporary scribe.

Needless to say, this bald summary does poor justice to what is a tremendously rich, beautifully observed and often extremely funny text. However, it forms a useful basis for a discussion of some themes vital to an understanding of Hampaté Bâ's place in Malian life.

Hampaté Bâ's 'Double Heritage'

As seen above, the author describes himself as the product of a clash between two groups of Muslims. The confrontation between Futanké and Maasinanké is one of the most controversial episodes in Malian history, certainly as far as the losers' descendants are concerned. Even now, there are strong and little-researched oral traditions of resistance in various parts of Maasina. These traditions stress the Islamic illegality of 'Umar's action in going to war against the *Diina* in defiance of the Koranic injunction that Muslim shall not attack fellow Muslim. 'Umar's destruction of an already-weakened *Diina* is generally ascribed to greed and pride, sometimes to simple evil. The 'Umarian descent groups would stress – following al hajj 'Umar himself – that by allying with the Segu empire against the jihad that threatened the region's stability, the *Diina* had committed the unforgivable sin in Islam of allying with pagans against Muslims. The evidence for the *faama* (king) of Segu, Ali, having 'truly' converted after having sworn allegiance to the *Diina* is at the centre of the argument, which is still live in Mali and recently surfaced in connection with the 1992 presidential campaign of Mountaga Tall (a direct descendent of al hajj 'Umar). The depredations and violence of the invading Futanké – as much a product of the movement's lack of coherence and prevailing economic circumstances as of their innate hostility towards 'apostate' enemies – are reflected orally in idioms ranging from family histories to simple aphorisms. This is heightened by the perception that both sides sprang from a common background – that of the Fulfudé-speaking Fuuta Tooro area. Thus, Hampaté Bâ's double heritage is of great importance in forming an approach to his life's literary output.

Amkullel: the Tall and Their Opponents

In addition, as we have seen, Hampaté Bâ's adoptive father was a Thiam. The Thiam and the Tall were at the core of the jihad and are linked by both marriage and a tension that can only be described as structural, which goes back to eighteenth-century Fuuta Tooro. This tension has manifested itself repeatedly in Ségou, the other major centre of the jihad's survivors. The lengthy treatment of Tijani Thiam's deception by Aqib Tall and the privations Tijani undergoes as a result dominate the first half of the book. Tijani is doing his duty, collecting the *impôt* (head tax) in the villages of his area when he meets violent resistance in a non-Muslim village. Sending to Bandiagara for orders, he directs his messenger to Aqib – the king – and not directly to the French Commandant. In doing this Tijani is showing his respect for the son of al hajj 'Umar himself. Aqib notifies the Commandant, who specifies that Tijani has *carte blanche* to attack immediately, which Tijani's men do to great effect. Tijani is subsequently arrested and tried. Realizing that he has been duped by Aqib, he refuses – from honour – to say a word in his own defence at the tribunal, and the Commandant (who now understands precisely what has happened) has no option but to send him to prison, which he reluctantly does. Tijani then undergoes a long forced march and an initially horrendous stay in the Bougouni jail, until sympathetic members of the colonial administration, spurred on by the indefatigable Kadidja, ensure his parole and subsequent release. Throughout this passage, Tijani is portrayed as morally incorruptible, of great religious faith, physical strength and selfless stoicism – the victim of an amoral, machinating rival clan head. Aqib represents the opposite set of qualities, although Hampaté Bâ refrains from explicitly spelling this out in the text.

Cerno Bokar Salif Tall, a great nephew of al hajj 'Umar, also appears in *Amkullel*. He was Hampaté Bâ's spiritual master in the Tijani *tariq* until Cerno Bokar's death in 1940, and has been hailed as an African Islamic 'saint' of enormous stature by various European authors. Hampaté Bâ himself dedicated a book to 'le sage de Bandiagara,'[2] who also proved a fascinating character to the more cerebral type of French colonial administrator. Cerno Bokar was an exponent of *kabbe*, a simple, highly effective form of elementary Islamic education in Fulfudé, which helped him convert a large number of Dogon and

2. Hampaté Bâ (1980), *Vie et enseignement de Tierno Bokar: le sage de Bandiagara*, Paris: Seuil. See also Louis Brenner (1984), the excellent *West African Sufi: the Religious Heritage and Spiritual Search of Cerno Bokar Salif Tal*, London: Hurst.

other non-Muslim inhabitants of the Bandiagara area. More importantly, he sparked a major upheaval within the Tall by adopting in 1937 the variant of Tijani observance popularized by Cheikh Hamallah of Nioro, near the Mauritanian border. Ostensibly based upon a simple difference in ritual, the ramifications of what became known as 'Hamallism' led to one of the great tragedies of colonial Mali, when Hamallah, after having returned from exile, found himself persecuted for Islamic 'fanaticism' by the French at the insistence of various Tall subgroups who feared the challenge to their inherited supremacy over the West African branch of the Moroccan-based Tijaniyya.[3] In these circumstances, Cerno Bokar's adoption of Hamallah's form of prayer predictably led to ostracism by the Tall, and consequently trouble with the French authorities, which overshadowed his last years. His actions, which appear to have been exclusively influenced by a highly developed sense of religious duty, were defended by Hampaté Bâ's religious reputation and the enmity between himself and Soudan Français's most important single dynasty. In short, *Amkullel* is bound up with one of the major ideological crises among Malian Muslims this century. As seen below, Hampaté Bâ's Islamic position became inseparable from his political position in relation to the colonial state.

Hampaté Bâ and the Colonial State

As *Amkullel* reveals, the young Hampaté Bâ was selected for education in the new colonial school system. As with many other families within the Maasinké and Futanké élites, whose children were seen as crucial to French hegemony and therefore a target for 'voluntary' education in the French system, Hampaté Bâ's family were devastated by this development, as French education was seen as a sure route to impiety and damnation. However, the *toubab* school was also one of the most fundamentally important institutions of the colonial state, and had a huge effect upon Malian society. The products of these establishments were, in the early years, often from socially inferior groups. The existing Maasinanké and Futanké élites often did everything they could to keep their children away, even substituting family slaves' children for their own.[4] This, as many of their descendants now admit

3. See Alioune Traouré (1983), *Cheikh Hamahoullah: homme de foi et résistant*, Paris: Maisonneuve et Larose.
4. A superb fictional account of the dilemma Fulbé elites faced over this issue is Cheikh Hamidou Kane (1961), *L'Aventure ambiguë*, Paris: 10/18.

ruefully, rebounded upon them when they found vital positions in the state system staffed by ex-pupils of low birth but great local power, due to the backing of the French commandants, who relied on them for practically all their local intelligence. Both Hampaté Bâ and the quasi-fictional Wangrin, the interpreter (see below), were part of the social revolution. More generally, the narrative highlights in many places the perpetuation and modification of old social and ritual relationships, as the colonial 'economy of affection' came into being in the years around the First World War. I am coming to see these as perhaps the crucial years in Mali's modern history, when the bases of both social cohesion and social conflict were established, with consequences that have been visible ever since.

Hampaté Bâ's school career was the start of a lifetime spent, according to one's point of view, in two ways. The first, widely prevailing, interpretation is that of an intellectual and spiritual giant who straddled two discrete cultures: that of the Islamic civilization of the Middle Niger area, and that of the French colonial system. This view is, not surprisingly, widespread in France and in organizations such as Unesco, where Hampaté Bâ is seen as a figure of great ambiguity: the ambiguous position between the French colonial establishment and the African colonial subject was Hampaté Bâ's home ground throughout the colonial period. Each of these two institutions were, however, far from monolithic. Constantly evolving in relation to each other, they were also characterized by endless ambiguities that neither – the French then, many Malians now – wish to investigate too closely. The spaces where reality was negotiated and renegotiated between French and Africans were precisely the spaces Hampaté Bâ found himself occupying, and were unavoidably political, even – perhaps especially – after he became a full time historical researcher for the Institut Français d'Afrique Noire (IFAN). Metaphorically as well as literally, Hampaté Bâ was that classic figure of African ambiguity, the colonial translator. In *L'Etrange Destin de Wangrin* (1973), his only book that could be called a novel in the popular Western sense, an acute and hilarious picture is painted of the career of Wangrin, the interpreter, who with no more than native cunning and his French education, plays all ends against the middle, often quite outrageously, for the profit of himself and indirectly the poor and dispossessed of colonial Soudan. His hubris finally causes his ruin, at which point Wangrin – a figure up until now somewhere between Anansi and the English Robin Hood – is revealed as a fatalistic and deeply moral figure. There are obvious parallels in the later Wangrin with the qualities displayed in adversity by Hampaté Bâ's spiritual master, Cerno Bokar. Wangrin is a Malian culture hero who runs rings around the French and his local enemies, and quite possibly a new figure in Malian discourse.

Hampaté Bâ's Islamic heritage and his understanding of it led to a further set of consequences in the 1950s, when he became closely associated with the Bureau des Affaires Musulmanes and one of its officers, Marcel Cardaire. Cardaire is now remembered as the author of *Islam et le terroir africain* (1955), a penetrating and academically credible analysis of the changing face of Islam in Mali, at a time when reformist movements were on the rise and the Arabic language was becoming a symbolic issue for those Muslim intellectuals who objected to the recuperation of the colonial Muslim élite by the French colonizers. Cardaire, though genuinely interested in Muslim discourses, was anything but a detached academic. In particular, he fought a complicated battle against Sa'ad 'Umar Touré, who had opened a *medersa* (an Islamic school run on 'rational' lines compared with traditional esoteric forms of Koranic education) in Ségou, with the express intention of teaching Arabic to a high standard. Although not himself one of the scripturalist Arab-orientated reformers that were so worrying to the French, Sa'ad 'Umar's position was explicitly Arabist and anticolonial. He was also a central figure in the Ségou 'Umarian descent group and had very close links with Muntaga Tall, al hajj 'Umar's grandson and head of the 'Umarian Tijaniyya in Mali. In circumstances that are unclear, Hampaté Bâ became associated with Cardaire's battle against the *medersa*, going so far as to open an establishment (with government support) in Diafarabé, specifically geared to teaching Islamic theology but in Bambara and Fulfuldé. Both scripturalist reformers and the 'Umarians saw this as yet another example of Hampaté Bâ's collusion with the French against them. Probably due to his other commitments (he was doing research for *L'Empire peul du Macina* at the time), the experiment was a failure, whereas Sa'ad 'Umar's establishment continues to thrive. However, the episode – which could equally have had roots in Hampaté Bâ's endorsement of Cerno Bokar's *tafsir* in Fulfuldé – remains a source of bitter controversy, establishing Hampaté Bâ once and for all in the minds of many Malian Muslims as a tool of the colonial administration.

Hampaté Bâ, *Amkullel* and Oral Tradition

Amadou Hampaté Bâ always portrayed himself as an exponent of 'oralité couchée sur la page'. Further work must be done before his methods of composition can be understood but a more interesting question, and one highlighted by certain passages in *Amkullel*, is the influence his writings may have had upon the still-evolving oral traditions of the colonial period in Mali. One of the most interesting examples of this in the memoirs is the description of Tijani Thiam's insistence, in Kati, upon healing people suffering from mental illness, something he achieves in many cases. He is repeatedly warned, that in doing so, he risks visiting the same affliction upon members of his own family, and indeed this occurs. The Thiam of Ségou are locally credited with the same prowess with the mentally ill, and exactly the same unfortunate consequence. They had this reputation well before the publication of *Amkullel* and one wonders where this came from. Either Hampaté Bâ is faithfully relating a pre-existing tradition or, more intriguingly, the memoirs set down on paper a discourse about the Thiam that he received and then propagated orally among his own employees, colleagues and family. This would then make its way into the wider social discourse. I heard this view of the Thiam exclusively from people who had either worked for Hampaté Bâ, or from their descendants. Many of these people were and are in positions of social and political influence in Mali. Oral discourse, like any other, follows and responds to contours of power, and Hampaté Bâ many well have shaped oral discourse by the questions he asked in his wide-ranging field research on behalf of IFAN. The concept of 'feedback' from the written to the oral is a familiar one to oral historians. However, it would be worth investigating, if possible, whether Hampaté Bâ's oral discourse (he was, as one would expect, a compelling raconteur) itself shaped the understanding of colonial reality. As we have seen, he had plenty of opportunities to bend the ears of élites, local and French.

Amkullel and the Malian Present

Any serious examination of *Amkullel* would have to take into account the context of modern Mali into which the book comes. As noted above, *Amkullel* is set in a period of immense importance for the country's subsequent social history. How Malians, according to their position, would view Hampaté Bâ and his last book is a difficult question to answer. One certainty is that the remains of the 'Umarian élite, centring on the Tall family, will be no happier with this publication than they were with anything else involving Hampaté Bâ. I had first-hand proof of this when in Ségou I greeted a prominent young member of the lineage, forgetting that I had the book in my other hand. His reaction was abrupt. The 'Westernized' intellectual élite would probably hail *Amkullel* as a classic African text, which indeed it is. However, certain of them might have misgivings: quite apart from long-standing family feuds, Hampaté Bâ is seen by some Malian intellectuals as a 'Peul nationalist', embodying what was once described to me as 'the Peul superiority complex'. Islamists would, at a guess, have an equally ambiguous response: on the one hand, Hampaté Bâ epitomizes and has done much to promote the idea of a truly African Islam which has nothing to be ashamed of in front of its Arab equivalents. This is important in a country where Arab Muslims are often seen as arrogant, even racist, toward their African equivalents. However, Hampaté Bâ's Tijani mysticism, promotion of *tafsir* and known association with the French colonial state would mitigate this enthusiasm among many, regardless of other more personal reasons to dislike him.

In conclusion, it is clear that, when read against the landscape of recent Malian history and, above all, that of the period between the arrival of the Futanké jihad and 1960, Hampaté Bâ's works are a great deal more complicated – regardless of intrinsic literary merit – than may at first be apparent. They are in fact deeply political statements and must be understood as such. All forms of discourse about the past are of course political, and it would be an unwise historian who failed to understand this. However, Malian discourse about the past is especially charged in this respect, due to the country's current disastrous position and its colonial and Islamic legacies. Hampaté Bâ's works can only be fully appreciated as part of this political battle. *Amkullel* is no less problematic a text than the rest of the author's *oeuvre*. As with any other literary representation, an understanding of the context deepens and gives nuances to the text.

Afterword: Homecoming[1]

Mongo Beti

When writers are given the freedom to speak without constraint, a freedom so generously given to me today, they usually have great difficulty choosing which subject to talk about. I have had no difficulty whatsoever. My recent return to my country, Cameroon, still has me firmly in its grasp. This event had a very great effect upon me, not solely as the resolution – I was going to say as the crowning moment – of a seemingly endless exile (of which there can be very few examples, if indeed there are any others), but also because the welcome I received was so surprisingly varied, depending on the different parts of Cameroonian society I visited, and finally because, as you can imagine, I learnt a great many things.

The curse of exile is historically linked to those periods of a people's and, by extension, a continent's political and social transformation. As you know, African writers in exile are a contemporary phenomenon. Are there really that many African writers of my generation who have not been in exile at one time or another? I know this sounds like a contradiction, and perhaps it's because we are so used to it, but sometimes the exile of African writers can seem to be something we should be pleased about, precisely because these writers do bear witness to those upheavals I have just mentioned, upheavals which our peoples and societies have always needed and still need today. I suppose that things have to get shaken up to get better. There's a Chinese proverb (what else would it be?) which says that you can't make an omelette without breaking eggs.

In particular, what makes my own experience of exile remarkable is its length: thirty-two years! How can I successfully convey the incredible nature of something which, in abstract terms, is simply a lapse of time? Something of the experience of a man separated from the people who raised him, from his loved ones, from the places he

1. *Retour d'exil,* translated from the French by Trevor Norris.

saw when he opened his eyes for the first time, the places where he grew up, from the songs of his childhood and the sounds of his own language, and from his dreams of becoming himself?

Most of the journalists, both African and European, to whom I have entrusted the words, 'I have spent thirty-two years in exile', have ended up changing this figure in their final article, bringing it down almost instinctively. What they have written about me is that I have 'been in exile for about twenty years', 'for about thirty years' or even 'for a long time' or, better still, 'for a really long time'. The fact is, they simply couldn't believe me when I told them how long it had been, because it seemed so impossible to them that a man could have stayed away from his own country for such a long time without completely losing sight of his sanity or his identity.

And yet I am telling the truth. I have made a very thorough count of these thirty-two years away from Cameroon. And, as far as I can tell, given that delusion is the stock-in-trade of the schizophrenic, it seems that I have not lost my sanity and that I am still myself.

After 1951 I no longer lived in my country, although I did travel there from time to time, but it was in February 1959 that my third and last trip to Cameroon came to an end. This happened a year before the declaration of independence. Only in February 1991, after thirty-two years, almost to the day, was I once again able to set foot in my own country. For thirty-two uninterrupted years, I had to live amongst a people whose language I shared, but from whom I was separated by the colour of my skin, by their political prejudice and by their customs, if not by their culture itself. It has been, without doubt, an appalling experience. Let me tell you something of what it was like, living this nightmare. Every time a letter arrived from Cameroon (they still kept coming despite the censorship of the dictatorship) or a telegram or, since 1990, a phone call, my heart would start to pound furiously, because I could never be sure that I wasn't about to learn that my mother had died. During the years of Ahmadou Ahidjo's dictatorship, and again this involves my mother, I received not one word of the woman who had brought me into the world.

I still have bitter memories of the small Breton town where I was posted as a minor civil servant. The people there were welcoming, obliging and sometimes even eager to help and, on the whole, showed more indifference than contempt. In all honesty, the openness I felt from this little group of French people is something that I think cannot exist in many other places, but then it is true that they had gained something from their own recent past. I could see nothing here that reminded me of the cynicism and hypocrisy of people in positions of power, people who believe in nothing, ridicule everything, even the most fundamental values, but who are always careful to keep their thoughts to themselves. I should have been happy there. In fact, I must admit that I was happy to a certain extent. But looking back I still feel a slight shudder when I remember the weekends. At weekends the small town would empty completely: the pupils and teachers from the two schools went back home to their families in the surrounding villages, and I was left with these ordinary people who knew nothing about me. As an African intellectual, I had nothing to say to them and nothing to ask them. Having arrived there from Paris, where I had done the main part of my studies and which was a cosmopolitan city, I was forced to learn a basic trade of total solitude, and I was prevented from expressing my feelings to an extent that I could never previously have imagined. So I can safely say that I learnt to go without the things that are an essential part of an ordinary person's emotional life. As a result of this I achieved a formidable lack of sensitivity, which suited the political causes I supported as a young man, but perhaps this also caused me to sacrifice the love I had for those people to whom I owed the most.

Much later, I had cause to think long and hard about the moral pertinence of the path I had chosen. My mother's death in January 1992 is an example. Sadly, I was not there when she died, ten months after we had been reunited. I had never really doubted myself before but, God knows, maybe I have spent the last thirty-two years being tormented by the same siren voices that have seduced dictatorships and the institutions of neocolonialism to their surrender. Like a marble statue, I remained untouched by feeling because, having become so accustomed to my solitude, I reached that place where the person in exile can exist beyond the influence of anybody or anything. I became a kind of monster. Maybe I will be one for ever.

Anyway, I thought I had to all intents and purposes become inured to my feelings, but when I arrived in Cameroon in February 1991 I felt so many unforgettable things. For example, imagine my surprise at discovering there so many characters, scenes and situations that would normally be associated with the cinema and literature produced under Latin American dictatorships. There were military uniforms swarming all over the airport enclosure – I would later learn that these powerful little men had done me the honour of taking exceptional security measures as they were worried that my arrival would create some kind of trouble. I was also subjected to a very long and thorough search; this was carried out by some official thugs and it caused an outcry in the crowd who had gathered to greet me, a crowd which, incidentally, was mostly made up of journalists from Cameroon. Then there was the convoy of unmarked police cars which escorted me noisily to the friendly house in Douala where I was to be lodged. There was checkpoint after checkpoint on all of the roads. This is a feature of daily life in Cameroon: always having to show your papers, prove your identity and state the nature of your journey and your final destination. At least this made a change from the tedium of the daily grind in France. As all this was happening, I was beginning to emerge from my usual anonymous identity of minor civil servant. One by one the authorities cancelled the conferences organized for my benefit and their ludicrous persistence was lapped up by the newly created free press, which was full of articles laden with satire and heavy with irony. To compensate for these snubs, I was celebrated in company, behind the closed doors of universities, well-known thorns in the establishment's side. But it was the reactions that I saw among the ordinary African people that moved me the most. In the town which serves as the centre of the region where I was born, people crowded round and stared at me. Some of them, particularly the older men, who by no means made up the lesser part of my admirers, had never read a single line of my work, but their praise was no less forthcoming or less detailed. However, the younger ones started reciting entire paragraphs from *Ville cruelle*, which was the first novel that I wrote under the pseudonym of Eza Boto. When I arrived in my own village, twelve kilometres from the centre, I expected my appearance to be welcomed by gales of laughter and floods of tears. But it didn't happen, even though the villagers had already been informed of my arrival in the country and of my impending visit. Realizing that I was there, people came out of their mean houses, or slowly came back from the fields, one by one. They came up to where we were standing, me and my friends Célestin Monga and Ambroise Kom, in whose car we had arrived. I took the lead in greeting those villagers whom I recognized as the eldest. They seemed surprised that I should be calling them by name.

My mother, already infirm, was squatting in the gloom of her miserable house. She showed no sign of emotion as I approached her. First of all I thought this was because she had almost lost her sight. However I later learnt that she actually saw more than she let on. As she heard me she turned her head, looked at me glassily and said, 'Is it really you?'. Only then did I begin to understand the cautious nature of these people bound to their land, still as crude and superstitious as when I had first left. They later confessed to me that, at worst, they thought I was someone having a joke at their expense, or, at best, a kind of ghost, a zombie summoned from the dead by evil magic. For them I was dead and buried. They had wiped me from their memories, in the way that you do when a loved one has gone for ever, because you have to carry on dealing with the pressing demands of life. It was terrible. During the course of the day and the days which followed, and throughout the visits I made later on, I had to use a wealth of eloquent argument to persuade them that I wasn't dead, that I really was alive and that it really was me. It wasn't until the following summer that they came to terms with me as a real person, I had been around them so much because the government had allowed me a visa which authorized me to remain in the country for four long weeks. They said to me, 'What if you really had been dead? It would be a miracle. People could come back from the grave, like you. Wouldn't it be wonderful?' I replied sadly that, yes, it would be wonderful and I remembered the words of the great poet:

> Et j'ai dit dans mon coeur: 'Que vouloir à présent?
> Pour dormir sur un sein mon front est trop pesant,
> Ma main laisse l'effroi sur la main qu'elle touche,
> L'orage est dans ma voix, l'éclair est sur ma bouche;
> Aussi, loin de m'aimer, voilà qu'ils tremblent tous,
> Et, quand j'ouvre les bras, on tombe à mes genoux.'[2]

The simple memory of how confused and upset my family were is enough to make me advise anybody not to go into exile, whatever their reason. I now truly believe that nothing is worth a man finding himself in the midst of such a tragedy. This is what I say to all of the young people who waylay me when I'm over there, which is quite often nowadays, when they overestimate my influence and ask me to help them flee the country.

It is true that the reasons that men and women of my generation had to flee the country have been compounded by other more dramatic reasons perhaps, but ones which are still bound to the same basic cause: a greater power decides to impose a mastery which we do not want, which we have never wanted. It is this greater power which in Cameroon, and elsewhere, finances, encourages and supports a tyranny which has made the lives of young people in their own country impossible to bear.

Anybody who spends time there simply has to open his or her eyes, without prejudice or preconception, to understand that this is the reason for what is currently being acted out in Cameroon: the extreme destitution of the rural population; the shocking increase in urban

2. Alfred de Vigny (1822), *Moïse*, published in 'Livre Mystique' section of *Poèmes antiques et modernes* (1826).

poverty; the failure of the economy; tribal tensions; police brutality; political despotism; corruption running out of control. There is no other reason for the people's suffering.

If that petty dictator Paul Biya had not had the financial backing of Paris, he would have thrown in the towel a long time ago. After ten years of being in complete control, the man who has led the country into disaster can still think up whatever criminal plan he chooses and the support of Paris is guaranteed. Last October he allowed himself the luxury of fixing the presidential elections in the most scandalous way possible; yet, several weeks later, Paris granted him massive financial aid to pay his government staff. Neither the despair of the population (to which I can testify), nor the revolt of young people suffering wholesale unemployment and for whom any hope of a better future is impossible, nor the scandalous repression of the opposition, nor international condemnation can persuade Paris to relax its stranglehold on a country forced against its will into the cruel and humiliating destiny of being an accessory to its own future.

At the moment, the great struggle in which my fellow intellectuals in Cameroon are engaged is for free speech in the press, in the printed word, and for the right to hold non-violent demonstrations. This is something that is hard to imagine: while the Cameroonian diaspora can organize demonstrations in Paris, London or Washington, their brothers are not able to do it at home, that is, in their own country. The Cameroonian diaspora can criticize the French government in Paris, the British government in London, the American government in Washington; but in their own country their brothers are forbidden from even criticizing the dictator's golf-course, created at incredible cost while students at the national university are denied their pitiful grants, when the hostels that they pompously call hospitals go without resources, without sanitation even – like the one at Mbalmayo, my local town, where my own mother was sent when she was dying. Since I am going to visit my country more often and stay for longer and longer periods, I am determined to play my part in this struggle for freedom of speech, with all the risks that this involves.

As an old exile who has discovered by virtue of bitter experience that one's real life is perhaps the one that each person leads in the land of his ancestors, I want future generations in Cameroon to avoid knowing the tragedy that I have known. I want life to be livable for us, so that our children and grandchildren are no longer tempted to go into exile or emigrate in search of something that they cannot find at home.

Westerners with more than their fair share are always scandalized to see waves of brown and black immigrants invading their happy lands, threatening to wreck the mechanisms of alliance which they say have taken long centuries of hard work and great sacrifice to construct. So they erect insurmountable obstacles in the face of these new barbarian hordes whose needs are as strong as their desires – at least this is their view of us – I'm thinking of the recent Pasqua laws in France, for example. Personally, I would challenge the easy use of the term 'racism' to condemn what are understandable reflexes of collective defence. Human experience gives us plenty of examples of this throughout history. A human grouping is always legitimately tempted – even when the temptation is unfounded – to protect what it sees as the fruits of its labour and struggle. An ordinary family whose years of unstinting work and mutual sacrifice have resulted in a modest house surrounded by a small plot of land would not like to see a group of vagrants intrude and trespass on its land. And a nation is only ever a group, like a family, and it reacts in the same way. This is something you have to understand, without of course excusing the self-interest which in the West expresses itself in the shape of violent excess and miscarriage of justice.

Racism, as far as I am concerned, is at the heart of the following question: why do the same Westerners who exclude us from privileges which they say have been acquired at great cost strive to prevent us from developing in our own country? The first, if not the only, obstacle to the development of Cameroon is the dictatorship of Paul Biya. And yet, without Paris, Paul Biya's dictatorship would not exist. When I was a young man, colonialism was the accepted cause of exile. Today, it seems that Cameroon has its independence but the reality of people's lives has not improved. Perhaps it is even worse, and this is why, thirty-two years after me, other young people dream of leaving, of going into exile, of uprooting themselves. I cannot accept this. I will not accept it. I am convinced, old exile that I am, that everything must be done to prevent the young people of Cameroon from experiencing the unhappiness of exile. And since it is neocolonialism which is the cause of exile and emigration, we must fight this disaster which has befallen contemporary Africa with more conviction than ever before.

I have often heard it said that politics is no business for a writer, that militancy weakens the artist if indeed it doesn't cause him to shy from his true path for ever. As a teacher of literature, I hardly need to consult literary history in order to disprove this argument completely. I only have to examine my conscience to state that there is no greater calling for a man of letters than the defence of a great cause. And what more noble cause exists in all the world than a people's happiness and freedom?

Chronology

	Political and Historical Events	Non-fiction and Critical Works	Key texts (Fiction)
1817	French reoccupy **Senegal** (previously in British hands during Napoleonic wars)		
1830	French conquer **Algeria**		
1835	**Algerian** revolt led by Emir Abdelkader		
1848	Abolition of slavery in French territories		
1854	Constitution of 'Afrique Noire Française'		
	Colonial administration of **Senegal** founded by General Faidherbe		
1870	Onésime Reclus coins the word *francophonie*		
1877	Stanley's descent of River Congo		

1880	French establish protectorate in **Tunisia**	
1883	Bamako (**Mali**) captured by French	
1884	Berlin conference on African colonies	
1885	French occupy **Gabon**	
1891		M'Hamed Ben Rahhal, *La Vengeance du cheikh*
1893	French colonies of **Ivory Coast** and **French Guinea** officially established	
	French troops enter **Dahomey**	
1898	Fashoda crisis: France forced to withdraw from the Nile region by British troops led by General Kitchener	
	Upper Volta becomes a French protectorate	
1903	Beginning of French educational system in West Africa	
1904	Establishment of AOF (Afrique Occidentale Française)	

1910	Establishment of AEF (Afrique Equatoriale Française)		
1911	Franco-German Congo agreement		
1912	French establish protectorate in **Morocco**		
1914	Blaise Diagne (**Senegal**) elected to Chamber of Deputies in Paris	Chérif Benhabyles, *L'Algérie française vue par un indigène*	
1917	Blaise Diagne becomes Under-Secretary of State for colonies of metropolitan France		
1918	Former German colony of **Cameroon** comes under French control		
1919			J. Vehel, *Les Veillées de la Hafsia*
1920	Destour, **Tunisian** constitutional party is prohibited by the French	Arthur Pellegrin, *La Littérature nord-africaine*	Ben Cherif, *Ahmed Ben Mostapha, goumier*
1921			René Maran, *Batouala*
			Blaise Cendrars, *Anthologie nègre*
1924	Completion of Dakar–Kayès railway		Tahar Essafi, *Les Toits d'émeraude*

1925	**Moroccan** revolt in the Rif led by Abdelkrim		Abdelkader Hadj Hamou, *Zohra, la femme du mineur*
1926	ENA (Etoile Nord-Africaine) is founded in **Algeria**		
1929			Chukri Khodja, *El Eudj, captif des barbaresques*
1930	Centenary celebration of conquest of **Algeria**		T. Rivel, *L'Oeillet de Jérusalem*
	Berber Dahir (French law separating Arabs and Berbers in **Morocco**)		
1931		First number of the journal, *Légitime Défense*	
1933	Neo-Destour in **Tunisia**		Mahmoud Aslan, *Pages africaines*
1934			Jean Amrouche, *Cendres*
1935	Léopold Sédar Senghor is first African *agrégé*		Ousmane Socé, *Karim: roman sénégalais*
			T. Rivel, *Lumière de la hara*
1936			Mohammed Ould Cheikh, *Myriem dans les palmes*
1937	Riots in **Morocco** and abolition of Berber Dahir	E.F. Gautier, *Le Passé de l'Afrique du Nord: les siècles obscurs*	

	Establishment of PPA (Parti du Peuple Algérien, formerly ENA)	
1938		Paul Hazoumé, *Doguicimi*
1939		Jean Amrouche, *Chants berbères de Kabylie*
1942		Aïssa Zehar, *Hind à l'âme pure ou l'histoire d'une mère*
1943	Creation of Hizb Al Istiqlal (**Moroccan** party for independence)	Ferhat Abbas, *Manifeste du peuple Algérien*
1944	Brazzaville Declaration calling for reform of French colonial rule Uprising in Rabat (**Morocco**)	
1945	UN assumes responsibility for administration of former mandated territories of League of Nations Uprising in Sétif (**Algeria**)	
1946	Félix Houphouët-Boigny (**Ivory Coast**) founds RDA (Rassemblement Démocratique Africaine) headed in **Senegal** by Léopold Sédar Senghor, in	Léopold Sédar Senghor, *Chants d'ombre*

	Guinea by Sekou Touré and in **Mali** by Modibo Kéita		
	Creation of French Union		
1947		First number of the journal, *Présence Africaine*	Birago Diop, *Les Contes d'Amadou Koumba*
			Marguerite Taos Amrouche, *Jacinthe noire*
			Djamila Debèche, *Leila, jeune fille d'Algérie*
1948	Creation of committee of liberation of the Maghreb in Cairo	Jean-Paul Sartre, *Orphée noir*	Léopold Sédar Senghor, *Anthologie de la nouvelle poésie nègre et malgache*
1950		Aimé Césaire, *Discours sur le colonialisme*	Mouloud Feraoun, *Le Fils du pauvre*
		Octave Mannoni, *Psychologie de la colonisation*	
1951			Mohamed Dib, *La Grande Maison*
1952	Murder of Ferhat Ached in **Tunisia**	Frantz Fanon, *Peau noire, masques blancs*	
		L. Chenier, *Colonisation, colonialisme, décolonisation*	
1953	King Mohammed V of **Morocco** dethroned and forced into exile by the French		Camara Laye, *L'Enfant noir*
			Mouloud Feraoun, *La Terre et le sang*

			Albert Memmi, *La Statue de sel*
1954	Algerian war of liberation led by FLN (National Liberation Front)		Mongo Beti, *Ville cruelle* (pub. under name of Eza Boto)
	Battle of Diên Biên Phu, 75% of soldiers in front are African		Driss Chraïbi, *Le Passé simple*
			Ahmed Sefrioui, *La Boîte à merveilles*
			Mohamed Dib, *L'Incendie*
1955	Bandung Conference: 29 African and Asian states condemn colonialism		Tchicaya U Tam'Si, *Mauvais sang*
			Albert Memmi, *Agar*
	Founding of first university in French Africa (**Senegal**)		Mouloud Mammeri, *Le Sommeil du juste*
	King Mohammed V returns to **Morocco** from exile		
1956	Independence of **Morocco**	Malek Bennabi, *L'Afroasiatisme*	Mongo Beti, *Le Pauvre Christ de Bomba*
	Independence of **Tunisia**		Bernard Dadié, *Climbié*
	Code de la Famille in **Morocco** (marriage and inheritance placed under Sharia Law)		Ferdinand Oyono, *Une vie de boy*
			David Diop, *Coups de pilon*
	Tunisia prohibits polygamy and repudiation under Code de la Famille		Ousmane Sembène, *Le Docker noir*
	Creation of Union of African Workers		Kateb Yacine, *Nedjma*
			Driss Chraïbi, *Les Boucs*

(UGTAN), headed by Sekou Touré (**Mali**)

Civil war in **Cameroon** between communist and anti-communist groups (still unresolved in 1960 when the country becomes independent)

French government draws up the 'Loi Cadre' under which France keeps control of foreign policy, defence and economic development, while all other aspects of government become responsibility of individual colonies

1957		Henri Alleg, *La Question*	Assia Djebar, *La Soif*
		Albert Memmi, *Portrait du colonisé précédé du portrait du colonisateur*	
1958	Establishment of French Community	Bakary Traoré, *Le Théâtre négro-africain et ses fonctions sociales*	
	De Gaulle returns to Brazzaville to proclaim autonomy within the French Community of the colonies of AEF. This leads to unrest on Belgian side of Congo. De Gaulle also offers AOF colonies choice of	Himoud Brahimi, *L'Identité suprême*	

autonomy (self-
government) or
independence. Only
Guinea chooses
independence

Independence of
Guinea

Senghor and Sekou
Touré leave RDA

| 1959 | Uprising in Léopoldville (**Congo**) which led to the Congo Crisis (1960–5)

French colonies call for independence | Frantz Fanon, *L'An V de la révolution algérienne* | Bernard Dadié, *Un nègre à Paris*

Mohamed Dib, *Un été africain*

Malek Haddad, *Je t'offrirai une gazelle* |
| 1960 | First national elections in **Belgian Congo**. Patrice Lumumba elected Prime Minister. Some months later Lumumba is driven from power by Colonel Mobutu

Creation of Union of Central African Republics and Union of Sahel–Benin

Independence of **Dahomey, Central African Republic, Cameroon, Chad Congo, Ivory Coast, Gabon, Mali, Mauritania, Niger, Senegal, Togo, Upper Volta, Zaïre** | | Ousmane Sembène, *Les Bouts de bois de Dieu*

Djibril Tamsir Niane, *Soundjata ou l'épopée mandigue*

Marguerite Taos Amrouche, *Rues des tambourins*

Bel Hachmy, *Thouraya ou roman inachevé* |

Creation of
opposition parties in
Morocco

King Mohammed V
(**Morocco**)
condemns wearing
of veil

1961	Murder of Patrice Lumumba	Frantz Fanon, *Les Damnés de la terre*	Cheikh Hamidou Kane, *L'Aventure ambiguë*
	Creation of OAS (secret armed organization of *pieds-noirs*) in **Algeria**		Henri Kréa, *Djamal*
			Jean Senac, *Matinale de mon peuple*
	Massacre of Algerians in Paris		Hachemi Baccouche, *La Dame de Carthage*
1962	Mouloud Feraoun is murdered by OAS	Jacques Berque, *Le Maghreb entre deux guerres*	Nazi Boni, *Crépuscule des temps anciens*
	Independence of **Algeria**		Assia Djebar, *Les Enfants du nouveau monde*
1963	Creation of Organization of African Unity (OAU), headquarters in Addis Ababa	Lilyan Keseloot, *Les Ecrivains noirs de langue française*	
	First parliament in **Morocco**		
1964	Establishment of Charter of Algiers	Léopold Sédar Senghor, *Liberté I*	
		Jaqueline Arnaud et al., *Anthologie des écrivains maghrébins d'expression française*	

1965	Mobutu named President of **Congo-Léopoldville** Military coup in **Algeria**. Ben Bella put under house arrest Ben Berka (leader of **Moroccan** opposition) is murdered in Paris. Riots in Casablanca	Mohammed-Chérif Sahli, *Décoloniser l'histoire: introduction à l'histoire du Maghreb*	Mouloud Mammeri, *L'Opium et le bâton* Albert Bensoussan, *Les Bagnoulis*
1966	Military coup in **Upper Volta** led by Colonel Lamizana	Yves Lacoste, *Ibn Khaldoun* Germaine Tillion, *Le Harem et les cousins* First number of the journal *Souffles* (edited by Abdellatif Laâbi)	Kateb Yacine, *Le Polygone étoilé* Mourad Bourbonne, *Le Muezzin*
1966–7	Military coups in **Dahomey Togo** and **Upper Volta**		Francis Bebey, *Le Fils d'Agatha Moudio* Malick Fall, *La Plaie* Mohammed Khaïr-Eddine, *Agadir*
1968	President Kéita (**Mali**) overthrown by military coup led by Moussa Traouré Military coup in **Congo-Brazzaville** led by Capitain Ngouabi	Abdelkebir Khatibi, *Le Roman maghrébin*	Ahmadou Kourouma, *Les Soleils des indépendances* Yambo Ouologuem, *Le Devoir de violence* Mohamed Dib, *La Danse du roi*
1969	Proclamation of **United Congo Republic**	Frantz Fanon, *Pour la révolution africaine* Auguste Viatte, *La Francophonie*	Thérèse Kuoh-Moukory, *Rencontres essentielles* Abdellatif Laâbi, *L'Oeil et la nuit*

			Rachid Boudjedra, *La Répudiation*
1970			Mohammed Khaïr-Eddine, *Moi, l'aigre*
1971	**Congo-Léopoldville** renamed **Republic of Zaïre** Failed military coup against King Hassan II of **Morocco**		Abdelkebir Khatibi, *La Memoire tatouée*
1972	Marxist-Leninist republic established in **Benin** Failed military coup against King Hassan II Casablanca trial. Abraham Serfaty, Abdellatif Laâbi imprisoned	Stanislas Adotevi, *Négritude et négrologues* Mongo Beti, *Main basse sur le Cameroun*	Alioum Fantouré, *Le Cercle des tropiques* Pierre Bamboté, *Une fourmi dans l'eau* Driss Chraïbi, *La Civilisation, ma Mère!…*
1973			Amadou Hampaté Bâ, *L'Etrange Destin de Wangrin* V.-Y. Mudimbé, *Entre les eaux* Ousmane Sembène, *Xala* Tahar Ben Jelloun, *Harrouda*
1974		Jacques Chevrier, *Littérature nègre*	Mongo Beti, *Remember Reuben*
1975	Military coup in **Chad**. President François Toumbalaye's single-party government	Abdelwahab Bouhdiba, *La Sexualité en Islam*	Massan Makan Diabaté, *L'Aigle et l'épervier* M. a M. Ngal, *Giambatista Viko ou*

overthrown.
Toumbalaye
assassinated.
Northern Muslims
take control.

Moroccan Green
March to Western
Sahara. War with
Polisario (Sahrawi
army)

Abdallah Laroui,
*Crisis of the Arab
Intellectual*

Mohammed
Arkoun, *La Pensée
arabe*

Fatima Mernissi,
Beyond the Veil

*le viol du discours
africain*

Nafissatou Diallo, *De
Tilène au plateau*

Mostafa Nissaboury,
*La Mille et deuxième
nuit*

Rachid Boudjedra,
*Topographie idéale
pour une agression
caractérisée*

1976

Dorothy Blair,
*African Literature in
French*

Robert Cornevin,
*Littérature noire de
langue française*

King Hassan II, *Le
Défi*

Tahar Ben Jelloun,
*La Plus Haute des
solitudes*

Aïcha Lemsine, *La
Chrysalide*

1977 'Emperor' Bokassa's
self-coronation
(**Central African
Republic**)

Paulin Hountondji,
*Sur la philosophie
africaine*

1978

Awa Thiam, *La
Parole aux Négresses*

1979 French engineer a
coup to depose Jean
Bokassa (**Central
African Republic**)

Civil war in **Chad**
breaks out

Albert Memmi, *La
Dependance*

Abdelwahab
Meddeb, *Talismano*

Yamina Mechakra,
La Grotte éclatée

Mariama Bâ, *Une si
longue lettre*

Thierno
Monénembo, *Les
Crapauds-brousse*

Williams Sassine, *Le Jeune Homme de sable*

Sony Labou Tansi, *La Vie et demie*

Aminata Sow Fall, *La Grève des bàttu*

1980   Libyan forces invade **Chad**

Border disputes between **Senegal** and **Mauritania**

Berber uprising in Kabylia (**Algeria**)

Release of Ben Bella

Uprising in Casablanca and Rabat (**Morocco**)

Release of Abdellatif Laâbi after intervention of Amnesty International

Jean Déjeux, *Littérature maghrébine de langue française*

Abdellatif Laâbi, *Le Règne de barbarie*

Tchicaya U Tam'Si, *Les Cancrelats*

Jean-Marie Adiaffi, *La Carte d'identité*

Yodi Karone, *Le Bal des caïmans*

1981   **Cameroon** threatened by military intervention from Nigeria

Military coup in **Central African Republic**

Boubacar Boris Diop, *Le Temps de Tamango*

Mariama Bâ, *Un chant écarlate*

Ousmane Sembène, *Le Dernier de l'empire*

1982

Béji Hélè, *Désenchantement national: essai sur la décolonisation*

Jean Déjeux, *Dictionnaire des auteurs maghrébins de langue française*

Rachid Mimouni, *Le Fleuve détourné*

Abdellatif Laâbi, *Le Chemin des ordalies*

Henri Lopes, *Le Pleurer-rire*

			Emmanuel B. Dongala, *Jazz et vin de palme*
			Ken Bugul, *Le Baobab fou*
			Ibrahima Ly, *Toiles d'araignées*
			Abdelkebir Khatibi, *Amour bilingue*
			Leila Sebbar, *Shérazade*
1983	Beurs march for equality (from Marseilles to Paris)	Abdelkebir Khatibi, *Maghreb pluriel*	Antoine Bangui, *Les Ombres de Kôh*
			Werewere Liking, *Elle sera de jaspe et de corail*
			Véronique Tadjo, *Latérite*
			Djanet Lachmet, *Le Cow-boy*
			Edmond Amran El Maleh, *Aïlen ou la nuit du récit*
			Mehdi Charef, *Le Thé au harem d'Archi Ahmed*
			Abdelhak Serhane, *Messaouda*
1984	Foundation of SOS-Racisme by Harlem Désir	Bouzid, *La Marche, traversée de la France profonde*	Bernard Nanga, *La Trahison de Marianne*
	Upper Volta renamed **Burkina Faso**	Tahar Ben Jelloun, *Hospitalité française*	Tahar Djaout, *Le Chercheur d'os*
	'Révolte du pain' in **Tunisia**		Fettouma Touati, *Le Printemps désespéré*

Morocco withdraws
from OAU

Code de la Famille
in **Algeria** limits
women's rights

Creation of the Haut
Conseil de la
Francophonie

1985		Charles Bonn, *Le Roman algérien de langue française*	Mohamed Fantouré, *Le Voile ténébreux*
		Tahar Djaout, *Ecrivains francophones du Maghreb*	Mohamed Dib, *Les Terasses d'Orsol*
			Béji Hélè, *L'Oeil du jour*
			Tahar Ben Jelloun, *L'Enfant de sable*
			Leila Houari, *Zeïda de nulle part*
1986	Riots in **Gabon** in reaction to the austerity programme of the IMF (International Monetary Fund)		Assia Djebar, *L'Amour, la fantasia*
			Nabil Fares, *L'Exil au féminin*
	FLN establishes **Algerian** National Charter allowing multipartyism		Kateb Yacine, *L'Oeuvre en fragments*
			Azouz Begag, *Le Gone de Chaâba*
			Farida Belghoul, *Georgette!*
			Myriam Ben, *Sabrina, ils t'ont volé ta vie*
			Thierno Monénembo, *Les Ecailles du ciel*
			Tchichelle Tchivella, *L'Exil ou la tombe*

			Ahmed Kalouaz, *Point kilométrique 190*
1987	Assassination of President Thomas Sankara (**Burkina Faso**) President Bourgiba (**Tunisia**) overthrown in 'quiet coup'	Awa Thiam, *Continents noirs* Pierre Haski, *L'Afrique blanche*	Calixthe Beyala, *C'est le soleil qui m'a brûlée* Aminata Sow Fall, *L'Ex-père de la nation* Tahar Ben Jelloun, *La Nuit sacrée* Tahar Djaout, *L'Invention du desert*
1988	OAU peace-keeping force moves into **Chad**, following Libyan withdrawal Islamic fundamentalist uprising in Algiers	Daniel Rivet, *Lyautey et l'institution du protectorat français du Maroc*	Sony Labou Tansi, *Les Yeux du volcan* Mustapha Tlili, *La Montagne du lion* Albert Memmi, *Le Pharaon*
1989	Creation of UMA (Arab Maghreb Union) Legalization of FIS (Islamic Salvation Front) and RCD (Berberist party) in **Algeria** Kateb Yacine and Mouloud Mammeri die the same year The scarf affair (l'affaire du foulard) in Creil, France. Two Muslim sisters suspended from school for wearing headscarves	Mongo Beti and Odile Tobner, *Dictionnaire de la Négritude* Maxime Rodinson, *La Fascination de l'islam*	Abdellatif Laâbi, *Les Rides du lion*
1990	Marxist-Leninist regime abandoned in **Benin**	Paul Balta, *Le Grand Maghreb*	Ahmadou Kourouma, *Monné, outrages et défis*

Gilles Perrault, *Notre ami le roi*

Jean-Marie Adiaffi, *Silence, on développe*

Hinde Taarji, *Les Voilées de l'islam*

Ferudja Kessas, *Beur's story*

Mehdi Charef, *Le Harki de Meriem*

1991	Release of Abraham Serfaty

FIS win popular vote in first round of elections in **Algeria** | Alec Hargreaves, *Voices from the North African Community in France: Immigration and Identity in Beur Fiction*

Charles-Robert Ageron, *La Décolonisation française*

Benjamin Stora, *La Gangrène et l'oubli*

Farid Aichoune, *Nés en banlieue*

Djamila Amrane, *Les Femmes algériennes dans la guerre* | Nina Bouraoui, *La Voyeuse interdite*

Tahar Ben Jelloun, *Les Yeux baissés*

Driss Chraïbi, *L'Inspecteur Ali* |
| 1992 | Algerian government cancels national elections. Clashes between army and Muslim fundamentalists. Beginning of civil war in **Algeria**

Assassination of Mohammed Boudiaf in **Algeria**

Women's demonstration against Muslim fundamentalism in **Algeria** | Rachid Boudjedra, *Le FIS de la haine*

Fatima Mernissi, *La Peur-modernité* | Brahim Benaïcha, *Vivre au paradis: d'une oasis à un bidonville*

Rachid Mimouni, *Une peine à vivre*

Abdelhak Serhane, *Le Soleil des obscurs*

Khady Sylla, *Le Jeu de la mer* |

1993	Death of Houphouët-Boigny, long-standing president of **Ivory Coast**	Michel Laronde, *Autour du roman beur: immigration et identité*	Jean-Luc Istace-Yacine, *La Mauvaise Foi*
	Revision of **Moroccan** Code de la Famille	Fatima Mernissi, *Le Harem politique*	Rachid Mimouni, *La Malédiction*
	Murder of Tahar Djaout in **Algeria**	Fatna Aït Sabbah, *La Femme dans l'inconscient musulman*	Driss Chraïbi, *Une place au soleil*
	Creation of CISIA (International Committee for the Support of Algerian Intellectuals) in Paris presided over by Pierre Bourdieu		Stansilas Ouoham Tchidjo, *Par décret présidentiel*
1994	Devaluation of CFA by 50%	Zahya Daoud, *Féminisme et politique au Maghreb*	Tahar Ben Jelloun, *L'Homme rompu*
	Civil war in **Rwanda**	John Conteh-Morgan, *Theatre and Drama in Francophone Africa: A Critical Introduction*	Moncef Ghachem, *L'Epervier*
	Release of Abassi Madani (founder and leader of FIS)		Mohamed Berrada, *Le Jeu de l'oubli*
	Bayrou Law forbids wearing headscarves in schools (France)	Bruno Etienne, *Abdelkader*	Victor Fotso, *Le Chemin de Hiala*
	Requirement to use Berber languages in addition to Arabic and French in news broadcasts and schools becomes law in **Morocco**	Siradiou Diallo, *Houphouët-Boigny* Bernard Mouralis, *L'Europe, l'Afrique et la folie*	Pabé Mongo, *Nos ancêtres les baobabs*

Index

Abbas, Ferhat, 193
Abdelkader, Emir, 189
Abduh, Muhammad, 69–70
ACCT (Agence de Coopération Culturelle et Technique), 18–24
Achebe, Chinua, *Things Fall Apart*, 153
Ached, Ferhat, 194
Achour, Christine, 78n10, 79, 85
Adiaffi, Jean-Marie, 126, 133, 138
  Carte d'identité, La, 128, 130–1, 202
  D'éclairs et de foudre, 128, 129
  Silence, on développe, 128–31, 134, 206
Adotevi, Stanislas, 200
AEF (Afrique Equatoriale Française) 191, 196
Afrique Noire Française, 189
Ageron, Charles-Robert, 206
Agni, 129, 131
  see also language, Agni
Ahidjo, Ahmadou, 182
Aichoune, Farid, 206
Aidoo, Ama Ata, 139n3
AIMF (Association Internationale des Maires Francophones), 19, 23
AIPLF (Association Internationale des Parlementaires de Langue Française), 18, 23
Aït Sabbah, Fatna, 207
Alessandra, Jacques, 107, 109
Algeria, 193, 198, 199, 202, 204, 205, 207
  Algerian war, 9, 74, 206
    see also FLN
  Algerian women, 69–70, 74
  censorship in, 6
  colonization of, 189, 192
  independence of, 1, 3, 77
    see also ENA; FLN
  literature in, 2, 37, 69–81, 83–4
    women's writing in, 70–1, 74–5, 77–9

relations with francophone community, 11, 12, 15, 20, 24
Alleg, Henri, 196
Amin, Qasim, 70
Amrane, Djamila, 206
Amrouche, Jean, 192, 193
Amrouche, Marguerite Taos, 73, 78, 194
  Amant imaginaire, L', 71
  Jacinthe noire, 7, 70, 71
  Rue des tambourins, 71, 195
anti-Semitism, 95, 98
AOF (Afrique Occidentale Française), 190, 196
Arabic, 202
  see language, Arabic
  Arabic literature, 69
  Arabs, 192
Ardener, Edwin, 78n11
Arkoum, Mohammed, 201
Arnaud, Jacqueline, 7n22, 198
Artaud, Antonin, 86, 91
Aslan, Mahmoud, 192
assimilation, policy of, 3
Auden, W.H., 90, 91n15
AUPELF (Association des Universitiés Partiellement ou Entièrement d'Expression Française), 18, 23
autobiography, 8, 37, 73, 93, 94, 118
Awoonor, Kofi, 154

Bâ, Mariama, 8, 139–52
  Chant écarlate, Un, 139n2, 140, 141–4, 148, 149–52, 202
  Si longue lettre, Une, 6n19, 139, 140–1, 145–52, 201
Baccouche, Hachemi, 198
Bakhtin, Mikhail, 125
Balta, Paul, 205
Bambara, *see* language, Bambara
Bamboté, Pierre, 200
Bandung conference, 195

Bangui, Antoine, 203
Barthes, Roland, 60, 62, 63, 64
Bebey, Francis, 8
   Fils d'Agatha Moudio, Le, 153–62, 199
   Poupée ashanti, La, 161
   Roi Albert d'Effidi, Le, 161–2
Beckett, Samuel, 107
Begag, Azouz, *Le Gone du Chaâba*, 37–9, 204
Belamri, Rabah, 72n3
Belghoul, Farida, *Georgette!*, 38, 204
Belgium, 18, 19, 25
Bel Hachmy, 197
Ben, Myriam, 204
Benaïcha, Brahim, 40, 41n18, 206
Ben Bella, 199, 202
Ben Berka, 199
Ben Cherif, 191
Benhabyles, Chérif, 191
Benin, 25, 169, 200, 205
   see also Dahomey
Ben Jelloun, Tahar, 1n4, 200, 201, 203, 204, 205, 206, 207
Bennabi, Malek, 195
Ben Rahhal, M'Hamed, 190
Bensoussan, Albert, 199
Berber, 202
   see language, Berber
   Berber Dahir, 192
   Berbers, 192
   see RCD
Berrada, Mohamed, 207
Berque, Jacques, 198
Beti, Mongo, 2, 6, 200, 205
   Eza Boto, alias, 184, 195
   Ville cruelle, 184, 195
beur, 8, 33, 41, 42, 43, 203
'esprit beur', 35, 36
Radio Beur, 35
Beyala, Calixthe, 128, 138
   C'est le soleil qui m'a brûlée, 132–3, 205
   Petit prince de Belleville, Le, 132, 133
   Seul le diable le savait, 133
   Tu t'appelleras Tanga, 133
Bhiri, Slaheddine, 35
Bible, The, 130
   Song of Songs, 132
bildungsroman, 95
Biya, Paul, 186, 187
Black Panthers, 117
Blair, Dorothy, 2n5, 7n22, 201
Bokassa, Jean, 201
Boni, Nazi, 198
Bonn, Charles, 33, 85, 204

Boudhiba, Abdelwahab, 200
Boudiaf, Mohammed, 206
Boudjedra, Rachid, 4n10, 8, 206
   1001 années de la nostalgie, Les, 76
   Répudiation, La, 76, 200
   Topographie idéale pour une agression caractérisée, 45–58, 201
   Vainqueur de coupe, Le, 76
Boulal, Jamila, 38
Boumediene, 24
Bouraoui, Nina, 79, 206
Bourbonne, Mourad, 199
Bourdieu, Pierre, 207
Bourguiba, Habib, 18, 19, 205
Bouzid, 203
Brahimi, Himoud, 196
Breton, André, 106
Bryce, Jane, 139n3
Bugul, Ken, 203
Bulgaria, 25
Bunting, Basil, 108
Burkina Faso, 25, 172, 174, 203, 205
   see also Upper Volta
Burundi, 25

Cambodia, 18, 25
Cameroon, 6, 25, 169, 181–7, 191, 196, 197, 202
   literature in, 154
   society, 181–7
Canada, 14, 19, 25
Cape Verde Islands, 25
Cardaire, Marcel, 178
Cendrars, Blaise, 191
censorship, 5–6, 128, 182
Central African Republic, 25, 197, 201, 202
Césaire, Aimé, 2, 106, 110, 118, 194
   Cahier d'un retour au pays natal, 109, 132
Chad, 25, 197, 200, 201, 202, 205
Chaillot summit, 21
Cham, Mbye Boubacar, 151
Charef, Mehdi, 206
   Le Thé au harem d'Archi Ahmed, 41, 42, 203
Cheikh, Mohammed Ould, 192
Chenir, L., 194
Chevrier, Jacques, 2n5, 200
Chou En-Lai, 103
Chraïbi, Driss, 1, 4n10, 8, 206, 207
   Civilisation, ma mère! . . ., La, 61, 200
   Passé simple, Le, 46, 59–67, 110, 195
   Succession ouverte, 59, 62, 63
CILF (Conseil International de Langue

Index

Française), 19, 23
CISIA (International Committee for the Support of Algerian Intellectuals), 207
Collin, Jacques, 167
colonialism, 2, 11, 12, 19, 24, 145n18, 187
  administration of, 178, 189
  oppression, 113
  traditions of colonizer, 144, 146
colonization, 45, 51, 95
Comoro Islands, 25
Condillac, abbé de, 100
Congo, 25, 189, 191, 197, 199, 200
Conteh-Morgan, John, 5n13, 207
Cornevin, Robert, 201
cosmology, 154–162
Creole, *see* language, Creole

Dadié, Bernard, 2n6, 126, 195, 197
Dahomey, 190, 197, 199
  see also Benin
Daoud, Zahya, 207
Davies, Carole Boyce, 151
Debèche, Djamila, 73
  Leila, jeune fille d'Algérie, 7, 70, 71, 194
  Aziza, 71
decolonization, 18
de Gaulle, Charles, 19, 24, 196
Déjeux, Jean, 7n22, 34, 42, 202
Deleuze, Gilles, 43
Diabaté, Massan Makan, 200
Diagne, Blaise, 191
Diallo, Nafissatou, 6n19, 201
Diallo, Siradiou, 207
Dib, Mohammed, 70–1, 197, 204
  Danse du roi, La, 73
  Grande maison, La, 72, 194
  Incendie, L', 72, 195
  Métier à tisser, Le, 72
Diên Biên Phu, battle of, 195
Diina, 171, 174
Diop, Birago, 2, 3
  Contes d'Amadou Koumba, Les, 3n8, 125n1, 194
Diop, Boubacar Boris, 202
Diop, David, 195
Diori, Hamami, 18, 19, 20
Diouf, Abdou, 166
Djabali, Hawa, 78
Djaout, Tahar, 1n4, 6, 203, 204, 205, 207
Djebar, Assia, 1n4, 5, 7, 196
  Amour, la fantasia, L', 7n21, 73, 75, 80, 204

Enfants du nouveau monde, Les, 73, 198
Loin de Médine, 75
Ombre sultane, 75
Djeghloul, Abdelkader, 34
Dominican Republic, 25
Dongala, Emmanuel B., 203
Dorfman, Ariel, 105
Dostoevsky, Fyodor, 105, 110, 119
Dumont, Pierre, 127
Duras, Marguerite, 129

Egejuru, Phanuel Akubueze, 142n11
Egypt, 11, 18, 25, 69
El Maleh, Edmond Amran, 203
Emecheta, Buchi, 139n3
ENA (Etoile Nord-Africaine), 192
  see also PPA
Equatorial Guinea, 26
Essafi, Tahar, 191
ethnography, 39
  ethnographic literature, 1, 40
  ethnographic posture, 39
Etienne, Bruno, 207

Faidherbe, General, 189
Fall, Malick, 199
Fanon, Frantz, 106, 110, 197, 198, 199
  Peau noire, masques blancs, 143–4, 194
Fantouré, Alioum, 200, 204
Fares, Nabil, 204
feminism, 139–40, 144–7, 163
  feminist theory, 8
Feraoun, Mouloud, 39, 46, 71, 198
  Fils du pauvre, Le, 1n1, 70, 194
Ferry, Jules, 13
FIPF (Fédération Internationale des Professeurs de Français), 19, 23
FIS (Islamic Salvation Front), 205, 206, 207
Flaubert, Gustave, 70
FLN (National Liberation Front), 2–3, 195, 204
  see also Algeria
Fotso, Victor, 207
francocentrism, 15
francophone community, 18–25, 28, 29
francophonie, 8, 11–15, 21, 28, 189
  institutionalization of, 5, 29
Frank, Katherine, 144
French, *see* language, French
French Academy, 13
French community, 196
French Revolution, 103, 104
French union, 194

Freud, Sigmund, 60, 86, 131
Fulbé, 171, 172, 173, 180
    see also Peul
Futanké, 172, 174, 176, 180
Fuuta Tooro, 171, 172, 174, 175

Gabon, 26, 190, 197, 204
Gaelic, *see* language, Gaelic
GATT(General Agreement on Tariffs and Trade), 29
Gautier, E.F., 192
Genette, Gérard, 59
genital mutilation of women, 6
Ghachem, Moncef, 207
Ghana, 161, 167
Gide, André, 94
Giscard d'Estaing, Valéry, 20
Gontard, Marc, 107, 109
Gorky, Maxim, 103, 105
Graves, Anne Adams, 151
griot, 129, 130, 135
Guattari, Félix, 43
Guérin, Jean-Yves, 100n7
Guinea, 20, 26, 190, 194, 197
Guinea-Bissau, 26

Haddad, Malek, 8, 83–91
    Dernière impression, La, 83, 87, 89
    Je t'offrirai une gazelle, 84, 87, 88, 90, 91, 197
    Quai aux fleurs ne répond plus, Le, 85, 89, 91
Hadj Hamou, Abdelkader, 69
Haiti, 19, 26
Haley, Alex, 154
Hamallah, Cheikh, 176
    hamallism, 176
Hamou, Abdelkader Hadj, 192
Hampataté Bâ, Ahmadou, 8
    Amkullel: l'enfant peul, 171–80
    Empire peul du Macina, L', 172n1, 178
    Etrange destin de Wangrin, L', 177–8, 200
Hargreaves, Alec G., 33n1, 40n16, 41n20, 206
Harlem Désir, 202
Harlem Renaissance, 2
Harrell-Bond, Barbara, 139, 140, 147n28, 148n31
Haski, Pierre, 205
Hassan II, King, 200, 201
Haut Conseil de la Francophonie, 204
Hazoumé, Paul, 2, 193
Hefferman, Michael J., 40n16

Hegel, G.W.F., 130
Hélè, Béji, 202, 204
Hélou, Charles, 18
Henry, Jean-Robert, 40
historiography, 94
Houari, Leila, 204
Hountondji, Paulin, 201
Houpouët-Boigny, Félix, 193, 207
hybridity, 108, 128–9

IFAN (Institut Français d'Afrique Noire), 177, 179
Imaginary, the, 99
IMF (International Monetary Fund), 204
imperialism
    cultural imperialism, 5
    imperialist oppression, 83
intertextuality, 130–1
Islam
    abuse of, 165
    Arabo-Islamic world, 71
    fanaticism, 176
    fundamentalism, 6, 7, 205
    islamic civilization, 177
    islamic law, 174
    islamic society, 165
    see also Koran
Issaad, Ramdane, 41
Istiqlal, 193
Ivory Coast, 25, 128, 169, 190, 193, 197, 207

JanMohamed, Abdul R., 43n26
Jay, Salim, 42
Joyce, James, 108

Kalouaz, Ahmed, 43n26, 205
Kane, Cheikh Hamidou, 142n11
    Aventure ambiguë, L', 125, 129, 176n4, 198
Kant, Immanuel, 130
Karone, Yodi, 202
Kateb, Yacine, 1, 46, 78, 199, 204, 205
    Nedjma, 5, 73, 195
Kéita, Modibo, 194, 199
Kessas, Ferrudja, *Beur's Story*, 75, 78, 206
Kesteloot, Lilyan, 2n5, 198
Khadda, Naget, 72, 73
Khaïr-Eddine, Mohammed, 1n4, 199, 200
Khatibi, Abdelkebir, 1, 4n9, 7, 199, 200, 203
Khodja, Chukri, 192
Kikuyu, *see* language, Kikuyu

Index

Kitchener, General, 190
Kom, Ambroise, 184
Koran, The, 166
  Koranic education, 6, 72, 178
  Koranic law, 174
  see also Islam
Kourouma, Ahmadou
  Monnè, outrages et défis, 127, 128, 133–8, 205
  Soleils des indépendances, Les, 127, 134, 199
Kréa, Henri, 198
Kuoh-Moukoury, Thérèse, 199

Laâbi, Abdellatif, 1n4, 103–21, 200, 202, 205
  Brûlure des interrogations, La, 107, 108
  Chemin des ordalies, Le, 103, 104, 105, 118, 202
  Chroniques de la citadelle d'exil, 118
  Ecorché vif, L', 109, 120, 121
  Histoire des sept crucifiés de l'espoir, 118, 119
  Oeil et la nuit, L', 109, 199
  Règne de barbarie, Le, 110–17, 202
  Souffles, 107, 110, 117, 199
Lachmet, Djanet, 78, 203
Lacoste, Yves, 199
La Fontaine, Jean de, 130
language, 3–5
  Agni, 129
  Arabic, 1–5 *passim*, 38, 43, 50, 56, 86, 178, 207
  Bambara, 4
  Berber, 4, 38, 43, 86, 207
  bilingualism, 4, 15
  Creole, 127
  French, 3–5, 13–15, 19–20, 84–7, 126, 127, 136
    standardisation of, 13
  Gaelic, 112
  Kikuyu, 5
  linguistic policies, 12, 13, 14, 22
  monolingualism, 14
  multilingualism, 4, 15, 18, 28
  Wolof, 4, 142
Laos, 26
Laplanche, Jean, 60, 65
Laronde, Michel, 35, 36, 207
Laroui, Abdallah, 201
Lartéguy, Jean, *Les Centurions*, 36, 47
Laye, Camara, 2, 194
Lebanon, 18, 19, 26
Léger, Jean-Marc, 18

Légitime Défense, 192
Leiner, Jacqueline, 86
Lemsine, Aïcha, 201
Le Pen, Jean-Marie, 36
Literature *see* Algeria, Cameroon, Morocco, Orientalism
Levi, Primo, 105
Lloyd, David, 43n26
Lobbo, Shehu Ahmad, 171
logopoeia, 112
Loi Toubon, 22, 28
Lopes, Henri, 29, 30, 132, 202
Louisiana, 14
Lumumba, Patrice, 197, 198
Luxemburg, 18, 19, 26
Ly, Ibrahima, 203

Maasinanké, 172, 174, 176
MacDiarmid, Hugh, 112, 113
Madagascar, 19, 26
Madani, Abassi, 207
Mali, 26, 167, 171–80, 190, 194, 196, 197, 199
  see also Soudan Français
Malinke, 134, 135, 136
Mammeri, Mouloud, 37, 46, 70, 195, 205
  Colline oubliée, La, 71
  Opium et le bâton, L', 36, 71, 199
Mannoni, Octave, 194
Maran, René, 2, 191
Martinique, 2
Marx, Karl, 110
Marxism, 8, 163–9
Mauritania, 26, 176, 197, 202
Mauritius, 22, 26
Mauritius Summit, 12n2, 15
Mauron, Charles, 59, 61
Mechakra, Yamina, 77, 78, 201
Meddeb, Abdelwahab, 1n4, 201
Mehrez, Samia, 41n17
melopoeia, 112
Memmi, Albert, 1, 8, 93–100, 201, 205
  Agar, 100, 195
  Ce que je crois, 94, 99
  Portrait du colonisé, 4n9, 100, 196
  Statue de sel, La, 93–100, 195
Mernissi, Fatima, 7, 201, 206, 207
metaphor, 59, 67
metonymy, 67
Mill, John Stuart, 100
Miller, Elinor S., 143
Mimouni, Rachid, 1n4, 77, 202, 206, 207
Mitterrand, François, 12, 21, 22

Mobutu, Colonel, 197, 199
modernism, 110
Mohammed V, King, 194, 195, 198
Monaco, 26
Monénembo, Thierno, 201, 204
Monga, Célestin, 184
Mongo, Pabé, 207
Montaigne, Michel de, 94
Morocco, 26, 200, 201, 204, 207
  colonization of, 61, 191
  independence of, 1, 195
    see also Istiqlal
  literature in, 103
  politics in, 198
  publishing, 6n7
  repression in, 117–8, 200
  uprisings in, 192, 199, 202
Mortimer, Mildred, 149
Mouralis, Bernard, 207
Mudimbe, V.-Y., 200

Naamane-Guessous, Soumaya, 77
Nanga, Bernard, 203
Negritude, 2, 3, 132, 167
neocolonialism, 12, 183, 187
Neo-Destour, 192
Neruda, Pablo, 108, 117
Ngal, M. a M., 200
Ngouabi, Capitain, 199
Niane, Djibril Tamsir, 197
Niger, 18, 20, 26, 197
Nigeria, 167, 169, 202
Nissaboury, 201
Nwachukwu-Agbanda, J.O.J., 140n7

Oakley, Ann, 145n19
OAS (Organisation de l'armée secrète), 198
OAU (Organization of African Unity), 198, 204, 205
Obeichina, Emmanuel, 157n4
OCAM (Organisation Commune Africaine et Malgache), 19
Ojo-Ade, Femi, 139, 140n4, 145–6, 147–8, 150–1
oral history, 179
oral tradition, 3, 96, 171
Orientalism, 8, 46, 49
  oriental literature, 1, 51
Other, the, 45–55 *passim*
Ould Cheikh, Mohamed, 69
Ouologuem, Yambo, 142, 199
Ousmane, Sembène *see* Sembène, Ousmane

Oyono, Ferdinand, 2, 153, 195

Pascal, Blaise, 126
Pasqua law, 187
Paton, Alan, 153
Pellegrin, Arthur, 191
Perrault, Gilles, 206
Peul *see* Fulbé
phanopoeia, 112
polygamy, 6, 140–1, 144, 146, 157, 163
Pompidou, Georges, 20
Pontalis, J.-B., 60, 65
Pound, Ezra, 108, 112, 118, 119, 120
PPA (Parti du Peuple Algérien), 193
Présence Africaine, 194
proverbs, 130
psychoanalysis, 8, 60–5 *passim*
publishing, 5–6

Quebec, 14, 18, 22, 25, 107

Rahman, Fazlur, 166n6, 168n17
Rank, Otto, 61
Raspail, Jean, 36
RCD (Berberist party), 205
RDA (Rassemblement Démocratique Africain), 193, 197
realism, 109, 126
Reclus, Onésime, 14, 15, 189
Rezzoug, Leïla, 79
Rispault, Ghislain, 106n1
Rivel, T., 192
Rivet, Daniel, 205
Robinson, David, 172
Roche, Anne, 39
Rodinson, Maxime, 205
Romania, 26
romanticism, 91
Rushdie, Salman, 107
Rwanda, 26, 207

Sahli, Mohammed-Chérif, 199
Said, Edward, 46
Saint Lucia, 26
Sanankoua, Bintou, 172
Sankara, Thomas, 205
Sartre, Jean-Paul, 100
  Orphée noir, 3, 127, 194
Sarvan, Charles Ponnuthurai, 151n33
Sassine, Williams, 202
Sebbar, Leïla, 35, 75, 203
Sefrioui, Ahmed, 1n1, 195
Segat-Kuo, François, 156
Segu empire, 171, 174

Sembène, Ousmane, 2, 8, 163–9, 195, 197
  Ceddo, 4
  Dernier de l'Empire, Le, 163, 164, 166–7, 202
  Guelwaar, 164
  O Pays, mon beau peuple, 127
  Xala, 163, 164, 165–6, 200
Senac, Jean, 198
Senegal, 26, 164, 171, 173, 195, 202
  caste system in, 146, 149
  colonization of, 189
  independence of, 197
  language in, 4
  politics in, 166–7, 169, 191, 193
Senghor, Léopold Sédar, 192, 194, 198
  poetry of, 2, 3, 4, 154, 193
  politics of, 12, 15, 18–21 *passim*, 29, 166, 193, 197
Serfaty, Abraham, 200, 206
Serhane, Abedelhak, 203, 206
Seychelles, 26
Sihanuk, Norodom, 18
slavery, 189
Sony Labou Tansi, 4n10, 7, 202, 205
SOS-Racisme, 203
Soudan Français, 171, 172, 173, 174, 175, 176–9, 180
  see also Mali
Sow Fall, Aminata, 6n19, 163–9
  Appel des arènes, L', 164
  Ex-père de la nation, L', 163, 164, 166–7, 169, 205
  Grève des bàttu, La, 6n19, 163–4, 165–6, 168, 202
  Revenant, Le, 6n19, 164
Stegeman, Beatrice, 146
Stora, Benjamin, 206
story-telling, 3
stream-of-consciousness, 38n13
surrealism, 108
Switzerland, 18, 19, 20, 26
Sylla, Khady, 206
Symbolic, the, 99

Taarji, Hinde, 206
Tadjo, Véronique, 203
Tall, 175, 176
Tall, Cerno Bokar Salif, 173, 175, 176, 177, 178
Tchidjo, Stansilas Ouoham, 207
Tchivella, Tchichelle, 204
Thiam, 175, 179
Thiam, Awa, 6, 141, 201, 205

Third-Worldism, 117
Tijaniyya, 176
Tillon, Germaine, 199
Tlili, Mustapha, 205
Tobner, Odile, 205
Togo, 26, 167, 169, 197, 199
Touabti, Hocine, 35, 42
Touati, Fettouma, 78, 203
toubab, 137, 144, 172, 176
Toumbalaye, President François, 200, 201
Touré, Sékou, 194, 196, 197
Traoré, Bakary, 196
Traouré, Alioune, 176
Traouré, Moussa, 199
Tournier, Michel, *La Goutte d'or*, 35, 45–58
Tunisia, 18, 27, 194, 195, 203, 205
  colonisation of, 190
  independence of, 1, 191, 192, 195
  see also Neo-Destour

UAM (Union Africaine et Malgache), 19
UMA (Arab Maghreb Union), 205
'Umar, al hajj, 171, 172, 174, 175, 178
UNESCO, 177
Upper Volta, 190, 197, 199, 203
  see also Burkina Faso
U'Tamsi, Tchicaya, 2n6, 195, 202

Vallejo, César, 108
Vanuatu, 27
Vehel J., 191
Viatte, Auguste, 199
Vietnam, 18, 27
Vigny, Alfred de, 185

Wa Thiongo, Ngugi, 5
Werewere Liking, 4n10, 7, 203
Whitman, Walt, 111
Williams, Raymond, 79, 80n13
Williams, William Carlos, 108
Wolof, *see* language, Wolof
Women's writing, 6–7
  see also Algeria; feminism

Yacine, Jean-Luc, 41, 207
Yacine, Kateb *see* Kateb, Yacine
Yeats, W.B., 108
Yétiv, Isaac, 1

Zaïre, 27, 197, 200
Zehar, Aïssa, 69, 193
Zemouri, Kamal, 43n26
Zitouni, Ahmed, 35